Union Public Library
1980 Morris Avenue
Union, N.J. 07083

P9-CFV-998

Chefs, Farmers
& Artisans

West

ELISABETH PRUEITT, *Tartine Bakery & Cafe,* San Francisco, California, and **SUE CONLEY & PEGGY SMITH,** *Cowgirl Creamery,* Point Reyes Station, California

GREG HIGGINS, *Higgins Restaurant & Bar,* Portland, Oregon, and **CAROL & ANTHONY BOUTARD,** *Ayers Creek Farm,* Gaston, Oregon

NAOMI POMEROY, *Beast,* Portland, Oregon, and **DAVE HOYLE,** *Creative Growers,* Noti, Oregon

NANCY SILVERTON, *Osteria Mozza,* Los Angeles, California, and **MIMMO BRUNO,** *DiStefano Cheese,* Baldwin Park, California

VITALY PALEY, *Paley's Place,* Portland, Oregon, and **BARB FOULKE,** *Freddy Guys Hazelnuts,* Monmouth, Oregon

JASON FRANEY, *Canlis,* Seattle, Washington, and **TRACY SMACIARZ,** *Heritage Meats,* Rochester, Washington

GABRIEL RUCKER, *Le Pigeon,* Portland, Oregon, and **MANUEL RECIO & LESLIE LUKAS-RECIO,** *Viridian Farms,* Dayton, Oregon

CHARLES PHAN, *The Slanted Door,* San Francisco, California, and **ANDY GRIFFIN,** *Mariquita Farm,* Watsonville, California

DOUG KEANE, *Cyrus,* Healdsburg, California, and **LAEL FORD,** *Lola's Garden,* Healdsburg, California

VINNY DOTOLO & JON SHOOK, *Animal,* Los Angeles, California, and **JAMES BIRCH,** *Flora Bella Farm,* Three Rivers, California

MARIA HINES, *Tilth,* Seattle, Washington, and **JOE WHINNEY,** *Theo Chocolate,* Seattle, Washington

Southwest

TYSON COLE, *Uchi,* Austin, Texas, and **DAVID ANDERSON,** *Bluebonnet Hydroponic Produce,* Schertz, Texas

LACHLAN MACKINNON-PATTERSON, *Frasca Food & Wine,* Boulder, Colorado, and **BOB & MIKE MUNSON,** *Munson Farms,* Boulder, Colorado

DEAN FEARING, *Fearing's,* Dallas, Texas, and **TODD SMITH,** *Texas Quail Farm,* Lockhart, Texas

Northeast

ERIC WARNSTEDT, *Hen of the Wood,* Waterbury, Vermont, and **MATEO & ANDY KEHLER,** *Jasper Hill Farm,* Greensboro, Vermont

MATTHEW GENNUSO, *Chez Pascal,* Providence, Rhode Island, and **KARL SANTOS,** *Shy Brothers Farm,* Westport Point, Massachusetts

DEREK WAGNER, *Nicks on Broadway,* Providence, Rhode Island, and **PAUL BAFFONI,** *Baffoni's Poultry Farm,* Johnston, Rhode Island

ROB EVANS, *Hugo's,* Portland, Maine, and **ROD BROWNE MITCHELL,** *Browne Trading Company,* Portland, Maine

BARBARA LYNCH, *No. 9 Park,* Boston, Massachusetts, and **CHRIS KURTH,** *Siena Farms,* Sudbury, Massachusetts

JODY ADAMS, *Rialto,* Cambridge, Massachusetts, and **MATT LINEHAN,** *Sparrow Arc Farm,* Kennebunk, Maine

TONY MAWS, *Craigie on Main,* Cambridge, Massachusetts, and **KOFI INGERSOLL & ERIN KOH,** *Bay End Farm,* Buzzards Bay, Massachusetts

BRIAN LEWIS, *The Farmhouse at Bedford Post,* Bedford, New York, and **JOHN UBALDO,** *John Boy's Farm,* Cambridge, New York

MARK GAIER & CLARK FRASIER, *Arrows,* Ogunquit, Maine, and **TED JOHNSON,** Ogunquit, Maine

BILL TAIBE, *LeFarm,* Westport, Connecticut, and **ANNIE FARRELL & BETSY FINK,** *Millstone Farm,* Wilton, Connecticut

New York City

ERIC RIPERT, *Le Bernardin,* New York City, and **EBERHARD MÜLLER & PAULETTE SATUR,** *Satur Farms,* Cutchogue, New York

DANIEL BOULUD, *Daniel,* New York City, and **TIM STARK,** *Eckerton Hill Farm,* Hamburg, Pennsylvania

MICHAEL ANTHONY, *Gramercy Tavern,* New York City, and **ZAID KURDIEH,** *Norwich Meadows Farm,* Norwich, New York

JEAN-GEORGES VONGERICHTEN, *Jean Georges,* New York City, and **NANCY MacNAMARA,** *Honey Locust Farm,* Newburgh, New York

MICHAEL PSILAKIS, *Anthos,* New York City, and **PETER SKOTIDAKIS,** *Skotidakis Goat Farm,* St. Eugene, Ontario, Canada

APRIL BLOOMFIELD, *The Spotted Pig,* New York City, and **ROB THOMPSON,** *Thanksgiving Farm,* Harris, New York

DAVID SHEA, *applewood,* New York City, and **RIDGE SHINN,** *Hardwick Beef,* Hardwick, Massachusetts

PETER HOFFMAN, *Savoy,* New York City, and **MICHAEL YEZZI & JENNIFER SMALL,** *Flying Pigs Farm,* Shushan, New York

THOMAS KELLER, *Per Se,* New York City, and **KEITH MARTIN,** *Elysian Fields Farm,* Waynesburg, Pennsylvania

CHARLIE PALMER, *Aureole,* New York City, and **TOM JURGIELEWICZ,** *Jurgielewicz Duck Farm,* East Moriches, New York

DANIEL HUMM, *Eleven Madison Park,* New York City, and **STEVE & SYLVIA PRYZANT,** *Four Story Hill Farm,* Honesdale, Pennsylvania

WALDY MALOUF, *Beacon,* New York City, and **JON WALLACH,** *Eden Brook Fish Company,* Monticello, New York

TOM COLICCHIO, *Craft,* New York City, and **TRAVIS & RYAN CROXTON,** *Rappahannock River Oysters,* Topping, Virginia

JOHNNY IUZZINI, *Jean Georges,* New York City, and **RICK BISHOP,** *Mountain Sweet Berry Farm,* Roscoe, New York

DAN BARBER & ALEX GRUNERT, *Blue Hill,* New York City, and **RALPH ERENZO & BRIAN LEE,** *Tuthilltown Spirits,* Gardiner, New York

GINA DePALMA, *Babbo,* New York City, and **JODY & LUISA SOMERS,** *Dancing Ewe Farm,* Granville, New York

Mid-Atlantic

LEE CHIZMAR, *Bolete Restaurant & Inn,* Bethlehem, Pennsylvania, and **SKIP BENNETT,** *Island Creek Oysters,* Duxbury, Massachusetts

JOSÉ ANDRÉS, *minibar,* Washington, D.C., and **BEV EGGLESTON,** *EcoFriendly Foods,* Moneta, Virginia

MICHEL RICHARD, *Central Michel Richard,* Washington, D.C., and **MARK FURSTENBERG,** Washington, D.C.

MARC VETRI, *Vetri,* Philadelphia, Pennsylvania, and **TOM CULTON,** *Culton Organics,* Silver Spring, Pennsylvania

Southeast

MICHAEL PALEY, *Proof on Main*, Louisville, Kentucky, and **STEVE WILSON & LAURA LEE BROWN,** *Kentucky Bison Company*, Goshen, Kentucky

LINTON HOPKINS, *Restaurant Eugene*, Atlanta, Georgia, and **ALLAN BENTON,** *Benton's Smoky Mountain Country Hams*, Madisonville, Tennessee

SEAN BROCK, *McCrady's*, Charleston, South Carolina, and **GLENN ROBERTS,** *Anson Mills*, Columbia, South Carolina

MONICA SEGOVIA-WELSH & ANDREA REUSING, *Lantern Restaurant*, Chapel Hill, North Carolina, and **GEORGE O'NEAL,** *Lil' Farm*, Hillsborough, North Carolina

South

DONALD LINK, *Herbsaint Bar & Restaurant*, New Orleans, Louisiana, and **BILLY LINK,** *Link Crawfish*, New Orleans, Louisiana

JOHN BESH, *August*, New Orleans, Louisiana, and **STUART GARDNER,** *Gardner Ranch*, Cankton, Louisiana

MICHELLE BERNSTEIN, *Michy's*, Miami, Florida, and **GABRIELE MAREWSKI,** *Paradise Farms*, Homestead, Florida

FRANK STITT, *Highlands Bar & Grill*, Birmingham, Alabama, and **JASON & SHELLEY POWELL,** *Petals from the Past*, Jemison, Alabama

Upper Midwest

PAUL KAHAN, *Blackbird*, Chicago, Illinois, and **DAVID CLEVERDON,** *Kinnikinnick Farm*, Caledonia, Illinois

TORY MILLER, *L'Etoile*, Madison, Wisconsin, and **MATT SMITH,** *Blue Valley Gardens*, Blue Mounds, Wisconsin

LAURENT GRAS, *L20*, Chicago, Illinois, and **PETER KLEIN,** *Seedling Farm*, South Haven, Michigan

RICK BAYLESS, *Frontera Grill*, Chicago, Illinois, and **MARTY & KRIS TRAVIS,** *Spence Farm*, Fairbury, Illinois

CHARLIE TROTTER, *Charlie Trotter's*, Chicago, Illinois, and **LEE JONES,** *The Chef's Garden*, Huron, Ohio

PAUL VIRANT, *Vie*, Western Springs, Illinois, and **WILL ALLEN,** *Growing Power*, Milwaukee, Wisconsin

GALE GAND, *Tru*, Chicago, Illinois, and **JUDY SCHAD,** *Capriole Farm*, Greenville, Indiana

Harvest to Heat

Harvest to Heat

Cooking with America's Best
Chefs, Farmers, and Artisans

Darryl Estrine and Kelly Kochendorfer

Union Public Library
1980 Morris Avenue
Union, N.J. 07083

FOREWORD BY ALICE WATERS

The Taunton Press

Text © 2010 by DARRYL ESTRINE and KELLY KOCHENDORFER

Portrait photographs © 2010 by DARRYL ESTRINE; food photographs © 2010 ELLEN SILVERMAN

All rights reserved.

The Taunton Press, Inc.,
63 South Main Street, PO Box 5506, Newtown, CT 06470-5506
email: tp@taunton.com

Editor: CAROLYN MANDARANO
Copy editor: LI AGEN
Indexer: HEIDI BLOUGH
Jacket design: ERICA HEITMAN-FORD for MUCCA DESIGN
Interior design: ERICA HEITMAN-FORD for MUCCA DESIGN
Photographers: DARRYL ESTRINE and ELLEN SILVERMAN
Food stylist: SUSIE THEODOROU
Prop stylist: CHRISTINE RUDOLPH

The following names/manufacturers appearing in *Harvest to Heat* are trademarks:
Baggie®, Cabot®, Cadillac®, The Chef's Garden®, The Culinary Institute of America®, freshdirect®, Future Farmers of America®, Hershey's®, Home Depot℠, Hoover®, Insta Cure®, Silpat®, Tabasco®, Volvo®, Whole Foods®

Library of Congress Cataloging-in-Publication Data
Estrine, Darryl.
Harvest to heat : cooking with America's best chefs, farmers, and artisans / Darryl Estrine and Kelly Kochendorfer.
p. cm.
Includes index.
ISBN 978-1-60085-254-1
1. Cookery, American. I. Kochendorfer, Kelly. II. Title.
TX715.K723 2010
641.5973--dc22
2010011943

Printed in China
10 9 8 7 6 5 4 3 2 1

FROM DARRYL

With love, for Laura and Billie
To friends and family who supported this endeavor

FROM KELLY

To my mother Nanette and sister Kim,
whose passion for good food launched me into cooking.
For Christine, who has eaten my best and worst meals and
whose loving support helped to make this book possible.

Acknowledgments

"It takes a village to raise a kid," but it takes an army to produce a book like this. We want to thank all those who have supported us through the making of *Harvest to Heat* and who have put so much effort into making it a great book.

We cannot say enough kind things about our editor, Carolyn Mandarano. Her steady hand, great insight, and endless enthusiasm for this project gave us tremendous confidence and pushed us to places we didn't think we could go. Everyone should be so lucky to work with Carolyn. We love her.

The crew at Taunton Press took our vision and turned it into a book that outshines our wildest expectations. Thanks to Alison Wilkes and Katy Binder for their help in making *Harvest to Heat* look even better than we could have hoped for. Thanks to Pam Duevel and Allison Hollett for taking all of our crazy marketing ideas and channeling them into a solid plan to spread the word.

A few people came along on the ride for a learning experience and got more than they planned on. Thanks to Drake Patton, Devin Dugan, and Rachel Langosch for their help with the photo shoots

and for being great travel partners on all those long car rides. Thanks to Hannah Goldberg for editing and testing recipes and writing a few of the best sidebars about the artisans. And thanks to Cathy Vail for her top edit of our proposal. We look forward to a long relationship in the web world with Alistair Croll and Angela Chase of Red Nod. And finally a huge thanks to Francessca Messina for introducing us and believing we could make something great.

Trips to Boston, Chicago, San Francisco, Portland, Seattle, and many other places around the United States made for a lot of hotel rooms and airplane flights. We cannot thank enough Tara Carson and Lisa Borremeo of Jet Blue for believing in this project and supplying us with airplane tickets to cross the country and photograph the chefs and artisans who bring this book to life. A huge thanks to "The Hotel Saint" Chloe Mata Crane for making calls to every Kimpton Hotel along our path and making sure we had a place to rest our full stomachs.

Claudia Cross of Sterling Lord Literistic took on a couple of novices with a really good idea and

helped us get a publisher during the worst economy in 80 years; for her hard work and help in turning us into authors, we thank her.

This project started when Darryl went out to photograph local artisans near his home in the Hudson Valley, and while they are not featured in this book, they are much appreciated for their time and good wishes in making it. Thanks to Izzy Yanay of Hudson Valley Foie Gras, Ronny and Rick Osofsky of Ronnybrook Farm Dairy, Colin McGrath of Sprout Creek Farm, Tom Gray of Mountain Products Smokehouse, The DeMarias of Hemlock Hill Farm, and Keith Stewart of Keith's Farm.

Thanks to our family and friends for all of their enthusiasm and kind words of encouragement as we got this project launched and then kept it in the air for over two years.

And finally thanks to our chefs, artisans, and farmers for their contributions to this book and for trusting us with their recipes and stories.

Contents

Introduction

WE BOTH LOVE FOOD AND LOVE TO COOK—ALWAYS HAVE, ALWAYS WILL. We also have a huge curiosity for the way food is grown and how chefs turn it into amazing dishes. When we met on a photo shoot a couple of years ago, little did we know that what started as a casual conversation about our shared passion would turn into this celebration of the people who create great food.

Our first conversation was inspiring. We talked about great cheeses, small-batch bourbons, and even the best farmer for heirloom tomatoes (Tim Stark, whom we had both met separately at the greenmarket in New York City). We are like-minded—we wholly embrace the farm to table movement and recognize the amazing flavor of food grown locally and responsibly. We dig meeting farmers, food artisans and producers, and chefs to learn about their techniques, both Old World and modern, that help them to produce their work of art. These people are all truly craftsmen in their own right.

Our shared passion was clear, and those conversations soon morphed into a business proposition after we both shared our desire to write a book that would bring together two great loves: the best ingredients for cooking and the great restaurants we love to eat at. We knew that a coffee table book of pretty pictures was not enough, so the concept of this book was created over several more get-togethers that included grilled cheese sandwiches and bags of microwave popcorn. (Foie gras for brainstorming sessions seemed a little over the top!)

We ended up with what you have here: a collection of recipes by some of the best chefs in the country that highlight the artisans and farmers—and their products—on whom they rely for their restaurants. This cookbook tells the story of the respect and relationships between these craftsmen.

Getting to this place, though, was quite a journey. What we didn't realize at the time was that the thrill of the "yes, we love your idea" from four-star chefs across the country would be followed by email trails as long as Broadway. Needless to say, these chefs are all extremely busy running restaurants and creating masterpieces in their restaurant kitchens. The recipes you'll find in the pages that follow went through many refinements to make them suitable for a home kitchen, but none lack the creativity you would expect from a top-notch chef. And the artisans and producers are an amazing bunch of people who couldn't wait to get their message out and to show off their products.

So how did the folks featured in the book come to be included? First, we had to define artisan. We believe that an artisan can be the one who creates a smooth and luscious bourbon or a rich and creamy cheese or one who takes only the best pigs and cures and smokes them to perfection. An artisan also comes in the form of a farmer who knows his soil is just as important as his crop or a rancher who holds such deep respect for his animals that he treats them with the same love as he would his family. Even a butcher who has a strong belief in treating his medium with the utmost care is a great artisan to us. We fell in love with the artisans in this book because they are brilliant, cool, passionate, and have a strong belief in what they are doing.

Next, we had to pick chefs who are true to the belief that artisans create the best products and support them for it. This part was easy. Chefs know that the best ingredients will take their creations to new levels, and they know that small-batch artisans pour their hearts and souls into their products. We were very fortunate that the chefs we asked to participate in our project came to it with tremendous enthusiasm to show off their friends and suppliers with these great recipes.

A Volvo® with 100,000 miles and a very reliable GPS, a stripped-down lighting and camera kit, and the willingness to drive up and down the Eastern Seaboard got a good part of the book done. Then it was time to take the GPS, lights, and cameras across the country. We ate great meals at Jet Blue's Terminal 5 at JFK Airport before taking off to meet the chefs and artisans we had only known via email and a few calls. Getting out of New York to the Mediterranean climate of Oregon's Willamette Valley was great, but meeting Barb Foulke and Vitaly Paley and walking Barb's hazelnut orchards brought the project to life. We had such great talks about food, farming, politics, and our strange connections with so many of our contributors that it now seems like our families have expanded exponentially.

The best part of the project was the road trips, farm visits, and the amazing meals and products so generously given by the chefs and farmers to our small crew as we traveled around the country. Charlie Trotter sat us down in an empty restaurant and served us three stunning courses paired with great wines that sent us on the way to our next shoot very happy and kinda tipsy. Judy Schad gave us goat cheese so fresh it seemed to smell of the grass her goats had just eaten. Carol and Anthony Boutard fed us impossibly sweet grapes, and Mimmo Bruno gave us his burrata cheese that will make going back to mozzarella very difficult to do. Bev Eggleston gave Darryl a 2½-pound, grass-fed, 60 day–aged rib-eye packed in a homemade cooler of cardboard and ice for a long trip home. That steak was treated like a national treasure, and in the end it was a beautiful meal.

Like Bev's steak, all of the suppliers in *Harvest to Heat* are national treasures. We hope you take this book, cook from it, and enjoy some of the greatest food you'll ever taste.

Let's eat!

Foreword

WHEN WE OPENED CHEZ PANISSE, WE DIDN'T SET OUT TO BASE IT ON A philosophy of sustainability, organic farming, or even supporting local farms. We were searching for taste and striving to create a place where friends and family could gather at the table and share a simple meal. I wanted to find in California the flavors, smells, and sights of the markets of France that had opened up my senses. That search led us to the doorstep of local organic farms, along the coastline for fresh fish straight from the boat, and to the hills around the restaurant, where we foraged for mushrooms and nettles.

Over the years we have built beautiful and important relationships with the 85 fishermen, ranchers, farmers, and foragers who regularly supply the restaurant. We rely on them as they rely on us, and it is their work that drives our creativity and inspiration in the kitchen. Happily, we are not unique in this regard—there are many chefs and cooks around the country who do the same. The farm-to-table philosophy has grown immeasurably, with chefs and home cooks alike recognizing the value of sustainable local farming and fishing communities.

As we near the 40th anniversary of Chez Panisse, I look at how far we have come, in large part due to the heroes of the sustainable food movement, those people—

growers and cooks—who are shaping the way we think about food. *Harvest to Heat* embodies the spirit of collaboration both in the field and at the table.

There is a purity and simplicity about the recipes in this book that I love. Together, the artisans and chefs have taken food at its peak of seasonality and flavor and crafted recipes that showcase the flavors and textures of the ingredients. The simplicity of the recipes let the ingredients shine, and the accessible techniques place each and every recipe within reach of home cooks of all skill levels. My hope is that through these recipes and stories, more home cooks will embrace seasonality, support local economies, and in doing so build a sustainable future.

Harvest to Heat embraces the incredible regional diversity of our country while solidifying the connection between land and plate, and chef, farmer, and artisan. It represents a new generation of cookbook—for a new generation of cooks.

— ALICE WATERS

Starters

ERIC WARNSTEDT, *Hen of the Wood,* Waterbury, Vermont

MATEO & ANDY KEHLER, *Jasper Hill Farm,* Greensboro, Vermont (cheese)

Blue Cheese Tartine

Jasper Hill's blue cheese, Bayley Hazen, is a raw-milk blue with a flavor of nuts, grass, and, in some batches, hints of licorice. A tartine is just a fancy French name for an open-faced sandwich. This starter isn't fancy, but it is irresistible, thanks to the sweetness of honey, the smoky crunch of bacon, and the creamy tang of blue cheese.

SERVES 4

4 large slices rustic sourdough bread
2 tablespoons extra-virgin olive oil
¼ pound blue cheese, crumbled
8 slices thick-cut bacon, cooked until crisp
4 tablespoons wildflower honey
Freshly ground black pepper

1. Brush both sides of the bread lightly with olive oil, place on a baking sheet, and broil until golden on one side, about 2 minutes. Sprinkle the cheese on top of the bread and broil until slightly melted, about 1 minute.

2. Arrange the cheese toasts on a serving platter and lay 2 warm slices of bacon over each, then drizzle with the honey and grind some fresh pepper over the top. Cut each toast in half, if desired, and serve.

ELISABETH PRUEITT, *Tartine Bakery & Cafe,* San Francisco, California

SUE CONLEY & PEGGY SMITH, *Cowgirl Creamery,* Point Reyes Station, California (cheese)

Herb Gougères

Simple, savory cheese puffs have endless variations, from herbs to spices to the types of cheeses used. Cowgirl Creamery's Pierce Pt is a wonderful semisoft cheese produced only in the cold months and is washed in wine and rolled in dried herbs.

YIELDS 4 DOZEN

FOR THE CHOUX PASTRY
1¼ cups nonfat milk or water
10 tablespoons (1¼ sticks)
  unsalted butter
1 teaspoon coarse salt
1 cup all-purpose flour
5 large eggs

1 cup semisoft cheese (like Pierce Pt
  or Manchego), cut into small pieces
  or shaved with a cheese knife
2 teaspoons pimentón
  (smoked Spanish paprika)
½ teaspoon freshly ground
  black pepper

10 chives (each about 8 inches long),
  cut into ¼-inch pieces

FOR THE TOPPING
1 large egg
Pinch salt
Grated cheese for sprinkling (optional)

1. Heat the oven to 375°F. Butter or line two large baking sheets with parchment. Combine the milk, butter, and salt in a large saucepan over high heat, stirring, until the butter is melted. Reduce the heat to medium, add the flour all at once, and stir vigorously with a wooden spoon until the mixture pulls from away from the sides of the pan. Continue to stir for about 1 to 2 minutes. Remove from the heat and let cool for just 1 minute. Add the eggs one at a time and continue to stir, making sure to incorporate each egg before adding the next (the mixture may appear to separate but it will become smooth). After all the eggs have been added, the mixture should be thick, smooth, and shiny. Stir in the cheese, pimentón, pepper, and chives and mix well.

2. Using a rubber spatula, transfer the mixture to a pastry bag and pipe 1-inch mounds onto the baking sheet. Alternatively, you can use two tablespoons, one to level the batter and one to help turn out the batter onto the sheet. Leave 1 inch between each mound of batter.

3. To make the topping, whisk the egg with a pinch of salt and brush over each mound of batter. Lightly sprinkle each with a little cheese, if desired. If using a semisoft cheese, like Pierce Pt, make sure it's thoroughly chilled before it's grated. (Instead of cheese you can just add a bit of coarse salt.)

4. Put the gougères in the oven and bake until they're puffed, crisp, and golden, about 30 minutes. Continue to bake in batches until all of the batter is used. Serve hot or warm or let cool completely and store in an airtight container for up to a day. Gougères can be crisped in a 350°F oven for 5 minutes if they've been stored.

IN SUPPORT OF CHEESE

Sue Conley and Peggy Smith started Cowgirl Creamery with a dream of making cheese from their neighbor's organic milk. What they've managed to do, though, is spearhead a movement of artisanal cheese production on both sides of the country.

It was 1997 when their plan took shape and Cowgirl Creamery was born. The cowgirls started selling through their own retail outlet in Point Reyes Station, California, and their tremendous success led them to selling and distributing cheeses of other small artisans. When the Ferry Building in San Francisco reopened in 2003, it brought with it a mecca of food from the best farmers, artisans, and winemakers direct to the public on a daily basis. Cowgirl's cheeses were among those products in high demand.

Thanks to their success, Sue and Peggy have been able to step away from the day-to-day operation of the business in order to help in growing cheese production in both California and the Mid-Atlantic region. In California they have "casually consulted" one farm that wanted to transition from conventional milk to organic and into cheesemaking, another that is being started up by a winemaker with Ayershire cows, and a "city" friend that is setting up a goat farm. Sue adds, "Pennsylvania and Maryland produce the best milk in the country. The cattle are grass fed and completely organic. Now we are helping them produce, sell, and distribute their cheeses." While Sue says the cheese has a little way to go, she adds that "the milk is so good, the cheese easily will follow."

Elisabeth Prueitt

ERIC RIPERT, *Le Bernardin,* New York City

EBERHARD MÜLLER & PAULETTE SATUR, *Satur Farms,* Cutchogue, New York (zucchini flowers)

Crab-Stuffed Zucchini Flowers with Black Truffles

This dish is truly a joint creation. Eberhard and Paulette stuff zucchini flowers with two types of sweet crab, then Eric transforms them into an elegant dish with a black truffle butter and vinaigrette. You can buy truffle butter, whole truffles (jarred or canned), and truffle juice at specialty stores.

SERVES 4

FOR THE TRUFFLE BUTTER
8 tablespoons (1 stick) unsalted butter, softened
½ ounce fresh black truffle, shaved with a mandoline, or chopped canned black truffles
Sea salt and freshly ground white pepper

FOR THE TRUFFLE VINAIGRETTE
1 teaspoon Dijon mustard
2 teaspoons red-wine vinegar
2 teaspoons sherry vinegar
¼ cup olive oil
½ tablespoon chopped black truffle, fresh or canned, with juice if using canned
Coarse salt and freshly ground white pepper

FOR THE CRAB FILLING
½ pound peekytoe crabmeat, cleaned
4 ounces lump crabmeat, cleaned
Coarse salt
Crushed red pepper flakes

12 large zucchini flowers, stamens removed and brushed clean
1 tablespoon fresh chives, finely chopped, for garnish

MAKE THE TRUFFLE BUTTER
In a small saucepan, bring 1 tablespoon water to a boil and whisk in the butter. Add the truffle and mix until incorporated. Season to taste with salt and pepper. Cover the pan and keep warm over low heat.

MAKE THE TRUFFLE VINAIGRETTE
Combine the mustard and both vinegars in a bowl and drizzle in the oil in a slow, steady steam, whisking to incorporate. Add the chopped truffle and the truffle juice if using canned and whisk until just blended. Season to taste with salt and pepper. Cover and refrigerate until ready to use.

MAKE THE FILLING
Combine both crabmeats and ¼ cup of the truffle butter. Season with salt and red pepper flakes.

PREPARE THE ZUCCHINI FLOWERS
1. Have ready a bamboo steamer or lightly grease a steamer basket. Fill a large pot with 2 inches of water.

2. Using a teaspoon, gently stuff each zucchini flower three-quarters full with the crabmeat filling, then gently twist the top of the flower closed. Arrange the stuffed zucchini flowers in the steamer basket; lay them flat even if piled on top of each other. Place the basket in the pot; cover and steam until the crab filling is hot, about 3 minutes.

TO SERVE
Equally portion the remaining ¼ cup truffle butter among 4 plates and carefully arrange 3 steamed zucchini flowers on top. Spoon the truffle vinaigrette around the zucchini flowers and sprinkle with chives. Serve immediately.

GREG HIGGINS, *Higgins Restaurant & Bar,* Portland, Oregon

CAROL & ANTHONY BOUTARD, *Ayers Creek Farm,* Gaston, Oregon (corn)

Flint Corn Polenta Cakes with Heirloom Tomato Salsa

Ground flint corn is made from whole, hard corn kernels (also known as Indian corn) from several varieties, such as White Cap Flint, Seneca Nation, and Roy's Calais Flint. The Boutards not only grow the corn but also dry and grind their own cornmeal. Greg believes that the Boutards' fresh, ground cornmeal is as close as you can get to that found in Italy. These polenta toasts can be made in advance and kept in the refrigerator for 2 days before cutting and toasting.

SERVES 4

FOR THE POLENTA CAKES
1 cup ground flint corn or dry cornmeal
2 cloves garlic, minced
1 teaspoon whole cumin seeds
1 jalapeño, cored, seeded, and minced
½ cup grated Parmigiano-Reggiano
Coarse salt and freshly ground
  black pepper

FOR THE SALSA
2 large tomatoes, preferably heirloom,
  cut into ¾-inch dice (about 2 cups)
1 small red onion, finely chopped
3 hot and 3 mild chile peppers, such as
  jalapeño and serrano, cored, seeded,
  and minced
1 clove garlic, minced

½ cup fresh cilantro leaves, chopped
1 lemon, juiced and zested
½ teaspoon ground cumin
Coarse salt and freshly ground black
  pepper

3 tablespoons olive oil

1. To make the polenta cakes, in a heavy-bottomed saucepan, bring 3 cups water to a boil and slowly add the flint corn or cornmeal, stirring constantly. Lower the heat, add the garlic, cumin seeds, and jalapeños, and simmer over medium-low heat, stirring frequently to prevent lumps, until the polenta is thick and smooth, 20 to 25 minutes.

2. Stir in the cheese, season to taste with salt and pepper, and remove from the heat. Lightly oil a small, shallow pan (8 × 8 inches is a good size), then spoon the hot polenta into it, spreading it into an even, ¾-inch-thick layer. Refrigerate until firm, about 3 hours.

3. Meanwhile, make the salsa. Combine the tomatoes, onions, chile peppers, garlic, cilantro, lemon juice, zest, and cumin in a medium bowl. Season to taste with salt and pepper and set aside.

4. Cut the cooled polenta into 3-inch squares. Heat the olive oil in a large skillet over medium-high heat and cook the polenta squares until golden brown, 2 to 3 minutes per side. Transfer to a serving platter and top with the salsa.

MATTHEW GENNUSO, *Chez Pascal,* Providence, Rhode Island

KARL SANTOS, *Shy Brothers Farm,* Westport Point, Massachusetts (cheese)

Carrot Cannelloni with Soft Cheese and Pine Nuts

The beautiful Purple Haze carrot and mild milk cheese with an earthy flavor and creamy consistency are the inspiration behind this recipe. In the style of the Italian cheese-filled rolled pasta dish known as cannelloni, the carrot is used in place of the pasta and filled with cheese.

SERVES 4

6 medium carrots, preferably
   Purple Haze, peeled
2 teaspoons chopped fresh chervil
2 teaspoons chopped fresh tarragon
2 teaspoons chopped fresh flat-leaf
   parsley

2 teaspoons chopped fresh chives
¼ pound mild goat or farmer's
   cheese, broken into 16 small
   pieces if using 1 large piece (or
   16 thimbles if using Hannahbells)
5 tablespoons extra-virgin olive oil

2 tablespoons aged balsamic vinegar
Coarse salt and freshly ground
   black pepper
1 large head radicchio, cored
   and shredded
3 tablespoons pine nuts, toasted

1. Cut the carrots into 3-inch-long pieces and then using a mandoline or sharp knife, cut those carrot pieces into paper-thin lengthwise slices, for about 16 slices total. Lay them out flat on a large work surface or cutting board.

2. In a small bowl mix the chervil, tarragon, parsley, and chives. Press one side of each piece of cheese into the herb mixture to coat. Place one cheese piece on one end of a carrot strip and roll to encase the cheese, making sure to push the cheese in on both sides (the moisture from the carrot will seal the carrot closed). Lay the roll, seam side down, on a work surface. Repeat with the remaining pieces of cheese and carrot slices.

3. In a bowl, whisk 3 tablespoons of the olive oil with 1 tablespoon of the balsamic vinegar. Season with salt and pepper, add the radicchio, and mix well.

4. To serve, arrange 4 cannelloni in the center of a plate, arrange the radicchio around them, and drizzle the cannelloni with the remaining 2 tablespoons olive oil and 1 tablespoon balsamic vinegar. Top each serving with the toasted pine nuts. Season to taste with salt and pepper. The carrot cannelloni can be kept in the refrigerator in an airtight container with a damp towel covering them for up to a day.

FOUR SHY BROTHERS AND A SAVIOR

What are the odds of one family having two sets of fraternal twin boys? What are the odds of those brothers growing up to become farmers together? And finally, what kind of good luck does it take for two sets of fraternal twins who are brothers and farmers to find a business-savvy entrepreneur willing to invest her time and money to help them turn their declining family-owned dairy farm into a high-margin business of gourmet cheese production? This is the story of the Santos brothers of Shy Brothers Farm in Westport Point, Massachusetts.

Kevin, Arthur, Norman, and Karl Santos, three of whom are quite shy, are third-generation dairy farmers. All have their farm specialties and together can fix or grow just about anything. Kevin is the mechanic of the operation, while Arthur is the reliable feeder of the 120 cows (Holsteins, Ayrshires, and Jerseys); Norman likes milking, and Karl is the financial and marketing mind of the operation. They met Barbara Hanley and Leo Brooks a couple of years ago, when the couple approached the brothers and offered to help keep their business afloat. Barbara and Leo are interested in saving local farmland and preserving the landscape and realized that the best way to do this is through economic development.

With that in mind, Karl and Barbara spent two weeks in France learning the centuries-old craft of making the thimble-shaped cheese they call Han-nahbells, named after the Santos boys' mother. Once they returned to their farm, they rented space from the town's former butcher, but in the end they built a cheese house to better serve the highly exacting production needs of making their artisanal cheese. The semisoft cheese is aged for just 10 days and then is packaged for selling both direct to the public and wholesale to restaurants. The cheese flavors, from lavender to shallot to rosemary, are anything but shy and are delicious on pizzas, in salads, or alone as great hors d'oeuvres.

Karl Santos and Matthew Gennuso

DEREK WAGNER, *Nicks on Broadway,* Providence, Rhode Island

PAUL BAFFONI, *Baffoni's Poultry Farm,* Johnston, Rhode Island (chicken liver)

Sautéed Chicken Livers with Smoked Bacon and Roasted Grapes

The robust and hearty flavors of chicken livers and bacon are made into a wonderful canapé with the unlikely addition of roasted grapes. Try using a variety of the red, black, or green seasonal fall grapes you can find at your local market.

SERVES 4

1 cup green grapes, picked and rinsed
2 teaspoons extra-virgin olive oil
6 slices bacon
1 pound chicken livers, cleaned
and dried
Coarse salt and freshly ground
black pepper

1 tablespoon unsalted butter
½ cup thinly sliced red onions
(about 1 medium)
2 cloves garlic, sliced paper thin
2 sprigs fresh thyme
½ cup port
2 tablespoons aged sherry vinegar

Four ¾-inch slices brioche, buttered
and toasted right before serving
2 cups loosely packed mâche greens,
rinsed, and any large stems removed

1. Heat the oven to 400°F. Toss the grapes with the olive oil, spread out on a baking sheet, and roast until just wilted, about 5 minutes. Set aside and keep warm.

2. Cut 2 slices of bacon in half and cook until crisp in a sauté pan or in the microwave. Set aside and keep warm.

3. Season the chicken livers thoroughly with salt and pepper. In a large sauté pan, melt the butter on medium-high heat, then add the livers and sear on both sides until golden brown, about 5 minutes total. Remove from the pan and set aside.

4. Finely chop the remaining 4 slices of bacon, add to the pan, and brown slightly over medium-low heat, about 5 minutes. Stir in the onions and cook until lightly browned, about 8 minutes. Season with salt and pepper. Add the garlic and cook for another 2 minutes. Raise the heat to high, add 1 thyme sprig, then add the port and sherry vinegar and deglaze the pan. Cook until the liquid is reduced by half, about 3 minutes.

5. Return the chicken livers to the pan and heat through. Take the pan off the heat, remove the thyme sprig, and adjust the seasoning as necessary.

6. To serve, place a slice of toasted brioche in the center of each plate, mound the chicken liver mixture on top, and pile the mâche alongside. Lean a crispy bacon strip against the salad. Garnish the plate with the roasted grapes and small leaves picked from the remaining sprig of thyme. Spoon the pan juices over the plate and serve immediately.

NAOMI POMEROY, *Beast,* Portland, Oregon

DAVE HOYLE, *Creative Growers,* Noti, Oregon (dandelion greens)

Dandelion Tart with Sheep's Milk Ricotta and Grappa-Soaked Golden Raisins

Red dandelion is one of the few red leafy vegetables that keeps its deep color when cooked. It has a slightly bitter note, but the creamy sheep's milk ricotta balances its strong flavor. This tart uses no pan and is really more of a pizza in its presentation. You can make a border by twisting excess dough and placing it around the circle of dough or use the tines of a fork to create a pattern around the edge.

SERVES 8

2 cups all-purpose flour
½ teaspoon coarse salt
1½ sticks (12 tablespoons) unsalted
    butter, chilled and cut into
    ½-inch pieces
¼ pound pancetta or thick-sliced
    bacon, diced

4 tablespoons extra-virgin olive oil
1 medium onion, thinly sliced
3 cloves garlic, minced
2 pounds dandelion greens, trimmed,
    washed, and spun dry
¼ cup grappa
½ cup golden raisins

2 tablespoons capers, soaked
    and rinsed
4 anchovies in oil
Freshly ground black pepper
1 pound (4 cups) sheep's milk ricotta
Aged balsamic vinegar (optional)

1. Make the crust: In a medium bowl, combine the flour, salt, and butter pieces in the bowl of a food processor or in a medium bowl if blending by hand. Blend the butter into the dry ingredients quickly, making sure not to overmix (leaving some butter the size of peas is fine). Add 1 to 2 tablespoons water, again making sure not to overmix the dough, then turn the dough out on a cutting board and gently push it together into a ball. Wrap tightly with plastic wrap and refrigerate for 2 hours.

2. In a large skillet over medium heat, cook the pancetta for 10 minutes. Remove and drain on a paper towel–lined plate. In the same skillet, heat the olive oil over medium-low heat and cook the onions for 10 minutes until soft. Add the garlic and cook, stirring, for 1 minute. Add the dandelion greens, raise the heat to medium high, and sauté, stirring frequently, until wilted, about 2 to 3 minutes.

3. In a small saucepan, heat the grappa over low heat for 2 minutes. Remove from the heat and add the raisins to absorb the grappa; let sit for 15 minutes. With a slotted spoon, transfer the raisins and dandelion greens mixture to a blender; add the capers and anchovies with oil, and pulse until roughly chopped, about 4 pulses. Season to taste with freshly ground black pepper.

4. Line a baking sheet that will fit in your freezer with parchment. Lightly flour a work surface, then use a rolling pin to roll the dough into a 16-inch round. Transfer to the prepared baking sheet. Spread the ricotta over the tart, leaving a 2-inch border. Fold the edges of the dough around the cheese. Chill in the freezer for 30 minutes.

5. Heat the oven to 375°F. Remove the semi-frozen tart from the freezer and spread the dandelion mixture over the top. Bake for 30 minutes or until golden brown. Drizzle the aged balsamic vinegar over the top, if desired.

GROWING CREATIVE

Dave Hoyle, self-titled "food geek," has worked just about every aspect of the food cycle on his way to becoming a successful farmer in Noti, Oregon. Hoyle started his career in kitchens, working as everything from dishwasher to busboy. After becoming a member of the local CSA (Community Supported Agriculture), he was asked to help fill boxes when a CSA employee went missing. The CSA job turned into seven years of co-managing the farm.

Then in 1996, in a stroke of serendipity, Dave and his wife were made an offer by a local farm owner that they couldn't refuse. The offer was this: Work the farm for five years with no pay; live rent-free in a 20-foot yurt; and at the end of that time own half of the farm. The offer seemed pretty good. After all, the yurt was warmed by a "rockin' woodstove," and the couple received a small stipend of $400 a month, which paid for their minor expenses. Dave took the offer and ran. His Creative Growers farm has since become a supplier to local restaurants in Eugene, Corvalis, and Portland, thanks to his varieties of tomatoes, shelling beans, and 60 other crops that were not available locally.

Dave's plan was to get his seed from European dealers, pull seed from heirloom crops of his own, and occasionally smuggle in a few after a vacation in Europe. The main goal was to avoid "homogenized seed." These special products, along with his many other innovative techniques—like dropping off braising greens ready to cook, harvesting salad greens by cutting them in the field (easier to harvest, he says) and then triple-washing them at the farm, peeling onions, buffing eggplants and tomatoes, and generally saving chefs time—have made him very popular. Instead of employing a driver with no knowledge of the farm, Creative Growers' driver is also the packing manager, so he knows the product inside out and can talk with great experience about it when he delivers to finicky chefs.

Dave's relationship with his "power chef elite" is most rewarding when he sees his work turned into great meals and even better when he is invited to the table. He also loves talking to the folks who shop at farmers' markets and turning them on to new products to expand their palates.

Dave Hoyle, Naomi Pomeroy, and Mika Parades

ROB EVANS, *Hugo's,* Portland, Maine

ROD BROWNE MITCHELL, *Browne Trading Company,* Portland, Maine (scallops)

Maine Sea Scallop Ceviche

Diver scallops are those that are hand-harvested by divers who only pick large and mature scallops and leave the smaller ones to repopulate. Rob uses sea scallops and three types of citrus for his refreshing ceviche. Serve this as a light supper or in stemmed glasses as an elegant first course at a dinner party.

SERVES 4

2 medium red bell peppers
2 tablespoons extra-virgin olive oil
1 pound large fresh scallops
½ cup fresh lemon juice
¼ cup fresh lime juice
½ cup fresh orange juice
1 teaspoon soy sauce

1 teaspoon minced fresh ginger
1 clove garlic, minced
2 tablespoons thinly sliced scallions (white and green parts)
1 large tomato, peeled and finely chopped

2 tablespoons finely chopped fresh cilantro
1 teaspoon hot sauce, preferably Sriracha
4 cups mixed baby lettuces (optional)

1. Roast the red bell peppers: Heat the oven to 400°F. Rub the bell peppers all over with the olive oil and put on a baking sheet. Roast in the oven, turning a few times, until the peppers are lightly charred, 30 to 40 minutes. Transfer to a bowl and cover tightly with plastic wrap for 15 minutes. When the peppers are cool enough to handle, peel, seed, and finely chop. You should have about 1 cup of chopped roasted red peppers. Set aside.

2. Remove the tough white muscle attached to each scallop and discard. Cut the scallops into ½-inch pieces. Put the scallops in a medium saucepan, just cover with water, and poach in barely simmering water until opaque and firm, 30 seconds. Drain and allow to cool, then transfer to a large bowl.

3. In a medium bowl, whisk the lemon, lime, and orange juices, soy sauce, ginger, and garlic. Pour over the scallops, cover, and chill for 1 hour in the refrigerator. Mix in the roasted peppers, scallions, tomatoes, cilantro, and hot sauce. Serve chilled over a bed of mixed baby lettuces, if desired.

continued

BORN FOR THE SEA

It seemed natural that Rod Browne Mitchell would follow in his grandfather's footsteps and become a fisherman. After all, he was raised in Maine, fished and hunted from an early age, and learned what it takes to find and harvest the best seafood. So when he opened a wine and cheese shop it was as if he took a sharp left turn off the path of fishing. But it was there that he cultivated his appreciation for great food, and that, in turn, is how he ended up with Browne Trading Company.

While running the shop, Mitchell met Chef Jean-Louis Palladin in the early 1980s. This meeting spawned Mitchell's first business venture of supplying the chef with a litany of exotic fish and the luxury product Mitchell truly became known for, caviar. Mitchell's reputation grew as did the fish that he made available, including live urchins, live lamprey, and sweet Maine crabmeat, which he coined "Peekytoe."

Mitchell not only knows his fish, but he has been at the forefront of fishing techniques. His fish are caught by hook, not net, in order to reduce the amount of stress on a fish. He was the developer of diver scallops (those that are literally picked from cold water by divers, not scooped by a net) and is now leading the industry with his belief that sustainable fishing and farm-raised fish and caviar will keep the industry strong.

Rod's client list and business partnerships read like a who's who of fine dining. Eric Ripert, Charlie Trotter, and Daniel Boulud are but a few. Boulud's strong trust of Mitchell led them into business together, creating lines of smoked Scottish salmon and Chef Boulud's private stock caviar.

Rob Evans and Rod Browne Mitchell

DONALD LINK, *Herbsaint Bar & Restaurant*, New Orleans, Louisiana

BILLY LINK, *Link Crawfish*, New Orleans, Louisiana (crawfish)

Crawfish-Stuffed Deviled Eggs

The crawfish, or crayfish, season starts in Louisiana right after the New Year. Crawfish are essentially fresh-water shrimp and resemble tiny lobsters. Like their larger cousin, they're bought live and stored and cooked in the same manner. These stuffed eggs are made with seasonings and ingredients of the most authentic Louisiana cuisine.

SERVES 8

8 large eggs
2 tablespoons unsalted butter
½ small onion, finely diced
½ stalk celery, finely diced
1 small jalapeño, finely diced
½ small poblano chile, seeded and finely diced
½ teaspoon cayenne
1 teaspoon paprika

Coarse salt and freshly ground black pepper
½ pound crawfish tails, parboiled and peeled
2 teaspoons chopped fresh tarragon
1 tablespoon fresh lemon juice (from ½ lemon)

3 tablespoons mayonnaise, or a little more according to taste
1 tablespoon Creole mustard or spicy mustard
Paprika or cayenne, for garnish (optional)

1. Place the eggs in a medium pot and cover with cold water. Bring to a boil, then turn the heat down to a simmer and cook for 11 minutes. Let the eggs cool, then peel and cut them in half lengthwise, separating the yolks from the whites. Set both aside.

2. In a large skillet, melt the butter over low heat and add the onions, celery, jalapeños, poblanos, and spices. Season with salt and pepper. Cook for 4 minutes to sweat the vegetables. Add the crawfish and cook for another 5 minutes. Let the mixture cool, then add the tarragon and stir to combine.

3. Put the cooked egg yolks in a mixing bowl and mash them with a fork. Roughly chop the cooked crawfish mixture and add it to the bowl of mashed yolks, then add the lemon juice, mayonnaise, and mustard. Mix to combine.

4. Spoon the crawfish mixture into the cooked whites. Transfer to a serving platter and sprinkle with paprika or cayenne, if desired.

FLORA ROTATES TO FAUNA

Rice and crawfish run deep in the Link family. Billy Link's great-great-grandfather was the first to commercially grow rice in Louisiana, and his father has been raising crawfish since 1987. The Link family grows crawfish on about 700 of the 1,500 acres of rice they grow. The family grows 800 acres of soybeans as well.

Billy plants his rice crop in early spring, floods the fields around June, then drains the fields for harvest in late July or August, leaving about a foot of stubble from the rice plants as the perfect food for the crawfish to come. As the weather in Acadia Parish, Louisiana, starts to cool and thunderstorms move in, the fields are flooded again and ready for crawfish. If this is the first time the crawfish are being raised, the fields will have been sowed with baby crawfish in May; if the fields have been the home to them for years, they will pop up when the cool weather and rains come. Billy says, "Crawfish are kind of like cockroaches—they always come back." Billy can walk the fields after they have been drained in July to see if crawfish holes are abundant and get a pretty solid idea of how big the haul will be come the following February or March.

The crawfish are harvested from traps similar to lobsters and then picked up in boats that are custom made for harvesting in shallow waters. Finally, ducks, cranes, and other water fowl arrive by the thousands to clean up the land of the remaining crawfish and help ready it for the next rotation of rice.

Of course the best part of crawfishing is eating them. Billy likes to put them in a pot of boiling water, let the water come back up to a boil, and then dump them over ice and season them. He also adds, "My cousin Donald [Chef Donald Link] loves my crawfish, and he does a pretty good job with them, too."

Salads

DANIEL BOULUD, *Daniel,* New York City

TIM STARK, *Eckerton Hill Farm,* Hamburg, Pennsylvania (tomatoes)

Stuffed Cherry Tomatoes with Zucchini Pistou and Yellow Tomato Vinaigrette

This recipe capitalizes on three types of tomatoes used in three different ways: as a simple tomato salad, stuffed, and in a vinaigrette. The stuffed cherry tomatoes are great hors d'oeuvres for a party; stuff medium tomatoes with the pistou as a starter to a summer meal. Peeling tomatoes is an easy task: After blanching for 5 seconds, their skins slip right off.

SERVES 6

**FOR THE STUFFED
CHERRY TOMATOES**

18 large cherry tomatoes, assorted
　colors if available
1 tablespoon pine nuts
3 tablespoons extra-virgin olive oil
1 medium green zucchini, quartered
　lengthwise, seeded, and cut into
　¼-inch dice
1 clove garlic, lightly crushed
2 sprigs fresh thyme
1 cup fresh basil leaves
Coarse salt and freshly ground
　black pepper

**FOR THE YELLOW TOMATO
VINAIGRETTE**

3 small or 2 medium yellow
　heirloom tomatoes, chopped
　(about 1½ cups)
2 tablespoons extra-virgin olive oil
¼ teaspoon (small pinch)
　saffron threads
1 teaspoon cornstarch
Hot sauce
Coarse salt and freshly ground
　white pepper

FOR THE SALAD

3 to 4 pounds mixed heirloom
　tomatoes
1 shallot, finely chopped
3 tablespoons extra-virgin olive oil
1 tablespoon sherry vinegar
Coarse salt and freshly ground
　white pepper
3 cups baby arugula, washed and
　picked (about 6 ounces)
⅓ pound ricotta salata cheese, sliced
　thinly and cut in half for 18 narrow
　triangles
Micro basil leaves, for garnish

MAKE THE STUFFED TOMATOES

1. Bring a large pot of salted water to a boil and set aside a bowl of ice water. Remove the stems from the cherry tomatoes and score a very small "x" on their bottoms. Blanch the tomatoes in the boiling water for 5 seconds; transfer with a slotted spoon to the bowl of ice water to chill. Peel the skin from the tomatoes and slice about ¼ inch from the tops. Scoop out the inside of the tomatoes with a small melon baller.

2. Heat a dry skillet over medium heat and add the pine nuts, stirring for about 2 minutes until they just start to become golden brown and fragrant. Remove from the heat, transfer to a bowl, and set aside.

3. Heat 1 tablespoon of the oil in a small skillet over medium heat. Add the diced zucchini, garlic, and thyme. Cook, stirring, until the zucchini is tender, about 4 minutes. Discard the garlic and thyme and transfer the zucchini to a medium bowl. Combine the basil leaves, toasted pine nuts, and remaining olive oil in a blender and purée until smooth. Remove the purée from the blender and combine with the cooked zucchini; season to taste with salt and pepper. Fill the cherry tomatoes with the zucchini pistou when ready to serve.

MAKE THE VINAIGRETTE

Combine the yellow tomatoes, oil, and saffron in a double boiler or a heat-proof bowl on top of a pot of simmering water (be sure the bowl does not touch the water) over medium heat. Cook for 1 hour, allowing the tomatoes to break down. Strain the liquid from the tomatoes into a small saucepan and whisk in the cornstarch. Heat, while whisking, to a simmer (the mixture will thicken). Purée with the tomato pulp in a blender until smooth, then pass through a fine-mesh strainer. Season to taste with hot sauce, salt, and white pepper, then chill, covered, for at least 1½ hours.

MAKE THE SALAD

Bring a large pot of salted water to a boil and set aside a bowl of ice water. Remove the stems from the tomatoes and score a very small "x" on their bottoms. Add the tomatoes to the boiling water and blanch for 5 seconds; transfer with a slotted spoon to the bowl of ice water to chill. Peel the skin from the tomatoes and transfer to a medium bowl.

TO SERVE

1. Slice the tomatoes into ½-inch slices, sprinkle with salt, and lay on paper towels for 10 minutes. Combine the shallots, olive oil, sherry vinegar, and salt and pepper to taste. Dress the tomato slices lightly with the sherry vinaigrette and lay 1 slice in the center of each plate.

2. Top with a silver dollar–size spoonful of yellow tomato vinaigrette and arrange 3 stuffed tomatoes on top.

3. Dress the arugula with the remaining sherry vinaigrette and scatter it lightly around each tomato slice in a circle. Lay 3 triangles of ricotta salata on top of the salad.

continued

A FARMER GROWS
IN BROOKLYN

Writing fiction, working as a management consultant, and growing 3,000 tomato plants on the roof of a Brooklyn, New York apartment building, seemed like a good idea at first, but then the tomatoes got really good and the rejection letters from publishing houses kept on coming. Realizing that he was a struggling writer turning into a would-be farmer, Tim Stark brought two truckloads of his seedlings to his boyhood home in Pennsylvania, planting them at the house he grew up in.

Tim started growing other stuff, too, like peas, lettuce, carrots, beets, and sweet potatoes. While they all grew well on the land, they served only to feed the local deer population. The only things left standing were his beautiful tomatoes. The tomatoes looked like peaches, pears, and lemons, the colors of purple, pink, white, and green. They had great names like Cherokee Purple, Garden Peach, Green Zebra, and Radiator Charlie's Mortgage Lifter. Tim's first season of growing, now nearly 12 years ago, went great—he had 60 varieties of tomatoes and developed a strong following at the Union Square Farmers' Market in New York City. Soon the chefs who were market regulars started buying from him as well, and some of his customers included the best restaurants of New York City, including the empire of Daniel Boulud.

Today, Stark drives into Gotham from his recently purchased 58-acre farm twice a week with 2 tons of his heirloom tomatoes as well as onions and a few other vegetables. The variety of tomatoes has reached one hundred. Tim has become so well known for his tomatoes that the other vegetables just sit on the ground as an afterthought for customers who just happen to look below the rainbow of color on his selling tables. "I first sold my tomatoes in separate boxes by breed," Tim says, but he soon realized that by mixing them all up within one box meant he left town with an empty truck. A farmer's dream fulfilled.

Tim Stark and Daniel Boulud

TYSON COLE, *Uchi,* Austin, Texas

DAVID ANDERSON, *Bluebonnet Hydroponic Produce,* Schertz, Texas (salad greens)

Baby Romaine Salad with Edamame, Jalapeño Dressing, and Yellow Bell Pepper Pipérade

Mini red romaine lettuce is a unique variety of romaine, with a butter lettuce texture and deep red, shiny leaves. Hearty and healthy, the flavor of the edamame (soybeans) in the dressing sets off the sweetness of the yellow peppers. You can find kombu seaweed at most health-food stores.

SERVES 4

FOR THE SUSHI VINEGAR
½ ounce kombu seaweed
⅓ cup rice vinegar
2 tablespoons sugar
½ teaspoon coarse salt

FOR THE JALAPEÑO DRESSING
3 jalapeños, 1 finely chopped
¼ cup extra-virgin olive oil
1 cup shelled edamame (soybeans)
3 cloves garlic, roughly chopped

1 shallot, roughly chopped
1 tablespoon rice vinegar

FOR THE PIPÉRADE
½ cup extra-virgin olive oil
2 yellow bell peppers, diced
3 cloves garlic, minced
3 medium shallots, minced
½ teaspoon paprika
Coarse salt
1 tablespoon finely chopped fresh
  flat-leaf parsley

FOR THE ROMAINE SALAD
1 tablespoon fresh lemon juice
3 tablespoons extra-virgin olive oil
Coarse salt and freshly ground
  black pepper
2 heads baby romaine lettuce,
  leaves separated, kept whole,
  rinsed, and dried

MAKE THE SUSHI VINEGAR
Wipe the seaweed with wet paper towels until all salt sediment has been removed. Combine the seaweed, vinegar, sugar, and salt in a small saucepan and cook over medium heat, stirring constantly, until the sugar and salt have completely dissolved. Remove from the heat and discard the seaweed; let cool.

MAKE THE DRESSING
1. Over an open flame or in a 400°F oven, roast the 2 whole jalapeños until they're blackened and tender. Put them in a small bowl, cover with plastic wrap, and allow them to steam (this will make their skins easier to remove).

2. Heat the olive oil in a large sauté pan over medium heat. Add the edamame, garlic, and shallots, and cook until tender, about 5 minutes. Strain the mixture, reserving the cooking oil, and put the edamame mixture into a blender. Peel and seed the roasted jalapeños and add them to the edamame, along with the chopped jalapeños. Blend, adding just enough water to make a smooth purée. With the blender running, pour in the rice vinegar in a thin stream, followed by the reserved oil to emulsify. With the blender still running, add as much water as necessary to achieve a mayonnaise-like consistency for the dressing.

IT'S ALIVE!

Out in the hill country of Texas lie three greenhouses that contain some of the most beautiful, healthy, fresh, and soilless grown lettuces, basils, and microgreens a chef could ever hope for. In place of the soil is a constant stream of nutrient-rich water that comes to the plants instead of the plants using energy to find them. The water can be adjusted any time to raise or lower the pH balance so the plants can live at optimal nutrient uptake around the clock.

While the initial build took enough PVC pipe to make the crew of Bluebonnet Hydroponics the most favored customer of the local Home Depot℠, the carbon footprint and sustainability (water is recycled) of the farm make it an ideal way to work in the heat of Texas. The hydroponic growing system is also about nine times more efficient than growing in soil. Besides, there are no pesticides or herbicides, and the plants are shipped live to clients.

In a traditional situation, it may take a typical spring mix 5 days to arrive in Austin, Texas, from California, with its shelf life being only 2 more days after that. But because Bluebonnet's produce is pulled from the water and placed in a Baggie® with water (a rubber band secures it), the same typical spring mix will last 2 to 3 weeks in a chef's cooler. And not only does this extended life help the chef keep his costs from waste down but the greens have distinct individual taste. While a chef may not hang his reputation on a salad, he can create a personal mix that becomes more than just a delivery vehicle for getting dressing to your mouth.

Bluebonnet is also a great partner for a chef who wants to work closely with a grower. A chef can be jaded after years of seeing the same old greens, but the Bluebonnet greens usually make that same chef's eyes pop with excitement. When chef Tyson Cole of Uchi in Austin asked that the farm grow mizuna to full size (it's usually harvested as a microgreen for garnishes), the plant put out a unique serrated-edge leaf that the chef cooked with for its strong radish-like flavor. This kind of flexibility, consistency, and low environmental impact make Bluebonnet a great model for the future of farming.

MAKE THE PIPÉRADE

Heat the olive oil in a large skillet over medium heat. Add the bell peppers, garlic, and shallots and cook until tender, about 8 minutes. Remove from the heat and stir in the paprika. Season to taste with salt. When the mixture has cooled, stir in the parsley.

ASSEMBLE THE SALAD

Just before serving, dress the romaine salad. In a medium bowl, whisk the lemon juice and olive oil, season with salt and pepper, and add to the romaine; toss to coat. Portion the edamame jalapeño dressing evenly among 4 plates, stack the baby lettuce leaves on top of the dressing, and spoon the pipérade over the lettuce.

MICHAEL ANTHONY, *Gramercy Tavern,* New York City

ZAID KURDIEH, *Norwich Meadows Farm,* Norwich, New York (vegetables)

Warm Vegetable Salad

Michael's salad is an impressive use of vegetables, with various shades of beautiful colors. This dish uses the same vegetables cooked and raw for two different but distinct tastes. The tangy, creamy dressing enhances the sweetness of the carrots and beets while mellowing the peppery spice in the radishes.

SERVES 4

FOR THE WARM VEGETABLES
8 baby beets, preferably a mix
  of yellow, red, and chiogga, washed
Coarse salt
8 radishes, washed and thinly sliced
8 'Thumbelina' or tiny carrots, peeled
  and cut in half lengthwise
8 baby turnips, well scrubbed,
  trimmed, and cut into wedges
1 tablespoon honey
4 cups vegetable stock or water
1 clove garlic
1 sprig fresh thyme

FOR THE YOGURT WALNUT DRESSING
1 cup plain yogurt
¼ cup finely chopped mixed fresh
  herbs, such as flat-leaf parsley,
  dill, and tarragon
2 tablespoons walnut oil
2 tablespoons olive oil
2 tablespoons toasted walnuts,
  roughly chopped
Coarse salt
2 tablespoons fresh lemon juice;
  plus more as needed

FOR THE RAW VEGETABLES
6 large radishes, washed, trimmed,
  and sliced paper thin
1 small turnip, well scrubbed, peeled,
  and thinly sliced
1 small sunchoke, washed, peeled,
  and thinly sliced

1 tablespoon shaved Parmigiano-
  Reggiano, for garnish

COOK THE WARM VEGETABLES

1. Heat the oven to 375°F. Season the beets with salt and wrap them in aluminum foil. Roast the beets for 15 to 20 minutes (or until a paring knife easily slides in and out). Peel the beets, cut into wedges, and set aside in a medium bowl.

2. Combine all remaining ingredients in a saucepan and cook over medium heat until a syrupy glaze forms, about 7 minutes. Remove from the heat and keep warm.

MAKE THE DRESSING
Combine all ingredients except for the lemon juice. Use up to ¼ cup water to thin the dressing to the desired thickness; mix well.

TO SERVE

1. Evenly distribute the cooked vegetables in the center of 4 serving plates; surround with the raw vegetables. Garnish with the Parmigiano shavings.

2. Whisk the lemon juice into the dressing. Drizzle the dressing over the warm and raw vegetables (add more lemon juice to thin the dressing as needed) or serve alongside the salad. Serve immediately.

BARBARA LYNCH, *No. 9 Park,* Boston, Massachusetts

CHRIS KURTH, *Siena Farms,* Sudbury, Massachusetts (beets)

Beet Salad with Chèvre and Black Olive Croutons

Siena Farms grows stunning organic beets in many varieties. This simple yet sophisticated salad lets the beets' flavor shine, complemented by the tangy goat cheese and hearty croutons. Barbara and Chris say to choose whatever color and size beets you want based on your mood.

SERVES 4

2 pounds medium beets, scrubbed and stems trimmed

Coarse salt and freshly ground black pepper

4 tablespoons extra-virgin olive oil

1 tablespoon plus 1 teaspoon fresh lemon juice

1 thick slice country white bread, crusts removed and cut into ½-inch cubes (about 1 cup)

1 tablespoon tapenade or black olive paste

1 bunch baby lettuces, cut into 1-inch pieces (about 2 cups)

2 tablespoons finely chopped fresh flat-leaf parsley

½ pound chèvre or other goat's milk cheese, such as Bûcheron, at room temperature

1. Heat the oven to 425°F. Put the beets in an ovenproof pan, season with salt and pepper, and cover the pan with aluminum foil. Bake until the beets are tender when pierced with a paring knife, 50 to 60 minutes. Allow the beets to cool covered (steam helps the skin to loosen), then peel them and cut into 1-inch dice. Put in a medium bowl and mix in 1 tablespoon of the olive oil and 1 teaspoon of the lemon juice; season to taste with salt and pepper.

2. Heat the oven to 350°F. In a medium bowl, mix the bread cubes with the tapenade and 1 tablespoon oil. Spread the bread cubes on a baking sheet and bake until crisp and lightly golden brown, 10 to 12 minutes.

3. To serve, combine the remaining 2 tablespoons olive oil with the remaining 1 tablespoon lemon juice in a medium bowl. Add the baby lettuces, season with a little salt and pepper, and toss to lightly dress. Mix the parsley in with the beets. Portion the baby lettuces among 4 plates, evenly portion the beets on top of the lettuces, add the croutons, and crumble the cheese over the top.

GROWING A RAINBOW

After being raised on his family's farm in Sudbury, Massachusetts, Chris Kurth's parents advised him to not go into the farming business. They had first-hand experience with the endless work involved, the uncertainties of weather, and the ever-changing ways to make enough money to live on. But with 10 acres of family land rich from soils deposited by the Sudbury River and 40 more acres next door available for lease, there was no stopping Chris.

It didn't hurt that this soil was only 25 miles from Boston and home to a growing legion of farmers' market shoppers. Chris also had a card up his sleeve—his wife, Ana Sortun, the award-winning chef/owner of Oleana, who provided a link to other chefs in Boston, like Barbara Lynch and her market called Plum Produce. Four years later, Chris is now supplying 15 restaurants and a hearty CSA program along with the local farmers' markets.

Siena Farms is home to a variety of produce, including rainbow cauliflower, golden raspberries, yellow and purple carrots, tomatoes, fennel, and arugula, as well as sunflowers and dahlias that give the Siena booth at local farmers' markets its color. Diversity is the name of the game in farming, and Chris has figured out the game.

Chris only practices sustainable farming—he doesn't use any chemical herbicides, pesticides, fungicides, or fertilizers. The land is kept rich with a supply of naturally composted manure and plant matter as well as organic fertilizer. Chris believes that his farm's practices of growing organic, keeping the soil rich, and harvesting within 24 hours of sale keeps his produce at the highest level of quality for his clients.

Barbara Lynch and Chris Kurth

NANCY SILVERTON, *Osteria Mozza,* Los Angeles, California

MIMMO BRUNO, *DiStefano Cheese,* Baldwin Park, California (burrata)

Burrata with Speck, Peas, and Mint

Spring ingredients are added as a delicate addition to a rather simple meat and cheese pairing. Burrata was invented as a way to use leftover curds after making mozzarella. The mozzarella is formed into a pouch and filled with these creamy curds. Speck, an air-dried ham from northern Italy, is available at specialty shops.

SERVES 4

1½ cups fresh peas
½ cup medium-size mint leaves, julienned
2 tablespoons fresh lemon juice
4 tablespoons extra-virgin olive oil

8 tablespoons freshly grated Parmigiano-Reggiano
Coarse salt and freshly ground black pepper

1 pound speck (about 16 slices)
1 pound fresh burrata, cut into 8 slices (it may not cut into perfect slices)

1. Heat a small saucepan of water over medium-high heat; add the peas and cook for 2 minutes. Drain and cool under cold running water.

2. In a medium bowl, combine the peas, mint, lemon juice, olive oil, 4 tablespoons of the Parmigiano, and salt and pepper to taste. Mix well but gently until thoroughly combined.

3. Arrange 4 slices of speck in a circular pattern on 4 small plates; alternatively, you can arrange all slices of speck folded over on a large serving dish. Arrange 2 slices of burrata in the center of each plate of speck or evenly on the large dish, if using.

4. Pile the pea and mint mixture onto the burrata, allowing a bit to fall onto the speck. Sprinkle 1 tablespoon of Parmigiano evenly over the top of each plate or over the large serving dish.

LACHLAN MACKINNON-PATTERSON, *Frasca Food & Wine,* Boulder, Colorado

BOB & MIKE MUNSON, *Munson Farms,* Boulder, Colorado (sweet corn)

Chopped Salad with Corn Vinaigrette and Frico Cheese Crisps

Sweet corn with a subtle vinaigrette adds texture and taste to a salad of assertive greens. Frico is a northern Italian cracker served as a snack. Montasio vecchio is a traditional Italian cow's milk cheese and has a mild flavor like Swiss but with more of a texture like Asiago, an Italian hard cheese.

SERVES 4

2 tablespoons grape seed oil
1 small clove garlic, minced
½ cup fresh corn kernels
   (about 1 small ear of corn)
Coarse salt and freshly ground
   black pepper

3 tablespoons red-wine vinegar
1 medium lemon, juiced
1 tablespoon minced fresh chives
1 pinch chopped fresh oregano
2 cups grated Montasio vecchio
   or Parmigiano-Reggiano
¼ cup olive oil

6 cups mixed salad greens (arugula,
   radicchio, and frisée), washed well,
   dried, and roughly chopped
1 cup julienned hard salami
   (about ¼ pound)
1 cup chopped provolone (about
   ¼ pound)

GROWING HAPPINESS

Bob Munson's epiphany came to him more than 30 years ago as he was driving through Amish country in Pennsylvania on the tail end of a New York business trip. He crested a hill and came upon a farmer and his two young daughters working by the side of the road. The girls looked about the same age as his two boys. At that moment, he realized he really wanted to spend more time with his sons doing something wholesome and worthwhile, like this father was doing with his children. Bob got out of his car, introduced himself to this farmer, and walked the fields with the family. He knew then what he had to do. He went home to Boulder, Colorado, and bought a tractor.

Luckily, Bob knew what to do with a tractor, since he came from a line of farmers ten generations deep. He grew up on a big corn and soybean farm in Eastern Illinois and was always frustrated that his family's produce wasn't actually feeding anyone. When he started his own farm in 1975, he planted hearty things—corn, squash, pumpkins, and beans—and began to feed Boulder County.

Today, he runs the 100-plus-acre Munson Farms with his two sons, Mike and Chris, both of whom have returned to the farm after separate careers, like their father. Both sons maintain full-time jobs, like their father did before them, working the fields in the early morning and then again in the evening when they come home from their day jobs.

The Munsons grow a broad range of vegetables but are best known for their

1. Heat the grape seed oil in a medium skillet over medium heat, then add the garlic and cook for 1 minute. Add the corn and cook until tender, 3 to 5 minutes. Let cool, season with salt and pepper to taste, and then add 1 tablespoon of the vinegar, the lemon juice, chives, and oregano. Set aside.

2. To make the frico, heat a large nonstick skillet over medium heat, sprinkle one thin layer of cheese (approximately 4 inches in diameter) in the skillet, and cook for 1 to 3 minutes, or until the cheese is melted and golden brown. Alternatively, sprinkle the cheese in a thin, even layer on a microwave-safe plate and microwave on high for 1 minute, or until golden brown.

3. Using a spatula, carefully slide the cooked frico onto a paper towel to absorb any grease and to harden. Repeat until all the cheese is used. Once cool and hard, break each frico into medium-size pieces. The frico can be made a day ahead and stored in an airtight container.

4. In a bowl, whisk the remaining 2 tablespoons vinegar with the olive oil. Season with salt and pepper. Add the salad greens, salami, and provolone to the corn mixture, then pour the dressing on top and stir to combine. To serve, portion the salad among 4 plates and serve with the frico pieces on the side.

50 varieties of sweet corn and 60 varieties of winter squash and pumpkins. They sell the majority of their produce right from their own farmstand, but also vend at the farmers' market in downtown Boulder, in local supermarkets, and, in the last two years, directly to area restaurants, with that piece of the business spreading entirely through word of mouth.

There's still some incredulity in Bob's voice when he talks about Boulder, its remarkable growing climate and its blessed residents, whom he describes as the happiest, healthiest people you'll ever meet. He takes deep pride in his community and deep satisfaction in playing his part, in doing something tangible that helps the people of Boulder thrive. Walking though his fields in the morning, looking out at the mountains, he says, "This is as close as you'll get to paradise on this Earth."

JEAN-GEORGES VONGERICHTEN, *Jean Georges*, New York City

NANCY MacNAMARA, *Honey Locust Farm*, Newburgh, New York (baby greens)

Mesclun with Shrimp, Avocado, and Creamy Champagne Dressing

Nancy has made an art of growing mesclun, the mixture of young field salad greens. Her balance of the mix, which features both strong-flavored and mild-tasting greens, is admired by chefs. The dressing for this salad is a simple truffle vinaigrette, allowing the flavor of the greens to come through, with a decadent creamy sauce for the shrimp and avocado.

SERVES 4

1 shallot, minced
4 tablespoons plus 1 teaspoon
   Champagne vinegar
Coarse salt
1 cup heavy cream
5 tablespoons unsalted butter,
   chilled and cut in cubes
Cayenne

1 teaspoon soy sauce
1 tablespoon truffle juice
2 tablespoons fresh lemon juice
Freshly ground white pepper
5 tablespoons extra-virgin olive oil
1 pound jumbo shrimp (about 12),
   tails left intact

6 cups mixed baby greens, preferably
   baby Italian mixed greens, like
   escarole, radicchio, and arugula
2 large tomatoes, diced
¼ pound fresh enoki mushrooms
1 avocado, pitted and sliced

1. In a medium saucepan over low heat, combine the shallots and 4 tablespoons of the vinegar, season with salt, and cook until the liquid is reduced to just 1 tablespoon. Add the cream and cook until reduced by two-thirds, about 10 minutes. Add 4 tablespoons of the butter, piece by piece, continually whisking until each piece is completely incorporated. Whisk in the remaining 1 teaspoon vinegar and a pinch of cayenne. Keep the Champagne vinegar sauce warm.

2. In a medium bowl, combine the soy sauce, truffle juice, and lemon juice, and season with white pepper. While continuously whisking, slowly drizzle in the olive oil until emulsified.

3. Heat the remaining 1 tablespoon butter in a small sauté pan over medium heat. Season the shrimp with salt and pepper, then add to the pan and cook for 1 to 2 minutes per side, until just opaque; remove the shrimp from the pan to cool.

4. In a large bowl, combine and dress the mixed greens, tomatoes, and mushrooms with the truffle lemon vinaigrette. In a small bowl, season the avocado with salt and pepper. Divide the dressed mixed greens among serving plates and top with the avocado and shrimp. Drizzle the Champagne vinegar sauce over the shrimp.

WILD HERBS

It's unusual these days for a very small farm to be profitable. But thanks to her work with some A-list restaurants in New York City, Nancy MacNamara of Honey Locust Farm is doing just that. Contracts with restaurants including Corton, Morimoto, Nobu Fifty Seven, and Del Posto, as well as a long relationship with Jean-Georges Vongerichten, let Nancy focus her 2½ acres on herbs, heirloom tomatoes, and a few other specialty ingredients.

Nancy started by working the farm with her dad, who grew raspberries, lettuce, pansies, nasturtiums, and mesclun. She branched off on her own for creative reasons (Nancy is also an accomplished photographer) and to further her interest in Mexican ingredients as well as herbs for teas, which she now bags and sells at farmers' markets.

Nancy meets with her chef clients in January or February, when both the restaurants and her farm are quiet and resting. Together they plan what Nancy will grow for them, giving the chefs "a chance to previsualize the year" and Nancy a sound financial base with which to run her farm. The contracts with the chefs specify the dates that the produce will be available throughout the season.

Nancy first started working with Chef Vongerichten in 1985 as he was building his restaurant empire. As plans came together for his signature restaurant, Jean Georges, he knew he wanted to have a reliable herb grower to enhance the flavoring of his sauces and garnishes. Nancy was his go-to person for these wild herbs.

Nancy MacNamara and
Jean-Georges Vongerichten

ERIC RIPERT, *Le Bernardin,* New York City

EBERHARD MÜLLER & PAULETTE SATUR, *Satur Farms,* Cutchogue, New York (arugula)

Salted Cod Salad with Preserved Lemons and Arugula Pesto

Wild arugula, known as Sylvatica, has spiked leaves and a distinctive pungent taste, one that Satur Farms is known for and that European chefs love. This is a homemade salt cod, but you can also find it in specialty stores sold as bacalao. Smoked salt adds a unique, deep, smoky flavor.

SERVES 4

FOR THE SALTED COD SALAD
Two 6-ounce codfish fillets
1 teaspoon smoked salt (optional)
  or kosher salt
2 tablespoons plus ½ teaspoon
  extra-virgin olive oil
Freshly ground white pepper
Piment d'Espelette or cayenne
2 teaspoons finely chopped
  fresh chives
2 teaspoons minced red onions
  (about ¼ medium red onion)
2 teaspoons sherry vinegar

FOR THE OVEN-ROASTED TOMATO
1 medium tomato
Coarse salt and freshly ground
  white pepper
1 tablespoon olive oil
1 sprig fresh thyme

FOR THE ARUGULA PESTO
2 pieces Preserved Lemons (1 inch
  each, peel only), rinsed well
  (recipe follows)
¼ cup extra-virgin olive oil; more
  as needed

1 small bunch arugula, cleaned
  and trimmed (about 1 packed cup)
Coarse salt and freshly ground
  white pepper

FOR THE GARNISH
4 cloves garlic
Coarse salt
½ cup canola oil, for frying
¼ pound spicy Spanish chorizo,
  thinly sliced
¼ cup sliced almonds
Baby arugula leaves (approximately
  1 cup)

MAKE THE COD SALAD
1. To make the salted cod, season both sides of the cod with the smoked or kosher salt, and lay the fillets on a paper towel–lined plate. Cover and refrigerate for 3 hours.

2. Heat the grill or a heavy-bottomed skillet over high heat. Rinse and dry the cod, then lightly coat the fillets with ½ teaspoon of the olive oil and season with white pepper and piment d'Espelette or cayenne. Cook the cod for 3 to 4 minutes on each side. Take care not to overcook the fish; it should be medium rare. Transfer to a medium bowl and put in the refrigerator to stop the cooking. Once cool, gently flake the fish apart, then add the remaining olive oil, the chives, red onions, and sherry vinegar to the fish and mix gently, trying not to break the fish up too much. Season to taste, adding more salt if necessary. Return to the refrigerator and let marinate for at least 30 minutes.

MAKE THE OVEN-ROASTED TOMATO
1. Heat the oven to 250°F. Slice the tomato ½ inch thick and line a small baking sheet with parchment paper. Arrange the tomatoes on the paper. Season them with salt and pepper, drizzle with olive oil, and sprinkle with the thyme leaves.

2. Bake the tomatoes until they look like they've collapsed and flattened a bit as well as taken on a hint of color, about 1 to 1½ hours. Transfer to a plastic container and store in the refrigerator until ready to use.

MAKE THE PESTO

Fill a small saucepan with water, add the preserved lemons, and bring to a simmer. Cook for 5 minutes, then drain off the liquid. Put the cooked preserved lemons, the olive oil, and arugula in a blender and purée until smooth, adding a little more olive oil if needed for a smooth consistency. Season to taste with salt and pepper.

MAKE THE GARNISH

1. Slice the garlic cloves paper thin and lightly blanch in a small saucepan of salted water, for 10 seconds. Drain and pat the garlic slices dry. Heat the canola oil in a medium saucepan until it reaches 200°F on an instant-read thermometer or when it sizzles when a piece of garlic is added. Fry the garlic slices until golden and crisp, about 1 minute. Remove with a slotted spoon and drain on a paper towel–lined plate.

2. Heat a large skillet over low heat and gently render the oil from the chorizo slices until crisp, about 8 minutes. Strain, reserving the chorizo oil.

3. Wipe out the skillet, then add the sliced almonds and toast for 2 minutes, stirring, until lightly browned. Remove and set aside.

TO SERVE

Spoon a line of pesto down the center of each serving plate and lay the cod salad down the middle of the plate. Cut the oven-roasted tomato slices into ½-inch pieces and place them on each piece of fish. Sprinkle the toasted almonds and garlic chips over the cod; arrange the arugula on top of the cod salad and drizzle 1 teaspoon of chorizo oil around each plate. Serve immediately.

Preserved Lemons

5 cups coarse salt
5 tablespoons sugar
6 large lemons

1. Combine the salt and sugar and mix well.

2. Trim the ends off each lemon, then cut into quarters lengthwise.

3. Put half of the salt-sugar mixture in a medium bowl and add the lemons, tossing to coat.

4. Put about a quarter of the remaining salt-sugar mixture in a large plastic container. Press the lemons into the mixture, packing more of the salt-sugar mix between and around the lemons. Continue to layer the remaining lemons in the salt-sugar mixture until all the lemons are covered. Be sure to leave enough salt-sugar mix to completely cover the last layer of lemons.

5. Tightly seal the container. Refrigerate for at least 2 weeks before using, though the lemons are best after 3 months and will keep refrigerated for up to a year (keep them in the salt-sugar mixture until ready to use).

6. To use, thoroughly rinse the lemons with water. Cut away all of the flesh from the rind of the lemon; discard the flesh. Leave the rind whole, or mince or julienne as needed. Lightly blanch the rind (before cutting) if using as a garnish that will not be cooked.

continued

FROM CHEF TO FARMER

In the late 1980s, Eberhard Müller was part of the dream team heading up the kitchen at the highly regarded four-star restaurant Le Bernardin in New York City. After many years he moved to the next powerhouse of its time, Lutèce, where as executive chef he was charged with modernizing the menu and reinvigorating the restaurant back to its world-renowned status.

During one of his daily strolls in the dining room to greet guests, Eberhard stopped at a table and began chatting with local wine distributor Paulette Satur. Small talk eventually led to marriage (Paulette admits "I love food, that's why I married a chef"), which led the couple to buying a farm in Cutchogue, Long Island, New York.

Initially, the idea was that Paulette would return to her farming roots (she grew up on a farm in Pennsylvania) and Satur Farms would supply Lutèce and other four-star restaurants with local high-quality ingredients such as micro lettuces, wild herbs, and long, white European-style leeks. But the plan changed when the workload of farming on weekends, deliveries on Monday mornings, and full-time jobs all week felt like a recipe for an early death. So Paulette and Eberhard slowly expanded the farm and added staff and became full-time farmers.

Now, not only do they provide many of New York's best restaurants with their produce, but their products are sold to the public at specialty food stores on the East Coast as well as being featured by freshdirect®, New York City's high-quality grocery delivery service.

Eric Ripert and Paulette Satur

PAUL KAHAN, *Blackbird,* Chicago, Illinois

DAVID CLEVERDON, *Kinnikinnick Farm,* Caledonia, Illinois (arugula)

Crispy Smelts with Sun Gold Tomatoes and Arugula

Smelts are often fried and eaten whole, complete with head, fins, and tails. They are a sign of spring in the Great Lakes region of the United States. Paul loves the quick blast of heat from the peppery, nutty flavors of Dave's "strapleaf" arugula. Paul infuses his oil with garlic rather than adding fresh garlic to the aïoli.

SERVES 4

1 cup all-purpose flour
1 cup finely crumbled salt-and-vinegar potato chips
3 large eggs
32 tiny smelts, 3 to 4 inches in length, heads removed (about ½ pound)

4 to 6 cups vegetable oil for frying
Coarse salt and freshly ground black pepper
1 pint yellow cherry tomatoes, such as Sun Golds, halved
4 cups small arugula leaves, washed
4 small shallots, thinly sliced

2 tablespoons fresh lemon juice
3 tablespoons extra-virgin olive oil
Garlic Aïoli (recipe follows)
½ cup shaved Parmigiano-Reggiano, for garnish

1. In a medium shallow bowl, mix the flour and potato chip crumbs. In another medium shallow bowl, beat the eggs with ½ cup water. Dip the smelts in the egg mixture, shake off excess egg, and then dredge in the flour-potato chip mixture. Place on a plate; continue until all smelts have been coated.

2. Heat about 2 inches of vegetable oil in a medium skillet or 4- to 5-quart heavy-bottomed pot over medium-high heat to 375°F. Check that the oil is hot enough for frying by dipping the tail of one fish into the oil—it should sizzle. Fry the fish in batches (don't pack them in), cooking on one side until golden brown, about 1 to 2 minutes, and then turning over to cook the other side, about another 1 to 2 minutes. Remove the fish with a slotted spoon and drain on a paper towel–lined plate; season lightly with salt. Repeat until all the fish are cooked.

3. In a medium bowl, combine the tomatoes, arugula, and shallots. In a small bowl, whisk the lemon juice with the olive oil. Season to taste with salt and pepper. Pour the dressing over the tomato-arugula mixture and toss to coat.

4. To serve, spoon 1 to 2 teaspoons of Garlic Aïoli onto each serving plate. Top with 8 fried smelts and spoon the tomato salad on the side of the fish. Top each plate with a few pieces of shaved cheese.

continued

Garlic Aïoli

YIELDS 1 CUP

1 cup extra-virgin olive oil
6 cloves garlic
1 large egg
1 egg yolk

1 medium lemon, juiced and zested
1 teaspoon chopped fresh
   flat-leaf parsley
1 teaspoon chopped fresh chervil

Coarse salt and freshly ground
   black pepper

1. Combine the oil and garlic in a small saucepan. Bring to a boil over medium heat. Reduce the heat to low and cook the garlic until it is very soft, 10 to 15 minutes. Remove from the heat, cover, and let cool for 15 minutes.

2. In the bowl of a food processor, combine the egg and yolk and process for 30 seconds. Remove the garlic cloves from the oil and slowly drizzle in the oil with the machine running until the aïoli begins to thicken, about 1 minute. Add the lemon juice, zest, and herbs, and season with salt and pepper.

LIVING THE DREAM

Five old washing machines lined up outside a barn is a strange sight indeed. But when you look inside at the empty tub you realize that these are simply oversized salad spinners for drying leafy greens just picked and washed in the field. This is when you know you are on a different kind of farm.

Dave Cleverdon, owner of Kinnikinnick Farm, came to farming after years spent working in the rough and tumble world of Chicago politics, getting outsiders elected in a machine-run city. He also spent time working in the civil rights movement and did a stint on The Chicago Board of Trade. He calls himself and his workers "misfits with an incredible sense of agency" whenever he considers the kind of person who would take on the work of organic farming.

Dave fell in love with growing vegetables when he bought a weekend house in Wisconsin. The garden he started soon turned into what Dave called "an insane idea" of buying a 170-acre farm on the Kinnikinnick Creek in Caledonia, Illinois. The farm started slowly, with Dave and his wife Susan living in a trailer on the land as they readied the buildings and let the land show them the way it should be worked.

They made mistakes, growing too much variety, planting at the wrong time, and trying to grow difficult crops like corn, eggplant, and cucumbers (too many insects to fight without chemical help). Eventually they got the rhythm right and figured out how to get from seed to market with an efficiency

that has kept them busy and growing for 14 years.

The farm's philosophy is simple: Deliver beautiful vegetables to market and compost the rest. Dave takes great care to cool and hydrate all his most sensitive products as fast as possible to keep not only their beautiful color but also, and most important, their superior taste. His arugula has a fragrance and taste that make it practically jump out of a bowl, and his asparagus is so good straight from the ground that it's hard to stop eating it. Dave's eye for detail, love of his crops' freshness, and big personality have made him a favorite supplier to some of Chicago's best restaurants, like Paul Kahan's Blackbird.

Dave Cleverdon and Paul Kahan

TORY MILLER, *L'Etoile,* Madison, Wisconsin

MATT SMITH, *Blue Valley Gardens,* Blue Mounds, Wisconsin (asparagus)

Asparagus–Country Ham Bundles with Toasted Pecans and Citrus Vinaigrette

Tory features local ingredients on every menu at L'Etoile and embraces seasonal eating. Matt, known as the Asparagus Man because he grows jumbo green and white asparagus, shares Tory's commitment for high-quality food. In the spring Tory creates an all-asparagus themed tasting menu at L'Etoile with Matt's asparagus.

SERVES 4

FOR THE CITRUS VINAIGRETTE
1 medium lemon, juiced, and zest cut into fine julienne
3 medium oranges, juiced (½ cup), and zest of 1 cut into fine julienne
1 tablespoon sugar
1 teaspoon Dijon mustard
Coarse salt and freshly ground black pepper
6 tablespoons peanut oil
1 tablespoon finely chopped flat-leaf parsley

FOR THE ASPARAGUS-HAM BUNDLES
¼ cup pecan pieces
1 pound large asparagus spears (about 16), trimmed and peeled
½ pound thinly sliced country ham (about 16 slices)
½ pound goat cheese, crumbled (about 1 cup)
¼ cup fresh tarragon leaves, roughly chopped

MAKE THE VINAIGRETTE

1. Bring a small saucepan of water to a boil; add the lemon zest, cook for 30 seconds, and drain and set aside to cool. Put the orange juice, orange zest, and sugar in a small saucepan and cook over medium-low heat until reduced by two-thirds (you'll have about 3 tablespoons), about 3 minutes. Remove from the heat.

2. In a bowl, whisk together the lemon juice, mustard, and salt and pepper to taste. Whisk in the oil, then the reduced orange juice and zest. Just before serving, stir in the lemon zest and parsley.

PREPARE THE ASPARAGUS-HAM BUNDLES

1. In a medium skillet over medium heat, toast the pecans for about 3 minutes until fragment. Set aside.

2. Bring a large skillet of salted water to a boil and have ready a large bowl of ice water. Cook the asparagus for 2 minutes, then transfer to the ice water bath to stop the cooking. Drain and pat dry the asparagus. Wrap each asparagus spear in one slice of ham. Heat a sauté pan over medium-high heat and cook the asparagus-filled ham on all sides, about a minute total, until crisp.

3. To serve, place 4 asparagus-ham bundles on each plate with a bit of crumbled cheese and toasted pecans sprinkled over the top. Dress lightly with the vinaigrette and scatter the tarragon leaves over the top.

FEEDING THE NEXT GENERATION

Can an organic farmer be in a better place than Madison, Wisconsin? With the local university making Michael Pollan's *In Defense of Food* a mandatory read for freshmen, a farmer would seemingly have to just sit back and wait for customers to overrun him. While Matt Smith of Blue Valley Gardens would not go quite that far, he does admit that a smart university town with two Slow Food chapters, a couple of great restaurants, and a school full of college kids who cook is good for business.

Matt's farm has been certified organic for ten years, growing asparagus, raspberries, strawberries, mushrooms, and annuals like potatoes and onions. He also raises chickens and ducks as well as the biggest of all poultry, tur-

keys. Matt is quite proud of the heritage turkeys that he raises on pasture for 33 weeks (a double-breasted white tom grows to harvest weight in close to half the time, but the growth of edible meat is out of proportion to the growth of flavorful fats). Once again craft wins out over quantity when it comes to flavor. His local chef, Tory Miller of L'Etoile, is so fond of the birds that he packed them up and brought them to New York City for a James Beard House Thanksgiving meal.

Matt has seen the change in consumers' mentality firsthand at his local farmers' market. He says he now sees shoppers with long lists for a week's worth of food rather than just the special-meal shoppers. Over the last four years his new and repeat clients

include college students who are insisting on organic over conventionally grown produce.

Living in a climate with a short growing period does have a serious downside, though. Matt laments the fact that he has to work the most when the weather is the best. But he quickly adds, "It's better than punching holes in metal at a factory."

Soups

DANIEL BOULUD, *Daniel,* New York City

TIM STARK, *Eckerton Hill Farm,* Hamburg, Pennsylvania (tomatoes)

Chilled Tomato Soup with Aged Feta and Olives

Daniel uses a variety of tomatoes when available and likes Cherokee Purple, Aunt Ruby's, and Green Zebra for this soup. Sun Golds, a little cherry tomato, are Tim's favorite for garnish. The feta and olives add the extra salt needed to bring out the pure tomato flavor.

SERVES 6

3 pounds ripe tomatoes, preferably Sun Golds or other heirlooms, cored
3 tablespoons extra-virgin olive oil
1 small onion, diced
½ cup thickly sliced leeks, white part only (1 small leek)
¼ cup diced fresh fennel
¼ cup diced celery
1 large red bell pepper, split and seeded

3 large cloves garlic, chopped
Bouquet garni (2 sprigs fresh thyme, 1 bay leaf, and 2 sprigs fresh basil tied together with butcher's twine)
1 tablespoon tomato paste
3 cups chicken or vegetable broth
Hot sauce
Celery salt
Coarse salt and freshly ground white pepper

FOR THE GARNISH
⅓ cup feta cheese, preferably barrel aged, crumbled
⅓ cup black Taggiasche (Ligurian) or Niçoise olives, pitted and roughly chopped
12 fresh basil leaves, julienned
Extra-virgin olive oil

1. Bring a large pot of water to a boil and plunge in the fresh tomatoes for 1 minute. Drain and when cool enough to handle, slip off and discard the skins and seeds. Roughly chop the tomatoes, put in a bowl with their juices, and set aside.

2. Heat the oil in a large pot over medium heat. Add the onions, leeks, fennel, celery, red peppers, garlic, and bouquet garni. Cook until the vegetables are soft, stirring occasionally, about 15 minutes. Reduce the heat to medium, stir in the tomato paste, and cook for another 2 minutes. Add the chicken or vegetable broth, bring to a boil, and simmer for 20 minutes. Add the chopped fresh tomatoes, return to a boil, then lower the heat and simmer for 5 minutes.

3. Remove the vegetable-broth mixture from the heat and let cool. Transfer to a large bowl, cover, and refrigerate until cold, 1 to 2 hours.

4. Remove and discard the bouquet garni. In a food processor or blender, purée the soup (in batches if necessary) until smooth Season to taste with hot sauce, celery salt, and salt and pepper; cover and chill until ready to serve. The soup will keep in the refrigerator, tightly covered, for a few days.

5. To serve, ladle the soup into individual bowls or one large serving bowl and garnish with the feta, olives, basil, and a drizzle of olive oil.

MICHAEL PSILAKIS, *Anthos,* New York City

PETER SKOTIDAKIS, *Skotidakis Goat Farm,* St. Eugene, Ontario, Canada (yogurt)

Chilled Cucumber–Yogurt Soup with Candied Fennel and Lemon Gelée

Greek yogurt is thick and creamy and has a mild flavor because of the high fat content. Even the low-fat version is rich in taste. Michael builds on a variety of flavors and textures of sweet, tart, and creamy in this soup. Much of this dish can be made in advance.

SERVES 4

FOR THE SOUP
6 large English cucumbers, 3 peeled
1 tablespoon finely chopped fresh dill
1 tablespoon finely chopped fresh mint
1 tablespoon finely chopped fresh
    flat-leaf parsley
½ cup goat's milk yogurt
2 tablespoons extra-virgin olive oil
Coarse salt and freshly ground
    black pepper
1 tablespoon Champagne vinegar

FOR THE LEMON GELÉE
2½ teaspoons or one 7-gram packet
    unflavored gelatin powder
1 cup fresh lemon juice
1 tablespoon sugar
1 teaspoon coarse salt
1 teaspoon coriander seeds,
    lightly crushed

FOR THE CANDIED FENNEL
1 cup sugar
1 teaspoon fennel seeds
1 teaspoon black peppercorns
1 teaspoon coarse salt
6 heads baby fennel, bulb cut into
    quarters (reserve the fennel fronds
    for garnish; optional)

MAKE THE SOUP

1. Cut the cucumbers into large chunks. In a food processor, purée the cucumbers and herbs. Strain through a fine-mesh strainer into a large bowl and discard the pulp.

2. Whisk in the yogurt and olive oil. Season with salt and pepper. Place in the refrigerator for about an hour to chill completely. Add the vinegar just before serving.

MAKE THE GELÉE

1. Soften the gelatin in ¼ cup warm water. In a small saucepan, heat ½ cup of the lemon juice, the sugar, and salt over medium-low heat until just before boiling, then

pour over the gelatin and let sit until dissolved. Stir in the remaining lemon juice.

2. Pour the liquid into a shallow 9 × 9-inch baking dish and top with the crushed coriander seeds. Refrigerate, uncovered, for 1 hour, and then cut the lemon gelatin into 2-inch squares.

MAKE THE CANDIED FENNEL

In a medium pot, heat 1 cup water and the sugar. Bring to a simmer, then cook for 1 to 2 minutes, or until the sugar is completely dissolved. Reduce the heat to medium, then add the fennel seeds, peppercorns, salt, and fennel pieces. Cook for 3 minutes, or until the

GREECE VIA CANADA

"When you come from a traditional family that cooks and something new is better than your grandmother's, it has to far exceed your taste memory." That is how Michael Psilakis of Anthos remembers his first taste of Skotidakis yogurt. He was in his restaurant in New York when a distributor brought by a sample for him to try. "It just had an unparalleled taste profile." Psilakis attributes the taste to the mix of goat's milk, sheep milk, and Vermont cow's milk that goes into the Canadian product made near Montreal by the Skotidakis family. "The texture and layered composition of the flavors provide a palate experience that evolves with a beginning, middle, and end. Usually this would be the description of a wine, not a dairy product."

The Skotidakis farm is home to 3,000 goats that form the base of the farm's products that include Greek yogurt, feta cheese, ricotta, tzatziki, and a variety of flavored dips. The business started when Peter Skotidakis moved to Ontario from Greece and, after a stint in Montreal, felt the pull of the country life and purchased the farm in St. Eugene, Ontario.

The business has grown from Peter and his immediate family along with 20 goats to almost 45 full-time employees. "Our yogurt speaks for itself," says Peter. Chef Psilakis adds, "This yogurt speaks for Greece—it is the best representation of Greek yogurt in the United States *and* Greece."

fennel is tender and well-coated in the syrup. If the syrup isn't adhering to the fennel pieces, continue to cook for another 1 to 2 minutes. Transfer the fennel to a waxed paper–lined baking sheet and let cool at room temperature.

TO SERVE
Arrange 3 to 4 lemon gelée squares on the bottom of each shallow serving bowl; add 4 to 5 pieces of candied fennel. Pour about a cup of chilled cucumber soup over the top. Garnish with the reserved fennel fronds, if desired, and serve.

VITALY PALEY, *Paley's Place,* Portland, Oregon

BARB FOULKE, *Freddy Guys Hazelnuts,* Monmouth, Oregon (hazelnuts)

Pumpkin Soup with Crème Fraîche and Hazelnut Gremolata

Barb imported her roaster from Italy so that she could better control temperature, vibration, and time in perfecting her hazelnuts. Vitaly loves the deep nut flavor that her method produces. The nuts add flavor and texture to the gremolata, which is traditionally made without any nuts.

SERVES 4

FOR THE GREMOLATA
¼ cup dry-roasted hazelnuts, coarsely ground
Zest of 1 orange
¼ cup fresh flat-leaf parsley, finely chopped
2 cloves garlic, finely chopped

FOR THE SOUP
One 2-pound pie pumpkin, peeled, halved, and seeded, or 2 cups cooked, puréed pumpkin
4 tablespoons (½ stick) unsalted butter
Coarse salt and freshly ground black pepper

¼ cup hazelnuts, skinned and roasted
1 tablespoon canola oil
1 medium onion, thinly sliced
5 cloves garlic, finely chopped
4 cups vegetable broth
1 tablespoon fresh lime juice
½ teaspoon hot sauce

½ cup crème fraîche, for garnish

1. For the gremolata, mix all the ingredients in a small bowl. Cover and refrigerate until ready to use.

2. To make the soup, heat the oven to 350°F. If using a whole pumpkin, lay it cut side up on a roasting pan and put 1 tablespoon butter in the center of each half. Season generously with salt and pepper, cover loosely with aluminum foil, and roast in the oven until the flesh is very tender, about 40 minutes. When cool enough to handle, use a kitchen spoon to scoop the pumpkin flesh out and set aside. Discard the skins. In a small coffee grinder or food processor, process the nuts and oil into a paste.

3. In a large heavy-bottomed pot, melt the remaining 2 tablespoons butter over medium heat. Add the onions and garlic, season with salt and pepper, and cook, stirring, until the onions have softened and become translucent, about 8 minutes. Stir in the cooked pumpkin and the hazelnut-oil paste. Add the vegetable broth and bring to a simmer, stirring frequently to prevent sticking, about 10 minutes. Season with the lime juice and hot sauce. Carefully transfer the soup to a blender and liquefy (working in batches if necessary). Adjust with salt and pepper, if necessary.

4. Portion the hot soup into 4 bowls, garnish with a spoonful each of crème fraîche and gremolata, and serve.

LONG-TERM THINKER

Meeting the woman behind Freddy Guys Hazelnuts is like walking into the eye of a storm and being swept up in high winds of excitement, passion, and downright shrewd business thinking. Barb Foulke was a nurse running an Indian health clinic in eastern Washington State before she and her husband decided to buy an orchard of hazelnut trees in the Willamette Valley of Oregon. They knew nothing about nut farming, but luckily they had Uncle Ray.

Uncle Ray had been farming all his life and was a natural consultant for Barb as she and her family moved onto the farm and began production. Barb quickly realized that hazelnuts are a commodity crop that suffers from low prices due to flooding of the market from inferior producers in Turkey. Barb decided to take the whole process of growing, shelling, roasting, and selling into her own hands. In the process, she learned that this control gives her a superior product that local chefs and farmers' market shoppers love.

Hazelnuts are harvested once a year; the process takes about three weeks to complete as special tractors pick the nuts off the ground like a giant Hoover®. Barb has employed her college-aged kids and their friends for the harvest for a number of years, as she trusts them implicitly. The nuts are stored at the farm in their shells until they are needed for roasting (the shell is a perfect environment for the meat of the nut). Freddy Guys also produces flavored nuts, hazelnut butter, and hazelnut pancake mix, and sells hazelnuts to buyers in Vietnam, Hong Kong, and Europe in 44,000-pound quantities.

Barb is already on to her next great idea. While making a trip to the Piedmont area of Italy to buy a roaster, she noticed that olives were very happily growing right next to hazelnuts. While Barb doesn't expect to see Freddy Guys growing olives anytime soon, she knows it could be a good investment for her family and will keep her busy. Just how she likes it.

Barb Foulke and Vitaly Paley

Freddy Guys Hazelnuts, Monmouth, Ore.

LEE CHIZMAR, *Bolete Restaurant & Inn,* Bethlehem, Pennsylvania

SKIP BENNETT, *Island Creek Oysters,* Duxbury, Massachusetts (oysters)

Oyster Chowder

Chowder is as much a stew as a soup. Cream, bacon, and aromatic vegetables come together in a lively and flavorful soup, yet keep the essence of the oyster flavor. This is a special-occasion soup, though it's really quick to put together.

SERVES 4

¼ pound bacon (about 6 slices), cut into 1-inch pieces
1 tablespoon canola oil
1 medium white onion, finely chopped
4 stalks celery, finely chopped
1 leek (white and light green parts), finely chopped
1 small bulb fennel, cut into small dice
2 cloves garlic, thinly sliced
½ cup dry white wine

1 tablespoon unsalted butter
3 tablespoons all-purpose flour
5 sprigs fresh thyme
1 bay leaf
10 white peppercorns
1 russet potato, diced small
4 cups vegetable stock
1 cup heavy cream
1 teaspoon Worcestershire sauce

1 teaspoon hot sauce
20 oysters, shucked, with their liquor (juices)
1 tablespoon fresh lemon juice
1 tablespoon fresh flat-leaf parsley, finely chopped
2 tablespoons minced fresh chives
Coarse salt and freshly ground white pepper

1. In a large, heavy-bottomed pot over medium-low heat, render the bacon in the canola oil until crisp, about 10 minutes. Pour off all but 2 tablespoons of fat and set aside.

2. Add the onions, celery, leek, fennel, and garlic and cook over medium-low heat until the onions are translucent and soft, about 10 to 12 minutes. Increase the heat to medium, pour in the white wine, and reduce until the liquid is almost evaporated, about 5 minutes.

3. In a small saucepan, heat 2 tablespoons of the reserved bacon fat with the butter over medium heat. Whisk in the flour, stirring constantly to make a smooth paste. Cook without browning it, 2 to 3 minutes.

4. Wrap the thyme, bay leaf, and peppercorns in cheesecloth secured with string to make a sachet. Add to the soup pot, along with the diced potatoes, vegetable stock, cream, Worcestershire, and hot sauce. Stir in the flour mixture and bring the chowder to a boil, stirring constantly. Lower the flame and simmer the soup until the potatoes are tender, about 15 minutes.

5. Just before serving, add the oysters with their liquor, the lemon juice, parsley, and 1 tablespoon of the chives. Season with salt and white pepper, if necessary (the oysters and bacon have enough salt to season the chowder). Remove the sachet. Bring the chowder back to a simmer. To serve, ladle the soup into bowls and garnish the top of each serving with the remaining chives.

FARMER IN THE BAY

Oyster farming at Island Creek Oysters is just like produce farming, only not at all. The seeds of oysters are first grown in very controlled environments like a seedling crop. The difference is that the oysters are hidden in a chamber under boat docks and are force-fed fresh sea water to help them grow almost exponentially. Just as vegetables are moved to greenhouses for their next step, oysters are put into mesh bags when they are ¼ inch in diameter and moved to a shallow bay, where the constantly changing tides feed them the nitrogen they need as they grow and clean the bay at the same time. Finally, the oysters move to the field, and this one just happens to be a leased acre in Duxbury Bay, Massachusetts. There the oysters continue to grow for 18 to 36 months and are then harvested by claw-equipped bags dragged across the bottom of the bay. They're brought to a floating shed for culling—the act of deciding if the oysters are ready for market or need more time to grow—and finally are brought to land for bagging and shipping. Each oyster is touched about 15 times in the process of its growth.

Skip Bennett is the mastermind behind this farm. Skip started out trying to grow clams in the bay and soon found out that wasn't going to work. After meeting Christian Home, an oyster farmer in Freeport, Maine, they realized they could form the perfect alliance. Christian needed more farm space, and Skip needed oyster seed. With that, Island Creek Oysters was in business.

Island Creek has developed into a consortium of 12 farmers working in Duxbury Bay to grow the best oysters in the country. Once the oysters are ready to ship, Skip then takes over and uses his marketing prowess and logistics for shipping the fresh oysters to national clients like Per Se, Bolete, Le Bernardin, and even the White House.

There couldn't be a better ending.

Island Creek Oysters, Duxbury Bay, Mass.

Lee Chizmar and Skip Bennett

JODY ADAMS, *Rialto,* Cambridge, Massachusetts

MATT LINEHAN, *Sparrow Arc Farm,* Kennebunk, Maine (heirloom beans)

Heirloom Bean Soup with Lobster and Minestrone Vegetables

Steuben bean, a dried heirloom variety, is known by several names, such as Maine Yellow Eye, Molasses Face, and Butterscotch Calypso. These beans have a beautiful speckled color—brownish-red over white—and hold their shape when cooked. This soup pairs the classic combination of vegetables for minestrone with lobster, another New England favorite, which adds nice texture contrast to the vegetables.

SERVES 4

FOR THE SOUP
One 1½-pound lobster, steamed
½ cup extra-virgin olive oil
1 medium onion, cut into small dice
1 medium leek (white part only), washed, cut into small dice, and washed thoroughly again
1 stalk celery, peeled and cut into small dice
1 fennel bulb, cut into small dice
2 cloves garlic, minced
Coarse salt and freshly ground black pepper
2 cups Steuben beans, soaked overnight, or 2 cups navy or cannellini beans
2 bay leaves
1 teaspoon fennel seeds

¼ pound asparagus, ends snapped, peeled, and thinly sliced on the diagonal
1 cup fresh or frozen peas

FOR THE BASIL PESTO
1 cup lightly packed fresh basil leaves
⅓ cup extra-virgin olive oil
1 clove garlic, minced
2 tablespoons toasted pine nuts
2 tablespoons freshly grated Parmesan
1 tablespoon freshly grated Pecorino Romano
Coarse salt

FOR THE VEGETABLE GARNISH
Coarse salt and freshly ground black pepper
½ carrot, peeled and cut into ¼-inch dice
2 ounces green beans (about 12 to 15), cut in half
1 stalk celery, peeled and cut into ¼-inch dice
½ small leek (white part only), cut into ¼-inch dice and washed thoroughly
1 ripe plum tomato, peeled, seeded, and chopped
2 tablespoons extra-virgin olive oil
1 ounce thinly sliced prosciutto, preferably Parma, cut into fine julienne
1 tablespoon fresh flat-leaf parsley, chopped

1. Remove the lobster meat from the shells. Cut the shelled tails in half lengthwise and remove and discard the digestive tract (the dark vein-like structure). Cut the clawmeat into 1-inch pieces. Discard the shell. Cut the lobster tail meat into 1-inch pieces; cover and refrigerate. Remove the top shell and head from the body and discard. Rinse the body and break it into 3 pieces.

2. Heat the oil in a large stockpot over medium heat. When hot, add the onions, leeks, celery, diced fennel, and garlic; season with salt and pepper, and cook for 10 minutes, or until the vegetables are tender.

3. Drain the beans, then add them to the pot along with the bay leaves, fennel seeds, and lobster body pieces. Stir well and add enough water to cover. Bring to a boil,

reduce the heat to a simmer, and cook for 1 to 1½ hours, or until the beans are very tender. The amount of time this takes will vary based on the age of the beans. The younger they are, the less time they will need to cook.

4. While the beans are cooking, make the pesto. Put the basil leaves in the bowl of a food processor, add the oil in a thin steady stream, and process until the basil is finely chopped, about 1 minute. Add the garlic and pine nuts and process for another 20 seconds. The pine nuts should be finely chopped but not a paste. Transfer the pesto to a small serving bowl. Stir in the cheeses. Taste and season with salt as necessary.

5. Drain the beans and vegetables, saving the cooking liquid but discarding the bay leaves and lobster body pieces. Purée the beans in the bowl of a food processor. Return to the pot and add enough bean cooking water to make a thick soup. Taste and adjust with salt and pepper. Return the soup to low heat to keep warm. Add the asparagus and peas and cook for an additional minute, or until the vegetables are almost tender.

6. To cook the vegetable garnish, bring a medium pot of salted water to a boil. Add the carrots, green beans, celery, and leeks and cook for 2 minutes. Mix the semi-cooked vegetables, tomatoes, and lobster meat in a medium sauté pan with the olive oil. Heat slowly over medium-low heat. Season with salt and pepper. Just before serving, add the prosciutto and parsley.

7. To serve, ladle the soup into bowls and put a heaping tablespoonful of the warm vegetable-lobster mixture in the center. Drizzle with basil pesto. Serve immediately, with additional pesto at the table.

continued

Heirloom Bean Soup with Lobster and Minestrone Vegetables

DONALD LINK, *Herbsaint Bar & Restaurant*, New Orleans, Louisiana

BILLY LINK, *Link Crawfish*, New Orleans, Louisiana (crawfish)

Crawfish and Corn Stew

Donald has many aunts, uncles, and cousins contributing to the New Orleans food scenes. One aunt makes sausage, one uncle grows rice, and cousin Billy is a local fisherman who supplies crawfish to all three of his cousin's restaurants. Donald says this stew is best made a day in advance, to allow all the flavors to develop. Set the heat level to your particular taste by adjusting some of the red, white, and black peppers.

SERVES 8

2 sticks (½ pound) unsalted butter
1 cup all-purpose flour
1 medium onion, finely chopped
1 medium green bell pepper, finely chopped
1 poblano chile, seeded and finely chopped
1 jalapeño, seeded and finely chopped
3 stalks celery, finely chopped
4 cloves garlic, minced
¼ teaspoon cayenne, or more according to your taste

½ teaspoon ground white pepper
2 teaspoons freshly ground black pepper
2 teaspoons paprika
1 teaspoon dried thyme
Coarse salt
¼ cup red-wine vinegar
5 bay leaves
2 teaspoons hot sauce
2 tablespoons tomato paste
4 cups diced fresh tomatoes (about 3 medium tomatoes)

4 cups fresh corn kernels (about 2 very large ears of corn or 4 small to medium ears)
10 cups chicken stock or shrimp stock
2 pounds crawfish tails, peeled
Cooked white rice, for serving
⅓ cup finely chopped scallions (white and green parts)

1. Melt the butter in a large, heavy-bottomed pot or Dutch oven over medium-low heat. Add the flour and whisk constantly for about 10 minutes, or until the paste becomes golden brown.

2. Stir in the onions, bell peppers, poblanos, jalapeños, celery, and garlic and cook the mixture for 5 minutes. Add the spices, salt, vinegar, bay leaves, hot sauce, and tomato paste, and cook for another 5 minutes.

3. Add the tomatoes, corn, and stock; cook for 25 minutes over medium-low heat. Add the crawfish and cook for another 5 to 8 minutes. Adjust the seasoning for salt and remove the bay leaves.

4. Serve in individual bowls over warm white rice with a few chopped scallions.

APRIL BLOOMFIELD, *The Spotted Pig,* New York City

ROB THOMPSON, *Thanksgiving Farm,* Harris, New York (pork)

Smoky Pork and Apple Soup with Mustard

Ham broth makes this an intense soup. The union of apples and pork and the addition of fall vegetables make this a hearty cold-weather soup, a staple in the winter months at most English pubs. Use whatever kind of apples you like, and for a variation in flavor, add a dash of allspice or nutmeg.

SERVES 4

FOR THE STOCK
1½ pounds ham hocks (about 2)
2¾ cups apple cider
1 red onion, cut in half

FOR THE SOUP
½ cup extra-virgin olive oil
5 medium carrots, peeled and
    cut into ½-inch dice

7 medium parsnips, peeled
    and cut into ½-inch dice
3 small onions, cut into ½-inch dice
1½ pounds medium potatoes,
    such as Yukon Gold, cut into
    ½-inch dice

1 medium head garlic, peeled around
    the outside but kept whole
3 apples, preferably Granny Smith,
    cut into ½-inch dice
2 tablespoons mustard, preferably
    Dijon
Coarse salt

1. Make the stock: In large stockpot, combine the ham hocks, 3 quarts water, the apple cider, and red onion halves; simmer over medium heat for about 3½ hours, or until the meat is tender and falling off the bone. When cool enough to handle, remove the ham hocks and pull the meat off the bones and set aside; discard the bones. Reserve the cooking liquid (you should have about 2 quarts).

2. Make the soup: Heat the olive oil in large, heavy-bottomed pot over medium heat; add the carrots, parsnips, and onions, and cook until golden brown, about 10 minutes. Add the potatoes, garlic, apples, ham, and reserved liquid (if you don't have 2 quarts then add enough water to equal 2 quarts) and cook until the vegetables are tender, about 10 minutes. Stir in the mustard and season to taste with salt. Serve immediately.

JODY ADAMS, *Rialto*, Boston, Massachusetts

MATT LINEHAN, *Sparrow Arc Farm*, Kennebunk, Maine (heirloom beans)

Clam and Steuben Bean Soup with Fennel and Lemon

Steuben beans have a multicolored look, with reddish brown speckles. A good though less-colorful bean substitute is the Northern White bean, which has the same creaminess yet is light in its overall density. Fennel and lemon bring out the brininess in the clams while adding a subtle anise flavor. This soup is great as a main course but is equally satisfying as a starter.

SERVES 4 TO 6

½ cup dried heirloom Steuben beans, picked over for dirt, stones, and broken beans, and rinsed
½ cup extra-virgin olive oil
1 medium white onion, cut into ½-inch dice
1 small carrot, peeled and cut into ½-inch dice
½ stalk celery, cut into ½-inch dice

1 head fennel, trimmed of stalks and tough outer leaves, cut in half lengthwise, cored, and chopped into ½-inch dice
6 cloves garlic, chopped
1 teaspoon fennel seeds
2 bay leaves
3 cups fish stock (or 2 cups chicken stock plus 1 cup clam juice)

1 teaspoon chopped fresh thyme
Coarse salt and freshly ground black pepper
1 teaspoon minced lemon zest
¼ teaspoon red pepper flakes
40 littleneck clams, scrubbed
1 cup dry white wine
¼ cup chopped fresh basil

1. Put the beans in a medium saucepan, cover with 2 inches of water, bring to a boil, and turn off the heat. Cover and let them sit for 1 hour.

2. While the beans are soaking, heat ¼ cup of the olive oil in a large saucepan over medium heat. Add the onions, carrots, celery, fennel, and about two-thirds of the garlic, and cook until the vegetables are tender and beginning to brown, about 8 minutes. Add the fennel seeds and bay leaves and cook for another 2 minutes.

3. Drain the soaked beans and add them to the vegetable mixture. Stir well and cover with 2 inches of water. Bring to a boil and then reduce the heat to a simmer. Cook for 1 hour, adding more water if necessary. Add the fish stock and continue cooking until the beans are tender, about another 30 minutes. The mixture should

still be quite soupy when the beans are done; taste a few beans to confirm they are tender, and if not, add more water and cook for another 15 minutes. Stir in the thyme and season with salt and pepper.

4. Heat 2 tablespoons of the olive oil in a large sauté pan over medium heat. Add the remaining garlic and cook for 2 minutes. Add the lemon zest, red pepper flakes, clams, and white wine, then cover and cook until the clams have opened, about 5 minutes. Discard any clams that have not opened.

5. Remove the bay leaves from the bean mixture. Add the clams and the steaming liquid to the beans and stir in the basil. Taste and add salt and pepper if necessary. Ladle the soup into bowls, drizzle with the remaining 2 tablespoons olive oil, and serve immediately.

PROVIDING THE PALETTE

Sparrow Arc Farm owner Matt Linehan says his relationships with his restaurant clients are akin to those of a family. When he and his "family" meet, they talk about life and plan for the future, but what Matt likes best is when he brings out his farm's vegetables and fruit and the "family" goes nuts with excitement. That's how he describes the reaction of Rialto Chef Jody Adams and Sous-Chef Nuno Alves.

Matt started Sparrow Arc in 2005 and has had the good fortune to work closely with great chefs in Boston, Cambridge, and Portland, Maine, since the farm's inception. His 15-acre farm, 8 acres of which is tree fruit, combined with another 11 acres have been a testing and proving ground for his abilities to grow everything from Asian pears to Maine Yellow Eye beans. About the only things Matt doesn't grow are melons ("too cold") and sweet corn ("takes up too much land"). Matt recently bought his 80-year-old mentor's bean business and along with it a bean thresher from the 1930s that he affectionately says is "anarchy going through a field."

Matt's cooking tends to be simple and straight out of his fields. After researching Portuguese sea kale, Matt started growing it and then using it with chorizo and some potatoes and shallots from the garden. He adds, "Those are just the basics—you can throw anything in there that you like."

Matt continually reminds his crew of four that "Chefs are artists. We create the palette for them to work with." With this belief, his "family" will surely continue to grow.

Jody Adams and Matt Linehan

Main Courses

Meats

Chicken, Duck & Other Fowl

Fish & Shellfish

Tarts

Pasta, Grains & Rice

DAVID SHEA, *applewood*, Brooklyn, New York

RIDGE SHINN, *Hardwick Beef*, Hardwick, Massachusetts (beef)

Pan-Roasted Beef Rib-Eye with Fresh Red Currant Pan Sauce

applewood regularly has "meet the farmer" dinners, with four-course Hardwick beef tastings. Ridge speaks to guests about the importance of an all grass-hay diet to the health, well-being, and sustainability of his cattle, which produce a flavorful and well-marbled steak. Fresh red currants are fairly tart and usually need a boost of sugar or honey to cut the tartness. If you find them whole packed in syrup, give them a rinse and proceed with the recipe as follows, omitting the honey.

SERVES 2

Two 16-ounce, 1-inch-thick beef rib-eye steaks, trimmed
Coarse salt and freshly ground black pepper
2 tablespoons canola oil
¾ cup fresh red currants, stemmed and rinsed

1 large lemon, juiced and zested
2 sprigs fresh thyme
1 tablespoon honey
¾ cup veal demi-glace or strong beef stock

6 tablespoons (¾ stick) unsalted butter, softened
2 tablespoons fresh flat-leaf parsley, finely chopped, for garnish

1. Season the steaks with salt. Heat the oil in a heavy-bottomed skillet over high heat, add the steaks, and reduce the heat to medium high. Cook for 4 to 5 minutes per side for rare, if 1 inch thick. (Cook for an additional 2 to 4 minutes total for medium rare.) Remove the steaks from the pan, tent with foil, and let rest for 10 minutes.

2. Pour the excess fat from the pan and add the currants, lemon juice, lemon zest, thyme, and honey. Cook on medium high until the currants soften and begin to release their juices, about 1 minute. Add the demi-glace or beef stock, bring to a boil, and cook over high heat for 2 minutes.

3. Remove the pan from the heat and whisk in the butter, 1 tablespoon at a time. Season to taste with salt and pepper. Pour any juices that may have accumulated from the resting steaks back into the sauce.

4. Serve the steaks whole or carve into ½-inch slices. Place the steaks or sliced meat onto each plate and spoon a bit of the sauce over the top. Garnish with the parsley.

TONY MAWS, *Craigie on Main,* Cambridge, Massachusetts

KOFI INGERSOLL & ERIN KOH, *Bay End Farm,* Buzzards Bay, Massachusetts (herbs)

Grilled Skirt Steak and Beef Marrow Bones with Radish–Herb Salad and Pepper Purée

The peppery bite of radishes, an assortment of fresh herbs, and the smoky grilled meat are all brought together with the sweetness of the Cubanelle peppers. Tony serves this dish accompanied with grilled beef marrow bones for a rich component to a relatively light dish. Use the bones as soon as you purchase them, as they're quite perishable.

SERVES 4

4 cups mixed fresh garden herbs, such as flat-leaf parsley, cilantro, sweet cicely, baby mustard greens, baby sorrel, baby komatsuna, oxalis, mizuna, or watercress
11 tablespoons extra-virgin olive oil
Coarse salt and freshly ground black pepper

One 1½- to 2-pound skirt steak, preferably grass-fed
10 Cubanelle (Italian) peppers
Green hot sauce
1 tablespoon red-wine vinegar, such as Banyuls
1 pound mixed radishes, such as French Breakfast and White Icicle, cleaned and sliced

Four 2-inch-high beef marrow bones (about 4 pounds), refrigerated and soaked in water for 8 hours and changed at least once (optional)

1. In the bowl of a food processor, blend 2 cups of the mixed herbs with 3 tablespoons of the olive oil to make a coarse purée; season with salt and pepper.

2. Spread the herb purée on both sides of the steak. Marinate, covered, in the refrigerator for at least 30 minutes.

3. Meanwhile, roast the peppers: Heat the broiler. Coat the peppers with 2 tablespoons olive oil and arrange on a baking sheet or grill pan. Broil 2 inches from the heat, turning frequently until blistered and blackened, about 15 minutes. Transfer to a bowl and seal with plastic wrap until cool. When cool, peel and seed; discard the ribs and roughly chop the peppers.

4. Put the roasted peppers in the blender, along with a few dashes of the hot sauce and 2 tablespoons olive oil. Season the pepper purée with salt to taste.

5. In a medium bowl, whisk the remaining 4 tablespoons olive oil with the vinegar, then pour over the radishes and mix well to coat. Add the remaining 2 cups of garden herbs to the radishes. Season with salt and pepper.

6. In a cast-iron pan or skillet over medium-high heat, cook the steak for 2 minutes per side for rare or 3 minutes per side for medium rare. If cooking on a grill, heat the grill, put the skirt steak on the hottest part of the grill, and cook for approximately 2 minutes per side for medium rare. Remove the steak from the skillet or grill and let rest for 5 minutes. When cool, slice on the bias against the grain.

7. Season the marrow bones with salt and pepper and cook on the grill, covered, or roast in a 425°F for 15 to 20 minutes, or until the marrow is cooked through or a knife or skewer can pierce the marrow without any resistance.

8. To serve, spoon some of the pepper purée on serving plates, arrange the slices of skirt steak on top, and spoon a portion of radish-herb salad around the meat. Lay one roasted marrow bone on each plate, if using.

PRIDE AND TRUST

"We do our best to make the product as tasty and delicious as we can, and Tony does the same, so the two compound each other and we end up with an end product that is so good I can really be proud of it." These are the exact words of Bay End Farm's Kofi Ingersoll when he talks about his relationship with Chef Tony Maws of Craigie on Main in Boston. This kind of mutual satisfaction comes from individual passions that are respected and amplified by both Kofi and Tony. Kofi works very closely with Tony—when Tony asked for more baby lettuces, Kofi doubled the crop by planting every 6 inches instead of every foot and then harvesting every other plant for Tony.

Kofi runs Bay End Farm, located near Buzzards Bay, Massachusetts (on the way to Cape Cod), as a place to grow the best produce he can for his CSA customers, for a farmstand on the premises, and for his limited restaurant customers. He and his wife Erin are also raising their son Zeke on the farm. Kofi says that Zeke's vocabulary may differ from most 3-year-olds, with the recent request of "Dad, let's cultivate the chard" not the usual demand of a preschooler. This connection to the physical world is a happy reminder to Kofi and Erin that they made the right choice to live on the farm.

The farm has been in Kofi's family for three generations (it was once as big as 1,300 acres but reduced for trust and other reasons) and has at different times been home to chickens, pigs, cows, and ducks as well as an equestrian center. When Kofi came back to the farm, he decided to keep it simple (the soil is a challenge that will become better with age) and start by growing certified organic crops like lettuce, chard, herbs, eggplant, peppers, squash, and many others. Down the road, Kofi sees expanding the farm to be able to let areas go fallow for a regenerative season to break the pest and disease cycle, but right now he has his hands full with the 5 acres he is working, the 100 CSA members he is feeding, and the few restaurants he trusts to treat his produce with the respect he grows it with.

Tony Maws and Kofi Ingersoll

Bay End Farm, Buzzards Bay, Mass.

DAVID SHEA, *applewood,* Brooklyn, New York

RIDGE SHINN, *Hardwick Beef,* Hardwick, Massachusetts (beef)

Braised Short Ribs with Red Wine

Ridge is a tenacious beef farmer who raises top-notch beef with an unmatched quality and taste. David likes Ridge's flanken beef ribs, which are cut along the length of the cow's ribs. They make an incredibly flavorful braising liquid that is transformed into a rich sauce with little effort. Ideal accompaniments are mashed potatoes or buttered egg noodles.

SERVES 6

¼ cup canola oil

5 pounds beef short ribs, preferably flanken style

Coarse salt and freshly ground black pepper

2 large onions, chopped

4 large carrots, chopped

3 cups dry red wine, such as Merlot

1 bunch fresh thyme

1 head garlic, split in half and sliced

½ bunch fresh chives (about ¼ cup), chopped, for garnish

1. Heat the oil in heavy-bottomed pot on medium-high heat. Season the ribs with salt and pepper, then add to the pot and brown, turning frequently, until the ribs are nicely browned and caramelized on all sides, about 15 minutes. (You can also roast the ribs in the oven at 450°F for 20 minutes, turning a few times so all sides are evenly browned.) Adjust the heat if necessary so the meat doesn't burn.

2. Remove the ribs from the pot, remove almost all the fat from the pot except about 3 tablespoons, and add the onions and carrots; cook over medium heat until the vegetables soften and are lightly browned, 5 to 8 minutes.

3. Add the wine to the vegetables, turn the heat to high, and boil until the wine is reduced by about one-half, about 15 minutes.

4. Return the meat to the pot, then add the thyme, garlic, and 4 cups cold water or beef broth (or more if needed) so that the meat is just covered. Bring to a simmer, cover, and cook for at least 3 hours, or until the ribs are tender and the meat pulls away from the bone. Allow to cool completely in the liquid.

5. Transfer the ribs from the pot to a large serving plate, removing any excess vegetables from the meat; discard any loose bones and fat. Strain the liquid into a medium bowl. If serving right away, press out the liquid from the vegetable solids and discard the vegetables. If not using right away, refrigerate the liquid to allow the fat to rise to the top, then spoon off and discard with the vegetables.

6. Transfer the strained braising liquid back to the pot, and cook the sauce over medium-high heat until thickened or reduced by one-quarter, about 15 minutes. Add the short ribs and bring to a simmer over medium heat for 5 minutes to heat through. Season to taste with salt and pepper.

7. To serve, portion the ribs and sauce among serving bowls and sprinkle with the chives.

CHANGING MYTHS

"Grass-fed cows make the best burgers, period." This is Ridge Shinn's mantra. Ridge is on a mission to change the beliefs of American beefeaters to prove that grass-fed cattle produce a more flavorful meat than their grain-finished relatives and in the process are a boon to the environment. In his arsenal are the herd of Devon cattle that he shipped from New Zealand on two 747s in 2008 and the pure science that he uses to make his point.

The Devon cattle are the gentle giants of the farm that Ridge runs, and they are also the machine used to reinvigorate leased land that had been ruined by over-farming, herbicides, and other chemicals. The Devons eat grass whose roots have pulled carbon from the air; they then fertilize the land that they have been living on and within 2 to 3 years the land has been

revived. This is the kind of perfect balance that sustainable farmers are always looking for.

Ridge's goal is to increase the quantity of half-Devon cattle being raised by farmers and ranchers. His Bakewell Reproductive Center is the seed that he hopes will drive this goal. By developing herds of half-Devon cattle all over the United States, the quality of grass-fed beef will increase rapidly. He says "My bull's genes will push through, no matter the cow that it is bred with." The other upside of his breeding plan is that these grass-fed beauties will be ready for slaughter in 18 months rather than the usual 24 to 30 months for other grass-fed breeds, saving farmers from an extra winter's worth of expensive alfalfa.

Working with everyone from David Shea of applewood in Brooklyn, New

York, to scientists at Clemson University and Hardwick Beef, Ridge is getting the word out about his cattle and the advantages of raising an animal that helps the land and tastes great. Ridge loves to go to farmers' dinners to tell consumers about the advantages of his grass-fed beef, including studies from Clemson University that showed his steaks rated as "choice" by USDA standards. He is also proud to explain how his filets won a *Food Arts* magazine contest when put up against grain-finished beef from around the country. Ridge says, "Once consumers understand all the advantages of grass-fed beef, the only problem we'll have is getting enough supply to them." A good problem to have for any farmer.

Ridge Shinn

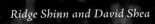
Ridge Shinn and David Shea

JOHN BESH, *August,* New Orleans, Louisiana

STUART GARDNER, *Gardner Ranch,* Cankton, Louisiana (beef)

Creole Beef Grillades and Cheese Grits

A grillade is a traditional beef or veal round cut into a square and then pounded thin to be tender. Beef round is the most suitable cut for this dish. Gardner Ranch calves are raised on a diet of grass and clover with the bare minimum of supplements, producing lean yet flavorful meat.

SERVES 6 TO 8

1 teaspoon paprika
1 teaspoon cayenne
1 teaspoon garlic powder
1 teaspoon onion powder
1 teaspoon dried oregano
1 teaspoon thyme
One 3-pound beef shoulder,
    sliced into ½-inch-thick cutlets
Coarse salt and freshly ground
    black pepper
2 cups all-purpose flour

¼ cup rendered bacon fat,
    or 2 tablespoons unsalted butter
1 large yellow onion, finely diced
1 stalk celery, finely diced
1 small red or green bell pepper,
    finely diced
3 cloves garlic, minced
2 cups canned chopped tomatoes
    with juices
2 cups beef stock
2 sprigs fresh thyme

1 teaspoon crushed red pepper flakes
1 bay leaf
1 tablespoon Worcestershire sauce
Hot sauce
Cheese Grits (recipe follows)
2 scallions (green parts only), finely
    chopped, for garnish

1. To make the Creole spices, mix the paprika, cayenne, garlic powder, onion powder, dried oregano, and thyme.

2. Season the beef with salt and pepper. Season the flour with the Creole spices, and reserve ¼ cup. Put the remaining 1¾ cups flour in a large, shallow bowl, and then dredge the beef in the flour, shaking off the excess.

3. Heat the rendered bacon fat or butter in a large skillet over medium-high heat. Cook the cutlets until golden brown, about 2 minutes on each side, making sure not to overcrowd the pan (you might need to cook in batches). Set aside the cooked cutlets on a paper towel–lined plate.

4. Add the onions to the same pan, lower the heat to medium, and cook until the onions are a deep mahogany color, about 10 minutes. Add the celery, bell peppers, and garlic, and cook for another 5 minutes. Add a tablespoon of the reserved seasoned flour to the pan and mix well.

5. Add the tomatoes and beef stock to the pan and bring to a boil. Reduce the heat to low and stir in the thyme, red pepper flakes, bay leaf, and Worcestershire sauce; return the beef cutlets to the pan. Cover and simmer for 45 minutes, or until the meat is fork-tender. Discard the bay leaf. Add hot sauce to taste and more salt and pepper as desired.

6. To serve, put a heaping spoonful of Cheese Grits on a serving plate, top with 2 or 3 pieces of beef, and spoon the sauce over the meat. Garnish with scallions.

continued

Cheese Grits

SERVES 6 TO 8

Coarse salt
1 cup stone-ground white corn grits
3 tablespoons unsalted butter

2 tablespoons mascarpone or
 cream cheese
¼ cup grated Edam or Swiss cheese

1. In a large saucepan over high heat, bring 5 cups of salted water to a boil while slowly whisking in the grits. Reduce the heat to medium low; cover and cook for 25 to 30 minutes, stirring occasionally and making sure the grits aren't sticking to the bottom of the pan; adjust the heat to low if the grits are cooking too quickly.

2. Remove the cooked grits from the heat and stir in the butter, mascarpone or cream cheese, and grated cheese. Season with salt to taste and serve warm.

KEEPING IT IN THE FAMILY

Holding onto a family farm is tough through the best of times, but with recent economic challenges, the job gets even rougher. Stuart Gardner recognized this problem and took charge by changing the way he markets his veal calves. While Stuart has always raised his mixed-breed (three-quarters Red Angus, one-quarter Brahma) babies for veal on a diet of only grass, he was mostly selling them to family, friends, and a few others who wanted these animals raised in a healthy, low-impact manner.

Stuart was introduced to John Besh of August by a mutual friend, and the rancher immediately recognized that direct marketing to restaurants was the way to keep the ranch (in Cankton, Louisiana) that had been in his family for four generations. Direct marketing, learning new farming techniques (Stuart is one of 25 student professionals chosen by Louisiana State University to study in their Agricultural Leadership Program), and a second job working for the USDA keep the farm going. The work that Stuart does for the USDA's Rangelands Management department keeps him up to date on the best practices of rotating grazing and keeping the best grasses in the fertile part of the "Cajun Prairie" ready for his cows.

The farm is a small one by most measures, 400 acres with 70 "mama" cows that breed about 60 to 65 calves a year. Stuart also manages the herds of a couple of friends to increase the amount he can have ready for area restaurants and one local meat market. With the price of a calf the same as it was in 1989 and the expenses about 5 to 10 times higher, being smart with the herd is a must. Stuart uses a local processor for his calves that also makes one run a week to New Orleans, saving the need for cold storage trucks and drivers. This kind of integration and expense cutting keeps the farm, as well as his mission, going. "I am serious about tryin' to stay on my family land and continuing to eat this good grass-fed beef," says Stuart with an earnestness that cannot be questioned.

APRIL BLOOMFIELD, *The Spotted Pig,* New York City

ROB THOMPSON, *Thanksgiving Farm,* Harris, New York (pork)

Roasted Pork Loin with Roasted Vegetables and Spicy Tomato Sauce

Pork is commonly paired with fruit, and the natural sweetness of tomato reminds us it is indeed a fruit. Rob won't reveal his pigs' diet and exercise regimen, but says they roam freely on a lovely pasture on his farm.

SERVES 4

FOR THE PORK
3 tablespoons fennel seeds, ground
2 tablespoons coarse salt
¼ teaspoon freshly ground
 black pepper
One 5½-pound pork loin with skin
 and bone
6 tablespoons olive oil

4 medium carrots, peeled and
 coarsely chopped
2 medium bulbs fennel, quartered
1 large red onion, peeled
 and quartered

FOR THE TOMATO SAUCE
2 tablespoons olive oil

1 dried red chile, pierced with a knife
7 cloves garlic, thinly sliced
1½ tablespoons ground coriander
¼ small stick cinnamon
1 large can (28 ounces) chopped
 tomatoes (about 3½ cups)
Coarse salt

1. Heat the oven to 400°F. In a small bowl, mix the fennel seeds, salt, and pepper. Score the pork with a pairing knife, making small incisions all over meat; press the fennel mixture into the incisions.

2. Put the pork in a roasting pan and rub all over with 2 tablespoons of the oil. Season with more salt and pepper all over, including the sides, ribs, and base of the loin. Let sit at room temperature for 20 minutes, then roast the pork for 1 hour.

3. Heat the remaining 4 tablespoons oil in a large skillet over medium-high heat; add the carrots, fennel, and onions. Cook the vegetables, stirring occasionally, until lightly browned on all sides, 7 to 10 minutes. Add the vegetables to the roasting pan with the pork and continue to roast for another 45 minutes, or until an instant-read thermometer inserted in the center of the pork reads 150°F for pork that's slightly pink. Remove from the oven and let cool for 15 minutes before slicing and serving.

4. Meanwhile, make the tomato sauce: Heat the olive oil in a large saucepan over medium heat. Add the chile and garlic and cook until the garlic is lightly browned, about 3 to 5 minutes. Stir in the coriander and add the piece of cinnamon. Cook for another minute. Add the chopped tomatoes and season with salt; stir and reduce the heat to medium low. Continue to simmer for 30 to 45 minutes on low heat until thick. Remove the cinnamon stick.

5. To serve, slice the pork into ½-inch pieces, surround with vegetables, and spoon the tomato sauce over the pork.

continued

INSPIRING DISCOVERY

Rob Thompson had been working on a 700-cow dairy farm and was starting to burn out when his mom showed him a "help wanted" ad for a farmer in New York's Catskill region. As Rob discovered, Thanksgiving Farm was no ordinary farm.

Thanksgiving Farm is a beautiful 350-acre farm that not only feeds the staff and students of The Center for Discovery but also educates residents and helps them find meaningful work. The Center for Discovery is the home for 350 special-needs children and adults ranging in age from 5 to 21 and a staff of about 1,400. The Center has changed the way families are able to interact with their children who suffer from multiple disabilities and need full-time care by making itself an open place built around families and not a warehouse for children to be left and not seen.

When April Bloomfield of The Spotted Pig met Rob and toured the farm, she knew this was a place she wanted to work with. Not only did Rob raise pigs of beautiful proportion and fat-to-meat ratios, but she "fell in love with the place and the work they do." April found Thanksgiving Farm and The Center for Discovery so inspiring that she comes back to cook for their fundraisers and looks forward to calls from Rob when he has extra pigs to supply her restaurant.

Rob finds the idea that famous chefs and food lovers know his name "entertaining." April invited him down to New York City a few times to eat at The Spotted Pig, and when he finally took her up on the offer, he said that her famous burgers were so good that he could have eaten two of the enormous creations. As Rob continues raising chickens, pigs, beef cows, and dairy cattle that are certified organic, he is also taking Thanksgiving Farm to the next stage by becoming certified biodynamic. With these new certifications, Rob is learning as much as he is teaching to the residents of The Center for Discovery.

Rob Thompson and April Bloomfield (left);
Peaches the pig (above)

PETER HOFFMAN, *Savoy,* New York City

MICHAEL YEZZI & JENNIFER SMALL, *Flying Pigs Farm,* Shushan, New York (pork)

Pork Osso Buco with Wild Mushrooms and Almond Piccata

This recipe has several steps but really isn't that complicated. Starting two days in advance makes the work easy and builds the complexity of flavors that makes this dish so wonderful. Serve the osso buco with mashed potatoes and sautéed hearty greens, such as kale or escarole.

SERVES 8

Twelve 2-inch-thick cross-cut pork
   shanks, about 4 pounds total
6 sprigs fresh thyme
2 tablespoons minced garlic
   (about 6 large cloves)
Coarse salt and freshly ground
   black pepper
1 carrot, peeled and roughly chopped
1 stalk celery, roughly chopped
2 bay leaves
3 large yellow onions, chopped

¼ cup extra-virgin olive oil
3 large tomatoes, chopped
1 cup dry white wine
¾ pound mixed fresh mushrooms
   (oysters, buttons, and chanterelles),
   cleaned and cut into
   1-inch pieces
2 teaspoons fresh lemon juice
2 tablespoons roughly chopped fresh
   flat-leaf parsley, for garnish

FOR THE ALMOND PICCATA
¼ cup almonds
¼ cup pine nuts
2 tablespoons extra-virgin olive oil
1 slice country-style bread
2 cloves garlic
½ cup fresh flat-leaf parsley,
   finely chopped

1. Put the shanks in a large bowl, then rub with the thyme, 1 tablespoon of the garlic, salt, and black pepper. Marinate overnight for the meat to develop flavor.

2. In a large pot or Dutch oven, spread the carrots, celery, bay leaves, and two-thirds of the chopped onions. Set the marinated shanks on top of the vegetables. Cover with water by 2 inches (about 2 quarts of water) and bring to a boil over high heat. Skim off any foam or impurities that rise to the top. Reduce the heat to medium low and simmer for 2½ to 3 hours. The meat should be tender and loose when pierced with a knife.

3. When the meat is done, remove the shanks from the pot, and strain the broth, discarding the vegetables and reserving the liquid. Allow the broth and meat to cool.

4. Heat the olive oil in a large braising pot or Dutch oven over medium heat and cook the remaining chopped onions for 10 minutes; add the remaining 1 tablespoon garlic and continue to cook for another 1 minute. Add the tomatoes and cook until the chunks of tomato begin to break down, about 5 minutes. Add the wine and 2 cups of the reserved braising liquid. Bring to a boil over high heat and cook until reduced by half, about 20 minutes. Add the reserved pork, cover with the rest of the braising liquid, and cook for 30 minutes.

continued

HOGS FOR CONSERVATION

Luckily, raising pigs has a low financial entry compared to other livestock. When Michael Yezzi and Jennifer Small of Flying Pigs Farm were still grad students at The University of Massachusetts, they cobbled together the money to buy the farm up the road from where Jennifer spent her summers at camp. The land had been a farm for multiple generations but was about to be turned into a housing development by a local builder. The prospect of seeing houses where animals grazed sent these two nonprofit specialists on the path that would become their passion—the conservation and protection of farmland. They also became great pig farmers, raising rare breed pigs like Gloucestershire Old Spots, Large Black, and Tamworths and supplying New York City restaurants like Savoy, Craft, and Telepan. The pigs are joined on the 150-acre farm by 1,500 laying hens as well as roasters.

Along with land preservation, Michael and Jennifer have another love: educating the restaurant industry about all aspects of farming. Jennifer, with support from the New York State Department of Agriculture, created "Farm Camp." Designed for chefs, line cooks, and just about anyone in the restaurant business, Jennifer takes students through the language of farming, the economics of land use, the processes of cheesemaking and dairy processing, and finally hands-on slaughtering and plucking, with students taking home their own chicken.

"Farm Camp is so awesome," says Jennifer. "Students leave here with a very passionate feeling for farming and farmers. They bond here and have started to get together for reunions in the City."

Michael and Jennifer sell their rare pigs via mail order, farmers' markets, and wholesale and have plans to add products like bacon and smoked hocks. But they continue to keep their eye on their ultimate goal of land conservation and educating food lovers about the need to keep valuable farmland and farmers in business.

Jennifer Small, Michael Yezzi,
and Peter Hoffman (left to right)

5. Meanwhile, make the almond piccata: Heat a medium skillet over medium heat and toast the almonds for 1 to 2 minutes, until fragrant; transfer to a bowl. Return the skillet to the stove, add the pine nuts, and toast for 1 minute, until they're just starting to turn brown; transfer to the bowl with the almonds.

6. In the same skillet, increase the heat to medium high and add the olive oil. Fry the bread on each side for 2 minutes, until golden brown. Transfer to a paper towel–lined plate and, when cool enough to handle, break up into small pieces. In the bowl of a food processor, add the garlic and roughly process. Add the bread pieces and toasted nuts and pulse to roughly chop again. Add the parsley and process again until chopped but not a paste.

7. Add the mushrooms to the pork and simmer for another 20 minutes, or until the mushrooms are soft and tender. Add salt to taste and then add the lemon juice. Add the piccata in small batches, stirring to thicken the sauce. Taste again for seasoning and adjust as needed. To serve, portion the pork pieces among 8 serving bowls, ladle broth over the top, and garnish with parsley.

PETER HOFFMAN, *Savoy*, New York City

MICHAEL YEZZI & JENNIFER SMALL, *Flying Pigs Farm*, Shushan, New York (pork)

Slow-Cooked Pork with Spanish Paprika and Sweet Spices

Peter loves the dense marbling of fat and the concentrated rich flavor of Flying Pigs' heritage breed pork. The meat has a smooth texture and distinct taste, and the slow-cooking process allows the spice mixture to add intense flavor. Serve with sautéed garlicky greens, stewed white beans, or simple mashed potatoes.

SERVES 6

2 bay leaves
8 cardamom pods
2 star anise
2 teaspoons coriander seeds

1 teaspoon cumin seeds, toasted
1½ teaspoons ground fennel
¼ cup extra-virgin olive oil
1 tablespoon pimentón
(smoked Spanish paprika)
2 teaspoons freshly ground
black pepper

5 cloves garlic, minced into a paste
2 tablespoons brown sugar
1 tablespoon coarse salt
One fresh 3-pound pork shoulder,
preferably with the skin on

1. In a coffee grinder, process the bay leaves, cardamom, and star anise until finely ground (you may have to grind in batches) and place in a small bowl. Grind the coriander and cumin until finely ground and add to the bowl; add the ground fennel to the bowl of spices as well. Mix in the olive oil, pimentón, pepper, garlic, brown sugar, and salt, mixing well to create a paste.

2. If the pork has the skin on, score the skin with a sharp knife in ½-inch intervals. Rub the paste evenly on the meat. Cover and let sit in the refrigerator for at least 4 hours and preferably overnight.

3. Heat the oven to 450°F. Scrape off the excess spice rub then put the pork on a rack in a large roasting pan, skin side up, and roast for 30 minutes. Cover the pan with foil then turn the oven down to 300°F, and cook for 3 hours. Add a bit of water in the bottom of the roasting pan, if there is no liquid, to keep the pork from drying out. Check after 3 hours; the pork should be fork-tender and very moist when done. If not, continue to cook until fork-tender.

4. If your pork has skin, slide the pan under the broiler for 3 to 5 minutes until the skin is crispy. If your pork doesn't have skin, remove it from the oven and allow it to rest for 10 minutes before slicing or pulling apart.

continued

*Slow-Cooked Pork with
Spanish Paprika and Sweet Spices*

BRIAN LEWIS, *The Farmhouse at Bedford Post*, Bedford, New York

JOHN UBALDO, *John Boy's Farm*, Cambridge, New York (pork)

Maple-Glazed Pork Belly, Sunny-Side Up Egg, and Pickled Chanterelles

This is Brian's version of the classic farmhouse bacon and eggs. Make sure you get a forkful of the pickled chanterelle, swished through the egg and grits, with a hunk of the pork belly for the full farm experience. The maple syrup cooked with assertive spices gives the pork meat a unique and well-rounded sweetness. John's Berkshire pigs happily forage in his back fields for 6 months until they reach a zaftig 250 pounds.

SERVES 4

FOR THE MAPLE PORK BELLY
One 1½-pound center-cut pork belly
2 heads garlic, roughly chopped
12 leaves fresh sage, roughly chopped
12 sprigs fresh thyme, stems on
   and roughly chopped
½ cup kosher salt
1 tablespoon freshly ground
   black pepper
½ cup sugar, preferably organic
1 tablespoon ground cinnamon
2 teaspoons ground star anise
½ teaspoon dried mustard
¼ cup pure maple syrup

FOR THE SCALLION GRITS
¾ cup grits, preferably heirloom
2 cups whole milk
1 cup heavy cream
Coarse salt and freshly ground
   black pepper
1 tablespoon farmstead butter
2 scallions (white and green parts),
   finely chopped
¼ cup Parmigiano-Reggiano,
   finely grated

FOR THE PICKLED CHANTERELLES
1 cinnamon stick
1 tablespoon coriander seeds
1 teaspoon black peppercorns
1 bay leaf
1 star anise

5 sprigs fresh thyme
½ cup sugar
1 cup apple-cider vinegar
½ pound fresh small to medium
   chanterelle mushrooms

FOR THE EGGS
1 tablespoon farmstead butter
4 large eggs
Coarse salt and freshly ground
   black pepper

FOR THE GARNISH
Pure maple syrup
Sherry vinegar
Coarse salt and freshly ground
   black pepper
2 tablespoons minced fresh chives

MAKE THE PORK BELLY

1. Put the pork belly on a clean work surface. Using the point of a sharp knife, score the top of the pork in a crosshatch pattern, which will allow the seasoning to penetrate the meat. In a medium bowl, mix the garlic, sage, and thyme, and set aside. In a small bowl, mix the salt, pepper, sugar, cinnamon, star anise, and dried mustard. Rub the pork thoroughly with the spice mix and then coat with the herbs. Cover and refrigerate for 12 hours to allow the pork to fully absorb the seasoning.

2. Heat the oven to 275°F. Rinse the herbs off the pork under running cold water. Thoroughly dry the pork with paper towels, then transfer to a baking pan with a wire rack. Bake, covered, for 3½ hours. After 3½ hours, remove the cover and pour the maple syrup over the pork and bake for another ½ hour. Remove from the oven, cover with aluminum foil to keep warm, and set aside.

MAKE THE GRITS

1. Put the grits in a medium bowl and cover with warm water; let soak for 1 hour, then drain. In a heavy-bottomed saucepan, heat the milk and cream and season with salt and pepper. Bring to a gentle simmer over medium-low heat and slowly whisk in the grits; cook over low heat, stirring occasionally, for 20 to 25 minutes, or until the grits are creamy and soft.

2. Heat the butter a medium skillet and sauté the scallions over medium-high heat for about 1 minute; season with salt. Add to the grits along with the cheese. Adjust the seasoning with salt and pepper. Remove from the heat but cover to keep warm.

MAKE THE CHANTERELLES

1. Make a spice sachet: Fill a 5 × 5-inch piece of cheesecloth with the cinnamon stick, coriander seeds, black peppercorns, bay leaf, star anise, and thyme. Tie it closed with butcher's twine.

2. In a large saucepan, combine 1½ cups water, the spice sachet, the sugar, and the cider vinegar and bring to a simmer; cook gently for 30 minutes.

3. Put the chanterelles in a large stainless-steel bowl, then place that bowl over another bowl filled with ice. Pour the hot pickling liquid over the mushrooms and stir to allow the mushrooms to absorb the aromatic flavors while cooling down the liquid. If using right away, set aside at room temperature. If storing, transfer the mushrooms with pickling liquid to an airtight container and refrigerate until ready to use or for up to 1 week.

MAKE THE EGGS

Just before serving, heat the butter in a large skillet, preferably cast iron, over very low heat. Break the eggs into the skillet, keeping the egg yolk right in the center, if possible. Cook the eggs as slowly as possible, avoiding any browning, until the whites look glossy and yolks look creamy, about 6 to 8 minutes. Season with salt and pepper.

TO SERVE

Slice the warm pork belly with the grain of the fat into four slices. Spoon the warm, creamy grits onto the center of each plate and top with a slice of pork belly. Drizzle the pork with maple syrup and a touch of sherry vinegar, then season with salt and pepper. Gently top the pork with a perfectly cooked sunny-side up egg, then garnish with the pickled chanterelles and chives.

continued

WALL STREET BULL FARMS PIGS

Twelve years as a national brokerage salesman on Wall Street was fun, says John Ubaldo, but it was only a stop along the way to his real goal of starting John Boy's Farm. John's brother is a chef, and he took John on a tour of the United States in search of the best ham. Along the way John fell in love with Berkshire pigs, "the nicest pigs ever," and the smoked products of legendary Allan Benton. Berkshires are the pig of choice for small artisan farmers as they produce beautiful, flavorful meat that chefs love and have a gentle personality that farmers appreciate.

John consults agricultural manuals from the 1920s that recommend raising a pig for 11 to 12 months to approximately 400 pounds. (Modern pigs usually go to slaughter at 240 pounds after about 7 to 8 months.) By length-

ening the growing time of his pigs, John is able to produce pork of beautiful red color that looks more like a steak than pork as we know it. He says, "It's like aging the meat. That extra time adds flavor and character." The extra time also gives the prime cuts of the pig time to get to a size that looks great on a plate.

John Boy's Farm started on a piece of land in Westchester County, New York, but soon the neighbors were less than happy to have a few pigs as well as chickens and ducks in their own backyard. So John moved and expanded his operation in the more rural Washington County, New York. The farm is now 185 acres with towering oaks, fields of non-genetically modified organism (GMO) alfalfa, and corn, as well as 130 pigs, fryer chickens, and ducks laying high-protein eggs. The

animals eat a healthy diet of grain as well as the occasional melon at the end of summer and pumpkins the day after Halloween. This tightly controlled diet and the fact that the meat is only sold fresh leads to raves from chef Brian Lewis of The Farmhouse at Bedford Post: "This product is so above and beyond the usual."

The businessman in John is looking to the future for his pigs. He intends to double the amount of Berkshires on his farm this year and become USDA certified to sell the bacon he is double smoking. And in the ultimate compliment, his brother said to him, "Finally, a bacon as good as Benton's."

John Ubaldo and Brian Lewis (below)

THOMAS KELLER, *Per Se*, New York City

KEITH MARTIN, *Elysian Fields Farm*, Waynesburg, Pennsylvania (lamb)

Lamb Saddle with Caramelized Fennel and Wild Mushrooms

This is a very tender, flavorful roast. A saddle of lamb is a double loin roast, which combines the loin roasts from each side of the lamb. Ask your butcher for the bones from the saddle to make the sauce. For the sauce, Thomas uses veal stock and reduces it for deep flavor, but here you'll use extra lamb bones for a more intense sauce. The sauce can be made a few days in advance. This is adapted from a recipe he serves at Per Se.

SERVES 4

FOR THE LAMB SAUCE
Canola oil
4 pounds meaty lamb bones, such as neck bones or shanks
2 medium onions, peeled and roughly chopped
2 large leeks (white and light green parts), split, washed, and roughly chopped
2 large carrots, roughly chopped
4 cloves garlic, crushed
8 cups veal stock or beef broth
1 tablespoon tomato paste
3 sprigs fresh thyme

Coarse salt
2 tablespoons unsalted butter

FOR THE LAMB
6 tablespoons canola oil
2 bulbs fennel, cut into 8 wedges and trimmed to 2 inches long by ½ inch wide
Coarse salt and freshly ground black pepper
4 hen-of-the-woods mushrooms, trimmed and cut in half or in quarters, if very large

1 lamb saddle (about 2 pounds), trimmed, boned (bones reserved), and tied
3 tablespoons unsalted butter
2 sprigs fresh thyme
2 cloves garlic, peeled
Fennel fronds, for garnish
Fleur de sel, for garnish

MAKE THE SAUCE

1. Heat the oven to 400°F. In a lightly oiled, large roasting pan, put the lamb bones, onions, leeks, carrots, and garlic. Roast, stirring occasionally to keep the vegetables from burning, for 30 minutes or until the bones are browned. Remove from the heat and transfer the bones and vegetables to a large pot.

2. Add 2 cups veal stock or beef broth to the roasting pan, scraping up the browned bits, then add this liquid to the pot with the vegetables along with the remaining 6 cups of stock or broth, the tomato paste, and the thyme. Bring to a boil over medium heat, then simmer gently, skimming off any impurities that rise to the top. Cook for 2 to 3 hours, or until the liquid is level with the bones. With tongs, remove the bones from the stock and discard.

continued

3. Pour the stock (in batches if necessary) through a fine-mesh strainer. If using right away, skim off the fat; if not, cool completely, cover, and refrigerate. When ready to use, scrape off the congealed fat from the stock and discard. You should have about 1½ cups of stock.

4. In a medium saucepan, heat the lamb stock over medium-high heat for 15 minutes, until the sauce is reduced by a third. Season with salt. When ready to serve with the lamb, whisk in the butter, 1 tablespoon at a time, until the butter is fully incorporated into sauce.

PREPARE THE LAMB

1. Heat 2 tablespoons of the oil in a large, deep, oven-proof skillet over medium-high heat. Add the fennel wedges and cook until lightly browned, about 3 to 5 minutes. Transfer the fennel to a plate and season with salt and pepper to taste. Repeat with the mushrooms, adding another 2 tablespoons oil to the skillet, seasoning with salt and pepper, and cooking for 3 to 5 minutes; transfer to the plate of fennel and set aside.

2. Season the lamb with salt and pepper. In the same deep skillet, heat the remaining 2 tablespoons oil over medium-high heat and brown the lamb on all sides, about 10 minutes total. Remove from the heat and add the butter, thyme, and garlic to the pan; turn the lamb to coat completely. Add the fennel and mushrooms to the pan around the lamb (without crowding) and baste with the flavored butter, making sure the fennel and mushrooms are well coated. Place the pan in the 400°F oven and cook for 10 to 15 minutes, or until an instant-read thermometer reads 120°F for rare or 130°F for medium rare.

3. Transfer the lamb to a plate and let it rest for 10 minutes, tented loosely with foil. When cool, cut the loin into 8 even slices and pour the juices over the meat.

TO SERVE

Arrange the fennel and mushrooms evenly among 4 serving plates. Place the sliced lamb over the fennel and mushrooms, then spoon the lamb sauce over the meat. Garnish with the fennel fronds and sprinkle with fleur de sel.

JOSÉ ANDRÉS, *minibar,* Washington D.C.

BEV EGGLESTON, *EcoFriendly Foods,* Moneta, Virginia (lamb)

Paella with Lamb Ribs

Rice is grown extensively in Spain, particularly in the swampy regions outside of Valencia. Within Spain, rice is graded by the amount of whole grains included in the weight. Calasparra rice, the rice José uses in his paella, is grown in a town near Murcia, where the rice plants grow slowly, forming a grain that is hard and absorbent, making it perfect for paella. Lamb ribs are a tough but flavorful cut and can make this a unique paella.

SERVES 4

FOR THE SOFRITO (ONION, GARLIC, AND PEPPER PASTE)
2 tablespoons olive oil
1 medium onion, diced small
1 Italian sweet pepper, cored, seeded, and diced small
1 small red bell pepper, cored, seeded, and diced small
6 cloves garlic, finely chopped
1 large tomato, seeded and diced small
Coarse salt

FOR THE SALMORRA (SMOKY TOMATO GARLIC SAUCE)
1 tablespoon extra-virgin olive oil
6 cloves garlic, peeled
3 dried nyora peppers or 1 small dried ancho chile, seeded and torn into pieces
1 can (14 ounces) plum tomatoes, drained and roughly chopped

½ teaspoon sugar
⅛ teaspoon pimentón (smoked Spanish paprika)
Coarse salt

FOR THE PAELLA
¼ cup extra-virgin olive oil
2 pounds lamb ribs, rack cross-cut into thirds, then cut into individual ribs
Coarse salt and freshly ground black pepper
1 pound fresh mushrooms, such as oyster, shiitake, and cremini, cleaned and cut into thick slices or bite-sized pieces
8 large cloves garlic, minced (about ¼ cup)
¼ pound cauliflower, florets cut into small pieces (about 2 cups)

1 small zucchini, diced (about 1½ cups)
¼ pound green beans, trimmed and cut into 2-inch lengths
1 teaspoon pimentón (smoked Spanish paprika)
½ pound fresh peas
½ cup dry white wine
4 cups lamb, chicken, or vegetable stock; more as needed
1¼ cups short-grain Spanish rice, such as calasparra or Bomba
8 medium asparagus spears (about ⅓ pound), cut into 2-inch lengths (about 1½ cups)
½ teaspoon saffron

1. Make the sofrito: Heat the oil over medium-high heat in a large, heavy skillet. Add the onions and cook, stirring often, for 6 minutes, or until light golden brown. Add the peppers and cook, stirring often, for 8 minutes, or until the peppers are softened. Stir in the garlic and cook for 1 minute. Add the tomatoes and cook, stirring often, for 8 minutes, or until the mixture is thick. Season with salt and set aside.

2. Make the salmorra: Heat the oil in a medium pot over low heat. Add the garlic cloves and sauté until soft, about 2 minutes. Add the chile peppers and cook, stirring, for 3 minutes, then add the tomatoes and sugar. Cook for 15 minutes, or until the tomato liquid evaporates. Stir in the pimentón. Transfer the mixture to a blender and purée. Pour into a bowl, season to taste with salt, and set aside.

continued

3. Make the paella: Heat 1 tablespoon of olive oil in a very large skillet or a 14-inch paella pan over medium-high heat. Season the lamb ribs with salt and pepper and sear on all sides until they are well browned and their fat is rendered, 10 to 12 minutes. Cook the lamb in batches, making sure not to crowd the pan and draining off the fat as they cook so that they brown rather than fry. Remove the lamb ribs, pour off the fat from the pan, and set aside but don't wipe out the pan.

4. Add 2 tablespoons of olive oil to the skillet and cook the mushrooms for 6 to 8 minutes, stirring frequently, until lightly browned. Add the garlic and continue to cook for another minute. Add the cauliflower and cook over medium heat for 3 minutes, stirring frequently, then add the zucchini and green beans. Cook for 2 minutes then add the pimentón, the sofrito, and the salmorra. Continue to cook for another minute. Add the peas and white wine. Cook for another 2 minutes. Add the stock and raise the heat to high.

5. Once the stock comes to a boil, stir in the rice, asparagus, and saffron, and return the ribs to the pan. Cook over high heat, stirring occasionally. After 6 minutes, lower the heat to medium high and cook for 20 minutes, uncovered, until the liquid is absorbed. (If the liquid evaporates too quickly you may have to add more stock. You want a nice brown crust on the bottom of the pan.) Don't stir the rice but rotate the pan partway through for even cooking.

6. Remove from the heat, cover with foil, and let the paella rest for 8 to 10 minutes before serving.

MAN ON A MISSION

Bev Eggleston is out to prove Michael Pollan wrong. Bev agrees with all of Pollan's mantras about sustainability and the need to eat fresh, simple, and well-cared-for food. He just has to prove Pollan wrong by staying in business with his new way of bringing pasture-raised meats to consumers through his own small slaughterhouse.

Bev took the enormous risk of building a million-dollar processing facility for the small amount of animals that he and his local farmers can supply. An industrial plant can slaughter 400 animals an hour while Bev may process as few as 8 in one day. While Bev's products are cleaner, safer, and more humanely treated, it is hard to fight the massive industrial machine. Pollan wrote in *The Omnivore's Dilemma*, "The industrial and artisanal econ-omies clash right here in Bev's packing plant, and sadly, it's not hard to guess which one will ultimately prevail." Bev believes that the fight is winnable, and he spends every weekend at Washington, D.C.'s farmers' market selling the message to his customers.

Bev runs EcoFriendly Foods, the first farmer-owned, multi-species, federally inspected, humane-certified slaughterhouse. "If you think that sounds complicated...it is," says Bev. Bev is way out in front of public policy on food, "pushing with my fork," he says. He considers the business of keeping small farmers in business and bringing new ones in as "the moral issue I can most contribute to." In an era of huge feedlots, inhumane conditions for animals, and a food economy that crushes small family farms, Bev is the "missionary man" for small farmers. His plan is to expand the farm-owned slaughterhouse model to 50 sites around the country so that 5,000 farmers will be able to take control of their own destinies. When he talks about his hopes and goals, the hair on his arm starts to stand up.

Bev's restaurant clients, including José Andrés and Michael Anthony, all credit his farm on their menus; even food critics like Frank Bruni, formerly of *The New York Times*, mentioned Bev's product in a review, calling it "outrageously fine swine." With the support of chefs, consumers, and even food critics, "The Mission" Bev is on stands a great chance for getting its message heard.

Bev Eggleston

JASON FRANEY, *Canlis,* Seattle, Washington

TRACY SMACIARZ, *Heritage Meats,* Rochester, Washington (sausage)

Roasted Lamb Loin with Yogurt Eggplant Purée and Merguez Sausage

Tracy makes sausage, charcuterie, and anything else a chef wants. The loin roast can come from either side of a lamb; when boneless and separate it's called a loin roll. Tracy makes merguez sausage specially for Canlis, but it's available from specialty food markets as well.

SERVES 4

FOR THE LAMB
2 tablespoons extra-virgin olive oil
2 boneless lamb loins, trimmed
(each side, about ¾ pound),
rolled and tied
2 tablespoons unsalted butter
1 sprig fresh thyme
1 clove garlic

FOR THE EGGPLANT PURÉE
Coarse salt and freshly ground
white pepper
1 small eggplant, peeled and diced
(about 2¾ cups)
½ cup sheep's milk yogurt
1 small clove garlic
1 to 2 tablespoon extra-virgin olive oil
1 teaspoon fresh lemon juice
Cayenne

FOR THE ARUGULA PURÉE
Coarse salt
2 bunches arugula, cleaned and stems
removed (about 5 cups leaves)
1 tablespoon extra-virgin olive oil
¼ cup white Balsamic vinegar
1 cup grape seed oil

1 tablespoon olive oil
8 links lamb merguez sausage
Taggiasca or Niçoise olives, pitted and
diced, for garnish

MAKE THE LAMB
Heat the oven to 300°F. Heat the oil in a large, heavy-bottomed skillet over medium-high heat. Place the lamb in the skillet; cook until browned. Transfer the skillet to the oven and cook the lamb until an instant-read thermometer inserted in the center reaches 125°F for rare or 130°F for medium rare, about 15 minutes. After 10 minutes add the butter, thyme, and garlic to the pan and baste the meat with the butter as it melts. Let rest for 10 minutes then cut each loin into ½-inch-thick slices.

MAKE THE EGGPLANT PURÉE
Bring a medium pot of salted water to a boil over high heat and cook the eggplant until tender, 3 minutes. Drain and cool, pressing gently to remove excess water. Place in a blender with the yogurt and garlic and purée. Add the oil and pulse until smooth. Season with lemon juice, cayenne, and salt and white pepper. Pass through fine-mesh sieve into a bowl and set aside.

MAKE THE ARUGULA PURÉE
Bring a medium pot of salted water to a boil over high heat and cook the arugula until wilted, about 20 seconds; drain and cool. Transfer to an ice bath then wring out the water. Place the arugula in a blender or food processor and purée. Add the olive oil and pulse until smooth. Season with salt. In a medium bowl whisk the vinegar and salt to taste. Slowly whisk in the grape seed oil until incorporated. Before serving, toss the arugula in the vinaigrette.

TO SERVE
Heat 1 tablespoon olive oil in a large skillet over medium-high heat. Cook the sausage until browned, about 4 minutes. Remove from the pan and slice each link on the diagonal into 2-inch segments. Spread a thin layer of eggplant purée on one side of each plate, and place 4 pieces of sausage on top of the purée. On the other side of the plate, spread a layer of arugula purée, top with the loin, and sprinkle diced olives on top.

A BUTCHER WHO SPEAKS "CHEF"

Tracy Smaciarz has been cutting pigs since the age of 17. After time away from the business, he took over the family butchering shop in 1996, and started to expand it by thinking in new ways. He searched for ranchers and growers who believed in "real pasture raising" for cattle and lamb, recognizing that the slaughter of animals should be done in a way that produces the least stress for the animals.

Determined to educate consumers about the vast difference in the quality between meat processed this way and meat from livestock slaughtered in a more production-oriented method, Smaciarz was keen on building a new kind of butchering business. He wanted to become the broker between ranchers and the public as well as between ranchers and restaurants.

His great idea came to fruition when he met Chef Jason Franey of Canlis in Seattle at a steak-tasting event. Tracy introduced Franey to Tom Schultz, a local Washington state lamb farmer. When the meat was delivered to the restaurant, the relationship was cemented.

Franey had just moved to Canlis after working in some of the best kitchens in New York and was looking to expand his purveyor list to include those that produced responsibly raised meats and fowl. The alliance Franey and Smaciarz have built continues to grow, with Heritage Meats now aging ducks for Canlis.

Smaciarz continues to innovate his business and the way "artisan meat" is produced. He has transformed a school bus depot into Heritage Meats,

going from 2,600 square feet at his original location to 5,000 square feet, adding smokers as well as full USDA processing facilities. Recently he started offering mobile slaughter as part of the Puget Sound Meat Producers Cooperative, and he's amped up his creative juices by smoking meat and making jerky.

Like a good movie script, this story comes full circle. The first time Smaciarz cut meat was at Tom Schultz's farm, and that was because Tracy's dad and Tom had worked together years before.

Tracy Smaciarz and Jason Franey

Tracy Smaciarz

THOMAS KELLER, *Per Se,* New York City

KEITH MARTIN, *Elysian Fields Farm,* Waynesburg, Pennsylvania (lamb)

Herb-Roasted Lamb Rib-Eye with Wild Preserved Mushrooms in Aromatic Oil

Although a rib-eye usually means a beef steak, here it's a boned rack of lamb. This recipe, an adaptation of a dish by Chef Keller, makes more mushroom conserva (mushrooms cooked and packed in the same oil) than you'll need, so use the extra in pastas or as a spread atop bread with a light cheese. Kept covered in oil, the mushrooms will keep for up to 1 month in the refrigerator.

SERVES 4

FOR THE MIXED MUSHROOM CONSERVA
2 pounds assorted fresh wild mushrooms (small shiitakes, morels, chanterelles, hen-of-the-woods, trumpet, and oyster)
2 cups extra-virgin olive oil

2 bay leaves
4 sprigs fresh thyme
1 sprig fresh rosemary
1 teaspoon coarse red pepper or piment d'Espelette
3 tablespoons sherry vinegar
Coarse salt and freshly ground black pepper

FOR THE LAMB
1 lamb rib-eye, about 2 pounds, tied
⅓ cup canola oil
Coarse salt and freshly ground black pepper
4 tablespoons unsalted butter
3 cloves garlic, split and crushed
4 sprigs fresh thyme
Sel gris

MAKE THE MIXED MUSHROOM CONSERVA

1. Prepare the mushroom conserva the day before you intend to serve it. Rinse the mushrooms to remove any dirt and remove and discard any stems that are tough, like those on shiitakes. Trim the ends of the other stems, as well as any bruised areas.

2. Cut the mushrooms into pieces. The size and shape will vary with the variety of the mushroom—small mushrooms can be left whole, larger mushrooms can be cut into chunks or into slices. Some mushrooms with meaty stems, such as trumpet mushrooms, can be cut lengthwise in half. Use the tip of a paring knife to score the inside of the stem in a crosshatch pattern. This will enable the marinade to penetrate the stem. The pieces of mushroom will shrink as they cook, but the finished pieces should not be larger than one bite. You should have about 1½ pounds (10 cups) of trimmed mushrooms.

3. Put the olive oil, bay leaves, thyme, rosemary, and red pepper in a large, wide saucepan over medium to medium-high heat. Place a thermometer in the pot and heat the oil until it reaches 170°F, stirring the aromatics in the oil from time to time. You may need to tilt the pot and pool the oil to get a correct reading on the thermometer. Adjust the heat as necessary to maintain this temperature for 5 minutes.

4. Add the mushrooms to the pot and gently turn them in the oil. When the oil reaches 170°F again, maintain the temperature for 5 minutes, gently turning the mushrooms from time to time. The mushrooms will not initially be submerged in the oil, but will wilt as they steep.

5. After 5 minutes, turn off the heat and stir in the vinegar and salt and pepper to taste. Let the mushrooms steep in the oil for 45 minutes. Put the mushrooms, oil, and herbs in an airtight container and refrigerate overnight.

COOK THE LAMB

1. Take the lamb out of the refrigerator 1 hour before cooking. Heat the oven to 375°F. Pour enough oil into a large skillet so that it's ⅛ inch deep and heat on medium high. Season the rib-eye with salt and pepper and sauté for about 3 minutes to brown the bottom. Turn it over and continue to cook for another 3 minutes. Rotate it to brown the sides, another 3 to 4 minutes. It should be well-browned but still slightly rare.

2. Remove most of the fat from the pan, then add the butter, garlic, and thyme, basting the lamb with the butter as it melts. Top the lamb with the garlic and thyme and put the pan in the oven for 10 to 15 minutes, or until the meat is medium rare; an instant-read thermometer should register 115°F to 120°F. Remove the pan from the oven, tent loosely with foil, and let the meat rest for 10 minutes.

3. Reheat the mushroom conserva in a sauté pan and spoon it and its sauce into 4 shallow bowls. Slice the lamb and arrange the slices over the mushrooms. Sprinkle with sel gris and serve.

continued

"THANK THE LAMB, NOT ME"

Keith Martin of Elysian Fields Farm talks with his lambs on a regular basis. They have a similar relationship to that of a pet owner, who knows whether his or her animal is happy, stressed, or ready to play. When the lambs talk to this farmer, they tell him that they like their vegetarian diet, their clean spring water, and the bedding that is continually changed. This farmer has a deep connection with his animals.

Speaking to Keith, human to human, is a lesson in the wholistic view of life, farming, chefs, and our connection to each other. Keith started Elysian Fields Farm in 1989 with the philosophy that he would grow it as the lambs told him. He wouldn't rush to grow his business, but was fortunate that the right chefs (sourcing was much more difficult pre-internet) searched him out and became an integrated part of his business. No chef proves this more than Thomas Keller of Per Se and The French Laundry.

"The guy who really brought us out was Thomas Keller. He was the one driving the integration of producers and chefs, and he was doing it so selflessly that it brought everyone along to improve the quality of food across the country." Keith and Tom started to work together in 1996 and have expanded their relationship into a business partnership, producing lamb that is source verified, data supported, and, most important to consumers, so good that they have never had anything like it.

Keith looks forward to the future when we are more connected to the sources of all of our food and modern barriers of the food industry have dropped away. As a rancher, Keith wants to see the respect and care that he gives to his animals continued as they go into our kitchens and onto our plates. "The animal gives itself up for the highest-quality product it can be," he says, so we should carry this forward by treating it with the reverence it deserves.

Thomas Keller and Keith Martin

MICHAEL PALEY, *Proof on Main*, Louisville, Kentucky

STEVE WILSON & LAURA LEE BROWN, *Kentucky Bison Company*, Goshen, Kentucky (bison)

Bison Pastrami "Hash" with Fingerling Potatoes, Fried Eggs, and Grilled Bread

Michael has raised national attention for Steve and Laura's bison as Kentucky's signature meat with his innovative dishes. Bison has slightly sweeter and richer flavor than beef but is much leaner. This humble and hearty meal is elevated with pickled ramps, but you could use jarred pickled onions or peppers as a substitute.

SERVES 4

1 pound fingerling potatoes, washed and cut in half
Coarse salt and freshly ground black pepper
4 tablespoons (½ stick) unsalted butter
1 tablespoon extra-virgin olive oil

1 small red onion, diced (about 1 cup)
3 cups loosely packed sliced and julienned Bison Pastrami (recipe follows)
½ cup finely chopped pickled ramps (optional)

½ cup finely chopped fresh flat-leaf parsley
1 lemon, juiced
8 large eggs
4 slices crusty country white bread, brushed with extra-virgin olive oil and grilled or toasted

1. Put the potatoes in a large saucepan, add water to cover, and salt generously. Bring to a boil, reduce the heat to a simmer, and cook the potatoes until easily pierced with the tip of a knife, about 10 minutes. Drain the potatoes and allow them to cool. When cooled, peel off the skin, if desired, and crumble them with your hands, breaking them into bite-size pieces.

2. Heat 2 tablespoons of the butter and the olive oil in a medium sauté pan over medium-high heat. Once the butter begins to melt, add the onions and cook for 5 minutes. Season with salt and pepper. Add the crumbled potatoes, julienned pastrami, and pickled ramps, if using, to the pan; cook until the potatoes begin to turn slightly golden brown, about 10 minutes.

3. Once the potatoes are browned and heated through, season with pepper. (The pastrami is heavily seasoned already, so taste first before seasoning.) Add the parsley and lemon juice. Remove from the heat and cover to keep warm.

4. In a sauté pan, melt the remaining 2 tablespoons butter, then cook the eggs sunny-side up or however desired (having the yolk runny helps to create the sauce). You may need to cook the eggs in batches depending on the size of your pan.

5. To serve, portion the hash evenly among 4 plates and top each portion with 2 eggs. Serve with the grilled or toasted bread.

continued

Bison Pastrami

Pastrami is made from the brisket cut, cured in a saltwater brine for several days. You can skip the brining and use corned bison or beef to make the pastrami. Insta Cure®#1 is a specialty salt with curing agents, such as sodium nitrite, and there is no substitute. The general rule for curing is 5 days per inch of thickness.

FOR THE BRINE
1½ cups kosher salt
1 cup sugar
1½ ounces Insta Cure #1

1½ cups packed brown sugar
¼ cup honey
5 cloves garlic
1 tablespoon pickling spice

FOR THE BISON PASTRAMI
One 8- to 10-pound fresh or thawed
   bison brisket or bottom round roast
2 tablespoons whole black peppercorns
2 tablespoons whole fennel seeds
2 tablespoons whole coriander seeds

1. Make the brine: Combine 1 gallon of water with all the ingredients in a large pot and bring to a boil. Once the salt and sugar are dissolved, take the pot off the stove and let cool completely.

2. Make the pastrami: Place the brisket in a large pot or roasting pan, then pour all of the cooled brine over the brisket and cover with a lid or plastic wrap. Refrigerate for 5 to 10 days, depending on the thickness of the brisket. To get the brisket evenly brined, you may need to turn it once a day if part of it does not stay submerged.

3. After the brining is complete, remove the brisket and rinse with water.

4. Combine the spices in a spice grinder and pulse to coarsely grind and combine. Rub the spice mixture into the rinsed brisket.

5. Preheat a smoker or, if you don't have one, an oven to 300°F. Roast the brisket, uncovered, until very tender, about 4 to 5 hours. Slice and julienne the brisket for hash or serve whole. The brisket will keep refrigerated for 1 week.

RESTORING LAND AND BEAST

Bison, the regal roamer of America's plains, is on a comeback in no small part due to the love and care of Steve Wilson, his wife Laura Lee Brown, and Steve's son J. B. Wilson. The Wilsons bought Woodland Farm in Oldham County, Kentucky, with the goal of restoring and preserving it from becoming yet another housing development. Coming from a family with farming in its roots, the Wilsons knew they wanted to farm and dis-

covered that bison was a perfect fit for their beliefs in nutrition and their vision of an alternative agriculture model.

The Wilsons set about restoring the farm and quickly realized they were grass farmers as much as they were bison ranchers—the rainfall in Kentucky provides for perfect grass to be harvested by the bison and the hay baler. Thanks to the lush grass, the bison-to-land ratio is one bison to 1 acre, whereas it could be 1:25 in drier climates.

With the help of chefs like Michael Paley of Proof on Main, consumers are more aware of the great taste and healthy protein bison provides. In fact, the Wilsons are in the enviable position of needing to raise more bison to fill demand. While chefs take the majority of prime cuts (about a third of the animal), ground meat, hot dogs, and bratwurst have become popular. It also didn't hurt that bison was on the menu at Kentucky's inaugural ball for President Obama.

CHARLIE PALMER, *Aureole,* New York City

TOM JURGIELEWICZ, *Jurgielewicz Duck Farm,* East Moriches, New York (duck)

Roasted Duck Breast with Farro "Risotto" and Caramelized Figs

The savory-sweet combination of duck and figs is a classic. The duck's crisp skin is seasoned with coriander, providing a counterpoint to the rich meat.

SERVES 4

2 tablespoons unsalted butter
1 small onion, finely chopped
2 cloves garlic, finely chopped
2 cups farro or barley
½ cup dry white wine
4 cups chicken stock

1 bay leaf
4 sprigs fresh thyme
Coarse salt and freshly ground
     black pepper
4 Pekin duck breast halves with skin,
     about 8 ounces each

1 tablespoon coriander seeds, toasted
     and ground
½ cup honey
8 fresh figs, halved lengthwise
¼ cup mascarpone cheese

1. Heat the butter in a large saucepan over medium heat. Add the onions and garlic and cook until tender, 5 minutes. Stir in the farro or barley, raise the heat to medium high, add the wine, and cook for 3 minutes. Heat the chicken stock and add it, the bay leaf, and thyme to the farro. Continue to cook the farro, stirring frequently, for about 20 minutes, or until the farro has a tender yet slightly chewy texture. Remove from the heat, season with salt and pepper, and set aside.

2. Trim the fat from only the flesh side of the duck breasts. Turn the breasts over and score the remaining fat in a close crosshatch pattern (this will help the fat render quickly and create a crisper crust). Season the breasts with salt, pepper, and 1½ teaspoons of ground coriander. Put the breasts in a large, heavy skillet, fat side down, and cook over medium-low heat for 12 to 15 minutes, or until richly browned. Turn the breasts over and continue to cook for 3 to 5 minutes for rare (an instant-read thermometer will register 125°F for rare or 135°F for medium rare).

3. Transfer the duck to a dish and carefully pour all of the rendered fat from the pan into the dish.

4. Return the pan to the stovetop and heat over medium heat. Add the honey and when hot, return the duck breasts to the pan; flip the breasts to coat both sides. Transfer the duck to a plate and cover loosely with foil to keep warm, about 5 minutes.

5. Put the figs, cut side down, in the pan in a single layer and cook over medium-high heat to caramelize them, about 1 minute or until lightly browned on the cut side. Turn the figs over, season with the remaining 1½ teaspoons of coriander and black pepper, and cook for about 30 seconds more (they should be tender but still hold their shape). Remove the pan from the heat and tent loosely with foil until ready to serve.

6. Return the farro to medium heat and heat through for about 1 minute. Stir in the mascarpone and season with more salt and pepper if needed. To serve, spoon the farro into the center of individual plates or on a large serving platter. Carve the duck breasts on an angle into ½-inch-thick slices (be sure to pour any juices over the duck when finished slicing) and arrange the sliced duck or whole breasts over the farro; arrange the figs around the duck or duck slices and serve immediately.

continued

Roasted Duck Breast with Farro "Risotto"
and Caramelized Figs

DANIEL HUMM, *Eleven Madison Park,* New York City

STEVE & SYLVIA PRYZANT, *Four Story Hill Farm,* Honesdale, Pennsylvania (poultry)

Roasted Chicken with Lemon Thyme and Summer Truffles

Less intensely flavored than white truffles, black truffles have a delicate aroma but a strong flavor. Mixed with butter and breadcrumbs, then stuffed under the skin of chicken, the truffles literally transform this dish. Four Story Hill's poulardes (fat hens) eat corn feed mixed with a bit of reconstituted powdered milk, which the Pryzants say makes the birds grow fatter and gives them a soft, tender skin.

SERVES 4

2 slices stale bread, preferably ½-inch-thick brioche
8 tablespoons (1 stick) unsalted butter, at room temperature
2 teaspoons chopped black summer truffles, with juices

1 tablespoon fresh lemon thyme leaves, picked from the stem
Coarse salt and freshly ground black pepper
1 whole chicken, about 3 to 4 pounds
10 sprigs fresh thyme

2 cloves garlic, peeled
1 lemon, cut in half

1. Heat the oven to 375°F. Make breadcrumbs from the bread by tearing it into 1-inch pieces and pulsing in a food processor until finely ground. (If your bread isn't stale, put it in a 300°F oven until crusty before tearing into pieces.)

2. In a medium bowl, make the truffle butter by mixing the butter and truffles with their juices with a fork until well combined. For stronger-flavored butter, blend in a food processor or blender until well mixed. Add the breadcrumbs and mix with a fork, making a paste. Add the thyme leaves and season to taste with salt and pepper.

3. Carefully loosen the skin from the chicken, using your hands to separate the skin from the meat but making sure the skin remains attached at the center of the bird. Stuff the truffle-breadcrumb mixture evenly under the skin of the breasts and legs, then smooth the skin back in place.

4. Season the inside of the chicken with salt. Stuff the thyme sprigs, garlic, and lemon halves inside the cavity. Truss the legs with butcher's twine, if desired. Cover the bird with plastic wrap and refrigerate for 20 minutes to chill the butter.

5. Put the bird on a rack in a large roasting pan and cook for 55 minutes, rotating the bird after 20 minutes and basting the skin with the melted butter from the pan. If the bird weighs 4 pounds, cook for about 10 minutes more. Check for doneness in the thickest part of the thigh. The bird is done when the juices run clear when pierced with a knife and an instant-read thermometer registers 165°F. Remove from the oven and let rest for 15 minutes before carving.

DEREK WAGNER, *Nicks on Broadway*, Providence, Rhode Island

PAUL BAFFONI, *Baffoni's Poultry Farm*, Johnston, Rhode Island (poultry)

Chicken Pot Pie

You can make the filling for this pie ahead of time and heat it just before topping it with the biscuits. Derek also recommends poaching a whole chicken with the vegetables, removing the meat from the bones, and using the liquid as your stock. Buttermilk in the biscuits adds flavor and acts like a tenderizer. The Baffoni family has been raising all-natural chickens for over 80 years, selling mostly to local residents who stop by the farm, but due to increasing popularity now also to restaurants. If you prefer a more mild biscuit, halve the amount of black pepper.

SERVES 6

FOR THE CHICKEN-VEGETABLE STEW
2 tablespoons unsalted butter
6 shallots, finely chopped
1 medium parsnip, peeled and cut
    into ¼-inch dice
1 medium carrot, peeled and cut
    into ¼-inch dice
1 Yukon gold potato, cut into
    ¼-inch dice
½ pound fresh shiitake or oyster
    mushrooms, wiped clean, stemmed,
    and sliced
Coarse salt and freshly ground
    black pepper

2 cloves garlic, minced
½ cup dry white wine
2 cups chicken stock
One 3-pound chicken, cut into
    8 to 10 pieces and skin removed,
    or 3 pounds chicken thighs, legs,
    and breasts, skin removed
2 cups fresh peas
1 cup heavy cream
3 sprigs fresh tarragon, leaves picked
    and chopped
1 tablespoon cornstarch

FOR THE BISCUITS
2 cups all-purpose flour
2 tablespoons baking powder
¼ teaspoon baking soda
½ teaspoon coarse salt
1 tablespoon freshly ground
    black pepper
8 tablespoons (1 stick) unsalted
    butter, cut into small pieces
1 cup buttermilk
¼ cup milk
Sea salt

MAKE THE STEW

1. Heat the butter in a large stockpot over medium heat and cook the shallots until softened, about 5 minutes. Add the parsnips, carrots, potatoes, and mushrooms, and season with salt and pepper. Cook until the vegetables are softened, about 10 minutes. Add the garlic, sauté for 1 minute, then pour in the wine. Continue to cook until the wine is reduced by half, about 5 minutes. Add the chicken stock; increase the heat to high and bring to a boil. Add the chicken pieces and cook for 10 minutes. Add the peas, cream, and tarragon; cook for another 5 minutes.

2. In a small bowl, mix the cornstarch with 2 tablespoons cold water. Stir into the pot until thoroughly combined, then continue to simmer until the stew is just thickened, about 3 minutes. Adjust the seasoning with more salt and pepper if needed.

MAKE THE BISCUITS

1. Heat the oven to 425°F. In a large bowl, mix the flour, baking powder, baking soda, salt, and pepper.

2. Add the butter and, using 2 knives or a pastry blender, mix it into the flour until small pea-size pieces are formed. Add the buttermilk and milk; mix with a wooden spoon until the dough just holds together.

3. With lightly floured hands, gather the dough and knead gently against the sides of the bowl a few times until any loose pieces of dough adhere. Transfer the dough to a lightly floured work surface and roll out the dough to ½ inch thick. Cut the dough into biscuits using a 2- or 3-inch lightly floured biscuit or cookie cutter. Reroll scraps of dough and cut out additional biscuits. You should have about 12 biscuits.

4. Arrange the cut biscuits on a nonstick baking sheet, about 1½ inches apart, sprinkle the tops with sea salt, and bake for 15 minutes, or until golden brown.

TO SERVE

Spoon the chicken mixture into large individual bowls and top with two warm split biscuits. (Alternatively, fill a 9 × 13-inch ovenproof serving dish with the chicken mixture and arrange uncooked biscuits on top of the chicken, tucking the edges into the sides of the pan if necessary. Cut a few 1-inch vent holes for a large pie or one 1-inch vent hole in smaller pies. Reduce the oven temperature to 400°F and bake for 20 minutes.)

continued

HAPPY CHICKENS

Ask Paul Baffoni what makes a great chicken and he'll give it to you straight: "A happy chicken is raised in clean conditions, fed good food, and raised close to your home." Paul would know—his family has been raising chickens (and turkeys) on their small but highly productive farm in Johnston, Rhode Island, for three generations. The chickens are slaughtered, cleaned, and sold in a small shop on the farm run by a number of Baffonis, including Paul's father, brother, cousins, and uncles. While Paul's generation of the family all hold full-time jobs elsewhere, they pitch in at the farm on a regular basis.

Paul sells his chickens and eggs to small local markets and local restaurants (like Derek Wagner's Nicks on Broadway), and he does about half of his business right out of the farm's shop. Rhode Island has a diverse culture, and Baffoni sells its Rhode Island Reds and Barred Rock breeds live to some of the local Asian community who like to cook the chicken from head to toe as well as to African and Spanish clients who have always thought the best-tasting chickens were brought home alive. Best to do if the chicken is local.

Derek Wagner and Paul Baffoni

DANIEL HUMM, *Eleven Madison Park,* New York City

STEVE & SYLVIA PRYZANT, *Four Story Hill Farm,* Honesdale, Pennsylvania (poultry)

Poached Chicken with Morels and Asparagus

In this amazingly simple yet elegant chicken dish, the meat becomes incredibly tender and moist as it's poached in the cream-chicken sauce. Vin jaune, an unusual wine from the tiny Jura region in France that literally means "yellow wine," will be well worth the trouble to find at specialty wine stores. If fresh morels are out of season, you can substitute the more available dried mushroom.

SERVES 4

5 tablespoons unsalted butter
1 small shallot, minced
1 pound fresh morels, wiped cleaned, dried, and cut in half if large
4 sprigs fresh thyme
¾ cup vin jaune (or ½ cup white wine and ¼ cup sherry)

2 cups heavy cream
2 cups chicken stock
4 chicken breasts, bone-in, skin removed, about 3 to 4 pounds
12 medium asparagus spears, about 1 pound, cut into 1-inch pieces
½ cup crème fraîche

Cayenne
Coarse salt

1. In a large sauté pan, heat 3 tablespoons of the butter over medium heat. Add the shallots and cook for 5 minutes; add the morels and thyme. Continue to cook for 5 minutes, or until the morels are browned and a slight crust has formed at the bottom of the pan. Deglaze the pan with the wine and continue to cook for 15 minutes, or until the liquid is reduced to a syrup consistency and only about 1 tablespoon is left in the pan.

2. Add the cream and chicken stock to the pan over medium-high heat; bring to a simmer. Add the chicken breasts and bring back to a simmer; cover, reduce the heat to medium, and cook for 25 minutes, or until the meat is cooked through or an instant-read thermometer reaches 165°F.

3. While the chicken is cooking, heat the remaining 2 tablespoons butter in a medium skillet over medium heat. Add the asparagus and sauté until just tender, 5 to 8 minutes. Set aside.

4. Remove the chicken from the sauce and transfer to a serving dish. Reduce the cream sauce for 10 minutes over medium-high heat (adjust the heat to a simmer if boiling). Whisk the crème fraîche into the mushroom sauce and heat over medium heat until just warm. Season to taste with cayenne and salt.

5. To serve, spoon the sauce over the chicken and arrange the sautéed asparagus around the chicken.

THROUGH THICK AND THIN

Steve and Sylvia Pryzant wanted to be farmers and nothing was going to stop them. The Pryzants met in Israel when Steve was in charge of milking the herd on the kibbutz he and Sylvia lived on. After their time in Israel, Steve and Sylvia decided to move to Pennsylvania and start their own herd. First problem: Dairy farms are expensive to start from the ground up. So the Pryzants decided to raise veal calves.

Although the mothers took care of feeding the calves for the most part, grain and maintenance were expensive. Steve estimates that out of 15 groups of calves he raised over 3 years, 2 of the groups were profitable (even though he was selling to the restaurant empires of Tom Colicchio and Daniel Boulud). Along the way, a barn collapsed from a massive snowstorm in 1993, which led to a weekend-only relationship for three years as Steve worked in Brooklyn, New York, to support the farm while Sylvia ran it.

Next plan. Wayne Nish had been buying veal from the Pryzants and was interested in getting Berkshire pigs finished on apples for his restaurant March. This was 1999, when heritage breed pigs were a rare commodity, but the Pryzants bought a couple of pigs so they could experiment for Nish. (During this time the Pryzants were also building the staple of their farm, a poultry business that fed the best restaurants in New York like Gramercy Tavern and Tabla.) The pig business took off and is now a major part of Four Story's income.

The Pryzants continue to raise Berkshire pigs, capons, Guinea hens, and Muscovy ducks and work other poultry into their rotation when one of their chef clients has a special request. Recently they started raising poulardes for Floyd Cardoz of Tabla, just like the ones he had in India as a child.

Steve Pryzant and Daniel Humm

CHARLIE PALMER, *Aureole,* New York City

TOM JURGIELEWICZ, *Jurgielewicz Duck Farm,* East Moriches, New York (duck)

Duck Meatballs with Pomegranate–Orange Glaze and Puréed Parsnips

With little seasoning, the pure duck flavor shines in these meatballs. They are unsurpassed in their ability to please crowds and have a sweet-tart glaze that adds a pleasant tang.

**YIELDS APPROXIMATELY 32 MEATBALLS;
SERVES 4 TO 6**

FOR THE MEATBALLS
1 tablespoon olive oil
1 cup finely chopped onions (about
   1 large onion)
1 tablespoon minced garlic
1 pound ground duck, preferably
   duck thighs and legs
1 to 2 tablespoons coarsely chopped
   fresh flat-leaf parsley
¼ cup panko-style breadcrumbs
3 large eggs
Coarse salt and freshly ground
   black pepper

FOR THE POMEGRANATE GLAZE
1 cup pomegranate juice
1 cup fresh orange juice
1 cup pomegranate molasses
1 cup chicken broth

FOR THE PARSNIP PURÉE
2 cups parsnips, peeled and chopped
   (about 2 large)
2 cloves garlic, minced
3 cups milk
Coarse salt and freshly ground
   black pepper

FOR GARNISH (OPTIONAL)
Orange segments
2 tablespoons grated orange zest
2 tablespoons chopped fresh chives

CROSS CULTURAL DUCKS

Jurgielewicz ducks have been roaming the farm in Moriches, New York, since 1919, when Tom Jurgielewicz's great-grandfather moved out to the then remote piece of land on Long Island after emigrating from Poland and living for a short stint in Brooklyn. Long Island became famous for ducks due in large part to the Jurgielewicz family and the 120 other farms that flourished there. But the demands of population growth and the high price of real estate have left only Tom and one other farmer in the area.

The White Pekin duck that Tom raises is known internationally for the beautiful breast meat it produces and skin that is unmarked with a gorgeous texture from being raised free-range. The animal, when raised outdoors, naturally produces an oil that makes Tom's ducks a favorite of Chinese chefs, who are his biggest clients. Tom's ducks are also a favorite with

MAKE THE MEATBALLS

1. Heat the oven to 325°F. In a medium skillet, heat the oil over low heat, then add the onions and garlic and cook until soft, about 5 minutes; let cool.

2. In a large bowl, combine the duck meat, cooled onions and garlic, the parsley, breadcrumbs, and eggs. Season with salt and pepper. Have ready a nonstick baking sheet. Shape the meat into roughly 1-inch meatballs and arrange them on the baking sheet. Bake for 10 minutes.

MAKE THE POMEGRANATE GLAZE

Combine all the ingredients in a large saucepan and cook over medium heat until the liquid is reduced by half, about 15 minutes. Remove from the heat, let cool, and set aside.

MAKE THE PARSNIP PURÉE

Combine all the ingredients in a large saucepan and cook over medium heat for 20 minutes, or until fork-tender. Transfer to a blender and purée until completely smooth (you might have to do this in batches). Season with salt and pepper to taste and set aside.

TO SERVE

1. Put the meatballs in a large skillet and pour the pomegranate glaze over them; turn to coat well. Glaze the meatballs over medium heat for 2 minutes. You might have to glaze the meatballs in batches.

2. Spread the parsnip purée on a large serving plate and top with the glazed meatballs. Garnish with the orange segments, grated orange zest, and chopped chives, if desired.

Jewish clients, as they are the only ducks raised in North America that are kosher.

Ducks are also known to produce fantastic eggs that are very popular with chefs and with some consumers who are allergic to chicken eggs. The eggs are up to 5 times higher in pro-tein than a chicken egg and produce a clear white and sunset-yellow yolk that is richer in flavor than those of chicken eggs.

While larger duck farms have mi-grated to Indiana, Pennsylvania, and California, Tom Jurgielewicz is sure that the superior taste and skin of his ducks will keep his customers happy and his business growing, especially as his Asian clientele continues to expand.

DEAN FEARING, *Fearing's,* Dallas, Texas

TODD SMITH, *Texas Quail Farm,* Lockhart, Texas (quail)

Apricot-Orange–Glazed Quail

Todd raises Coturnix quail, which grow rapidly and are the quail most prized by chefs for their tender and plentiful meat. A subtle apricot and orange glaze doesn't overwhelm the mild meat but instead complements its delicate flavor. Serve with any herbed grain and sautéed greens as side dishes.

SERVES 4 TO 6

2 cups dried apricots
1 medium onion, chopped
  (about 1 cup)
1 small jalapeño, seeds removed and
  finely chopped
1 tablespoon minced garlic

1 cup fresh orange juice
½ cup brown sugar
2 tablespoons malt vinegar
1 tablespoon Worcestershire sauce
½ teaspoon hot sauce

2 teaspoons fresh lime juice
Coarse salt and freshly ground
  black pepper
8 quail, about 4 to 6 ounces each
  (2½ to 3½ pounds total)

1. Make the apricot sauce: In a heavy saucepan over medium-high heat, combine all ingredients except for the quail and bring to a boil. Turn down the heat to a simmer and cook for 20 minutes. Remove the sauce from the heat and purée in a blender until the consistency is smooth. Adjust the seasonings and reserve about ⅓ cup to serve with the quail.

2. Heat the oven to 450°F. Season the quail inside and out with salt and black pepper. Place them on a rack in a roasting pan and fold the wingtips under the birds and tie the legs together with butcher's twine. Brush the apricot sauce over the birds evenly and roast for 10 minutes. Reduce the heat to 375°F and continue to cook for another 10 minutes, basting twice with the apricot sauce. Check that the birds are done, piercing the thickest part of the flesh with a knife; when the juices run clear, the birds are done. Remove from the oven, cover loosely with foil, and let rest for 10 minutes.

3. Warm the reserved apricot sauce. Cut the twine from the quail legs, and serve with the warm sauce.

BIG PLAN, LITTLE BIRD

A good professor can show a student a path; a good student listens and decides if that path will work for him. Todd Smith of Texas Quail Farm listened closely as his professor at Texas A&M steered him toward quail farming with the hint that "it seems like a pretty good untapped market."

Todd decided to run with the idea and started a quail farm using money from selling his breeding stock of cattle. The early days were filled with selling at farmers' markets in Austin, which also provided the opportunity to meet the cool chefs of a town whose unofficial motto is "Keep Austin Weird." Todd wasn't much for weird, but he was a fan of the chefs and happy that his quail were being used in great restaurants and his eggs were being cracked in sushi bars across Texas. Selling to Whole Foods® also fueled his growth.

The quail Todd raises, Coturnix quail (also known as Texas A&M Gourmet Quail), grow faster than other breeds, but more important to Todd, they have a beautiful meat that is light in color and very plentiful. The quail are raised in former chicken coops spread throughout Lockhart, Texas. The separation of the birds is good for keeping the possibility of damage to the whole flock from storms or disease to a minimum. The sentiment, "I don't like to have all my eggs in one basket," more than occasionally crosses the farmer's lips.

Todd wants to continue to expand his quail business, but he needs to find more eggs and chicks. "I am the only quail farmer that is inspected and licensed to process in the whole state of Texas." With his mix of business savvy and quality product, Todd will surely keep growing beyond the 25 employees he already has.

GABRIEL RUCKER, *Le Pigeon,* Portland, Oregon

MANUEL RECIO & LESLIE LUKAS-RECIO, *Viridian Farms,* Dayton, Oregon (peppers)

Chicken-Fried Squab with Stuffed Peppers

Gypsy peppers are a sweet pepper with a long curved shape, but similar in flavor to the more commonly known bell pepper. They're available in bright colors of orange, red, and green and often a pretty mix of two or three shades of colors. The cornbread stuffing is a wonderful partner to the crispy bird and spicy herbed vinaigrette.

SERVES 6

FOR THE STUFFED PEPPERS
3 tablespoons olive oil

1 medium red onion, finely chopped

8 Gypsy peppers, 2 thinly sliced
   and 6 with tops cut off, halved,
   and seeded

4 cloves garlic, minced

3 cups Cornbread, crumbled
   (recipe follows)

2 tablespoons unsalted butter, melted

¼ cup fresh flat-leaf parsley,
   finely chopped

Coarse salt and freshly ground
   black pepper

FOR THE CILANTRO-CHILE VINAIGRETTE
1 cup extra-virgin olive oil

1 teaspoon ground piment d'Espelette
   or red pepper

1 cup fresh cilantro leaves

⅓ cup sherry vinegar

Hot sauce

Coarse salt and freshly ground
   black pepper

FOR THE SQUAB
6 squab, about 1 pound each

Coarse salt and freshly ground
   black pepper

2 cups buttermilk

2 cups all-purpose flour

¼ cup cornmeal

1 teaspoon garlic powder

1 teaspoon dried mustard

¼ teaspoon cayenne

6 cups canola oil, for frying

1 lemon, for serving (optional)

Fleur de sel or other coarse salt,
   for serving (optional)

MAKE THE STUFFED PEPPERS

1. Heat the oven to 425°F. Heat the oil in a medium skillet over medium heat and cook the onions and sliced peppers for 5 minutes, or until softened. Add the garlic and cook for 1 minute more. Set aside to cool. In a medium bowl, mix the cornbread with the cooled onion-pepper mixture, the butter, and parsley. Season to taste with salt and pepper.

2. Bring a medium pot of salted water to a boil and cook the pepper halves for 2 minutes to soften; remove and let cool on a large dish. Fill each pepper half with the stuffing. Arrange close to one another in a 9 × 13-inch baking dish. Bake for 12 minutes just before serving.

MAKE THE VINAIGRETTE

In a small saucepan, warm the olive oil with the piment d'Espelette or red pepper over low heat for 2 minutes, then cover and let steep until cool. In the bowl of a food processor, combine the cilantro, vinegar, and a few drops of hot sauce. Process, adding the infused oil in a steady stream until emulsified. Adjust the seasoning with salt and pepper and set aside.

PREPARE AND COOK THE SQUAB

1. With poultry shears or scissors, cut each squab in half through the center of the breast (or have your butcher prepare the birds). Cut out the backbone completely and remove and discard it (or reserve it for making

stock). Season the squab with salt and pepper. Put the buttermilk in a large bowl and add the squab; turn to coat well and refrigerate for 30 minutes.

2. Combine the flour, cornmeal, and spices in a large brown paper bag or zip-top bag. Remove the squab pieces from the buttermilk, one at a time, and add to the bag; turn down the top and then shake vigorously to coat the squab with the flour-cornmeal mixture.

3. Heat the oven to 250°F. Add enough oil to a large, heavy-bottomed skillet to come 1 inch up the sides. Heat over high heat until an instant-read thermometer reaches 350°F or when bubbles come up the sides of the pan when a small corner of the squab is dipped into the oil. Carefully add the squab pieces to the hot oil and fry until browned on one side, about 3 minutes. Turn over and brown the other side, about 3 minutes. Remove the pieces and drain on a paper towel–lined plate. Fry in batches if necessary, making sure the oil remains a steady 350°F, and transfer the finished pieces to the oven to keep warm.

TO SERVE

Arrange two pepper halves on a plate with two pieces of squab alongside. Drizzle the vinaigrette over the squab and around the plate. Sprinkle with the juice of a lemon and fleur de sel, if desired.

Cornbread

SERVES 8

1½ cups ground cornmeal
¾ cup all-purpose flour
2 tablespoons sugar
2 teaspoons baking powder

½ teaspoon baking soda
2 teaspoons coarse salt
2 large eggs
1⅓ cups buttermilk

4 slices bacon, cooked until crisp and crumbled, with rendered fat

1. Heat the oven to 400°F. Combine the cornmeal, flour, sugar, baking powder, baking soda, and salt in a large bowl. In a separate bowl, whisk the eggs, buttermilk, and bacon. Pour the wet ingredients into the dry ingredients and stir just to combine.

2. Grease a 9 × 9-inch baking dish with the reserved bacon fat or butter, then add the cornbread mixture. Bake on the center rack for 30 minutes, or until a toothpick inserted in the center comes out clean. Let cool.

GABRIEL RUCKER, *Le Pigeon,* Portland, Oregon

MANUEL RECIO & LESLIE LUKAS-RECIO, *Viridian Farms,* Dayton, Oregon (peppers)

Halibut Poached in Pepper Butter with Roasted Corn Salad

Gently poaching fish in butter keeps it moist and velvety. Manuel and Leslie are known as authentic pepper farmers, and they buy their seeds in Europe and grow many varieties of peppers. Gabriel loves the challenge of using their various types of peppers and the subtle differences in each. You'll have extra red pepper butter from this recipe; it can be used atop other roasted or sautéed fillets, like cod, grouper, or red snapper.

SERVES 6

FOR THE PEPPER BUTTER
4 sticks (1 pound) unsalted butter
2 pounds mixed sweet peppers, such as banana, bell, or Doux Long des Landes, seeded and roughly chopped
1 red onion, sliced
2 cloves garlic, sliced
1 tablespoon chopped fresh oregano
½ teaspoon piment d'Espelette or coarse ground red pepper

Coarse salt and freshly ground black pepper

FOR THE CORN SALAD
6 ears yellow corn, kernels removed
2 tablespoons olive oil
Coarse salt and freshly ground black pepper
8 shallots, thinly sliced
1 pint cherry tomatoes, halved lengthwise

2 small sweet red peppers, julienned
15 fresh basil leaves, torn into small pieces
Juice of 2 limes
Dash of Tabasco®

Six 6-ounce halibut fillets
1 medium lemon
Coarse salt
2 scallions (white and green parts), sliced, for garnish

1. To make the pepper butter, combine all the ingredients except the salt and pepper in a medium saucepan and simmer, stirring frequently, for an hour. Remove from the heat and purée in a blender. Season with salt and pepper, then return to the pan to keep warm.

2. To make the corn salad, heat the oven to 350°F. Toss the corn kernels with the olive oil, season with salt and pepper, spread on a baking sheet, and roast for 20 minutes, or until tender. Remove from the oven and combine with 2 tablespoons of the pepper butter and all the remaining ingredients in a large bowl. Season to taste with more salt and pepper and portion the salad evenly in the center of 6 large serving plates.

3. To prepare the halibut, heat the pepper butter in a large, straight-sided skillet over low heat to 135°F (use a deep-frying thermometer). Gently lower the fillets into the butter and poach for about 15 minutes; the fish will become opaque within the first 5 minutes. The halibut should be firm when pierced with a knife and is completely opaque when cooked.

4. Carefully remove the fillets with a slotted spatula and lay them on top of the corn salad on each plate. The butter may separate. If it does, either whisk it until combined or use an immersion blender to emulsify the sauce. Drizzle each serving with a spoonful of the poaching butter. Season the fish with a squeeze of lemon and a sprinkling of salt, and garnish with the scallions.

SPAIN IN OREGON

A taste of Spain in Oregon? Although it might sound strange it's true, thanks to Viridian Farms and Manuel Recio and his wife Leslie Lukas-Recio. After being offered the opportunity to buy her family's farm in the Willamette Valley of Oregon, Leslie and Manuel wanted to figure out a way to make it work. Not only had they always wanted to run their own business, but they also wanted to bring their love of the food and culture of Spain to the business. It seemed the perfect time to make the dream a reality.

The couple had met while on a seven-month college stint in Spain (he came from Miami, she from Portland). After spending time traveling together and talking about their future, they knew they wanted to bring a piece of northern Spain home. It was decided that home would be Grand Island, Oregon, and growing produce from Spain on their new farm was a match made in heaven. Luckily the climate of northern Spain is similar to that of their farm in Oregon, where they decided to grow things like piquillo peppers, shelling beans, cannellini, and asparagus. With backgrounds in advertising (Manuel) and teaching (Leslie), they knew right from the start that they were going to need some help and so turned to Leslie's father, who grew berries, peaches, and apricots.

Getting into farming in the Portland area just as it was becoming a "food town" was a stroke of unplanned luck. Soon the farmers were taking their produce to restaurants and local farmers' markets. While at first they had to educate farmers' market shoppers and even some chefs about their exotic produce, it caught on and is now featured in restaurants from Miami to Portland, New York to Seattle.

Manuel Recio and Gabriel Rucker (top);
Gabriel's art (left)

WALDY MALOUF, *Beacon,* New York City

JON WALLACH, *Eden Brook Fish Company,* Monticello, New York (trout)

Roasted Trout with Herb-Champagne Vinaigrette

High heat creates a perfectly crisp skin with intense flavor, while chervil's subtle anise notes enhance the finished dish. Serve this fish with either boiled or steamed potatoes or any moistened grains with seasonings, such as barley with mushrooms or a simple rice pilaf.

SERVES 4

FOR THE VINAIGRETTE
1 cup chopped fresh chervil or chives
¾ cup chopped fresh flat-leaf parsley
3 tablespoons roughly chopped shallots
   (about 1 shallot)

3 tablespoons fresh lemon juice
2 tablespoons Champagne vinegar
   or white-wine vinegar
1 cup extra-virgin olive oil

Coarse salt and freshly ground
   black pepper

4 skin-on, boned whole trout, heads
   removed, about 12 to 14 ounces each

1. To make the vinaigrette, put the chervil or chives, parsley, shallots, lemon juice, vinegar, and ½ cup of the olive oil in a blender and purée. Transfer the mixture to a small bowl, stir in the remaining oil, and then season with salt and pepper to taste.

2. Sprinkle the inside of the trout with salt and pepper. Arrange in a glass baking dish and spoon about half of the vinaigrette over the trout, both on the inside and outside. Rub the vinaigrette into the fish. Wrap the fish with butcher's twine across the body to close the cavity. Cover the trout and refrigerate for 30 minutes.

3. Heat the oven to 500°F. Transfer the fish to a rack in a roasting pan and roast for 15 to 25 minutes, depending on the size of the trout, until the flesh is firm and translucent.

4. Serve immediately, with the remaining vinaigrette spooned over the top as a sauce.

continued

NOBLE FISH

Some fish, tilapia and catfish, for instance, can grow in just about any mud hole. Then there are trout, "the noble fish" as Jon Wallach of Eden Brook Fish Company calls them. Jon owns and farm-raises the fish in clear streams and ponds in Monticello, New York. "These fish really are the canary in a coal mine; if the ecosystem is not clean, they cannot survive."

The hatchery that Jon bought 20 years ago had gone into disrepair, but what still remained was a pristine piece of land. Jon saw a way to start and grow a business in his home state after going to school for aquatic biology in Santa Barbara, California. "From the beginning, my plan was to go to New York City and sell to the best chefs and restaurants I could find rather than stock sportsman's clubs like most trout farmers." He knew that locally grown fish that could be delivered immediately to chefs would be in great demand. He also knew that trout were associated with the romance of fly fishing.

The trials of a fish man are many. While the farm is only 100 miles outside of New York City, wildlife like black bears, minx, raccoons, and herons are always looking for a free juicy trout. In the other side of his business, Jon wholesales fish and lobster from boats (Jon calls these fishermen the hunters and gatherers of the last primitive food) and deals with the volatile worlds of weather, trends, and politics as well as supply and demand. "Fish prices move faster than just about any other commodity," says Jon, "and luckily my clients know this and we keep close to each other to weather the storms."

Whether the fish come from his ponds, the waters off the coast of Maine, or halfway around the world, Jon likes to say "every fish has a story."

MICHELLE BERNSTEIN, *Michy's,* Miami, Florida

GABRIELE MAREWSKI, *Paradise Farms,* Homestead, Florida (mangos)

Fish in Curry Mango Sauce

Green mangos have a slightly sour taste, which makes them a natural pairing in sweet-and-sour curry dishes. All mangos are green when unripe and some remain green when they ripen. Use mangos that are unripe but firm or that have a slight indentation when pressed with your thumb.

SERVES 4

4 cups Curry Mango Sauce
  (recipe follows)
Four ½-pound yellowtail, snapper,
  or grouper fillets, skin scored

1 green mango, cut into large chunks
½ cup mixed fresh cilantro, mint,
  and basil leaves, julienned, for garnish

1. Pour the curry sauce into a very large sauté pan and bring to a simmer. Heat on low, add the fillets, cover, and gently cook for 3 to 5 minutes, or until the flesh is opaque and flakes easily. Add the mango chunks to the warm sauce and remove the pan from the heat.

2. To serve, spoon some sauce onto each plate, lay a fillet in the center (or you may cut the fillets into smaller pieces), and top with more sauce and mangos; garnish with the mixed herbs.

continued

Curry Mango Sauce

3 tablespoons canola oil

2 shallots, thinly sliced

2 cloves garlic, chopped

One 2-inch piece fresh ginger, peeled and minced

1 tablespoon shrimp paste or anchovy paste

5 curry leaves (or 1 tablespoon Madras curry powder)

2 tablespoons mustard seeds

1 tablespoon fenugreek seeds

2 whole star anise

2 cloves

1 Thai chile, chopped (leave the seeds in for a spicier curry)

1 green mango, diced

1 beefsteak tomato, seeded and chopped

1 stalk lemongrass, hard exterior removed and chopped

1 medium onion, thinly sliced

1/2 cup tamarind purée, or 1/4 cup each fresh lime juice and white vinegar

One 14-ounce can unsweetened coconut milk

1 cup chopped fresh cilantro with stems

2 tablespoons soy sauce

2 tablespoons brown sugar

1. Heat the canola oil in a large saucepan over medium heat and sauté the shallots, garlic, and ginger, stirring, for 3 minutes. Add the shrimp paste or anchovy paste, curry leaves or curry powder, mustard seeds, fenugreek seeds, star anise, cloves, and Thai chile; cook for another 2 minutes. Add the mangos, tomatoes, lemongrass, onions, and tamarind purée (or lime juice and vinegar). Add 4 cups water and simmer for 5 minutes.

2. Add the coconut milk and cilantro. Simmer for 35 to 40 minutes. Strain the sauce and discard the solids, then add the soy sauce and brown sugar.

MARK GAIER & CLARK FRASIER, *Arrows,* Ogunquit, Maine

TED JOHNSON, Ogunquit, Maine (lobster)

Lobster Shortcakes with Vanilla Rum Sauce and Spicy Shallots

A rich dish, the spices complement the lobster's delicate flavor, with the shortcakes a necessary—and unique—vehicle for mopping up every bit of the decadent vanilla rum sauce.

SERVES 6

FOR THE CURRIED SHALLOTS
8 shallots, thinly sliced
1 tablespoon finely chopped fresh ginger
1 serrano chile, cored, seeded, and minced
1 teaspoon turmeric
1 tablespoon Madras curry powder
1 teaspoon coarse salt
1 cup rice vinegar

FOR THE SHORTCAKES
1½ cups all-purpose flour
1½ teaspoons baking powder
½ teaspoon baking soda
1 teaspoon fine salt
12 tablespoons (1½ sticks) unsalted butter, cubed and then frozen
¼ to 1 cup buttermilk
¼ cup heavy cream

FOR THE VANILLA RUM SAUCE
½ cup fresh lime juice; plus more to finish the sauce
½ cup rice vinegar
¼ cup dark rum; plus more to finish the sauce
¼ cup minced shallots (about 2 shallots)
1 serrano chile, cored, seeded, and finely sliced
One 1-inch cube fresh ginger, peeled and finely sliced
½ vanilla bean, split vertically
2 sticks (½ pound) unsalted butter, chilled and diced into ½-inch cubes
Coarse salt and freshly ground black pepper

3 lobsters, about 1½ to 2½ pounds each, cooked, cleaned, and lobster meat removed (about 2 pounds meat)
2 tablespoons chopped fresh cilantro, for garnish

1. Make the curried shallots: Combine all the ingredients in a small saucepan and bring to a boil. Take the pan off the heat and let cool.

2. Make the shortcakes: Heat the oven to 325°F and lightly grease a baking sheet. Whisk together the dry ingredients in a large bowl or pulse in a food processor. Cut the butter into the dry ingredients (use two knives if doing this by hand) until the mixture resembles coarse sand. Add just enough buttermilk to bring the mixture together and form a soft dough, being careful not to overwork it. Roll the dough out to a ½-inch thickness and cut out six 3-inch rounds using a biscuit cutter or cookie cutter. Arrange the rounds on the prepared baking sheet, brush the tops with cream, and bake until golden, approximately 15 minutes.

3. Prepare the sauce: Combine the lime juice, vinegar, rum, shallots, chile, ginger, and vanilla bean in a medium saucepan over medium heat and cook until the liquid is reduced by two-thirds, about 15 minutes. Let the mixture cool slightly, strain it through a fine-mesh strainer, and return it to the pan.

4. Over low heat, whisk in the chilled butter, a couple of cubes at a time, allowing them to emulsify before adding

more. Season with salt and pepper and more lime juice and rum to taste. The sauce can be held in a warm place for up to 1 hour.

5. Assemble the shortcakes: Put the lobster meat and a few tablespoons of sauce in a large saucepan, stirring to coat, and warm over medium-low heat for 1 to 2 minutes until heated through. Warm the shortcakes in a low-heat oven for a few minutes, split them in half horizontally, and place each bottom in the center of a plate. Portion the lobster meat evenly on top of the shortcake bottoms. Spoon some sauce over each shortcake and around the plate. Sprinkle with cilantro. Scoop the curried shallots out of their pickling liquid and pile on each plate next to the shortcake. Top with the remaining shortcake half and serve.

LOBSTER LAW

Ted Johnson, the main supplier of lobster to Arrows Restaurant in Ogunquit, Maine, likes to explain that the simple joy of cooking and eating a lobster comes after many years of that lobster shedding its shell (molting), being caught, being thrown back for being too small or too fertile, and finally being trapped and harvested somewhere near its home on the eastern seaboard.

While Americans think that majority of the lobster sold in this country comes from the cold waters off of Maine, the truth is that most of the lobster sold here comes from the waters off of Canada and Nova Scotia. The Canadian lobster industry reaps almost $1 billion in sales every year, making lobster that country's most valuable fishing export.

Because of the high value and cost of lobster, American and Canadian fishermen are highly regulated both publicly and privately. When caught, breeding females carrying eggs have their tales notched with a "v," which makes it illegal to harvest them for sale. Lobster rules along the East Coast vary by state. Massachusetts law allows small lobsters to be hauled in, but Maine requires that lobsters have a minimum of 3¼ inches of carapace (the upper section of the shell) and a maximum of 5 inches of carapace. Larger healthy lobsters are left in the water to continue successful breeding.

Ted is happy to follow the rules as well as give a little cooking advice: "Never eat a dead lobster, and make sure to salt the water in the pot—it keeps the flavor in."

Clark Frasier, Mark Gaier, and Ted Johnson

VITALY PALEY, *Paley's Place,* Portland, Oregon

BARB FOULKE, *Freddy Guys Hazelnuts,* Monmouth, Oregon (hazelnuts)

Sautéed Shrimp and Hazelnut Romesco

Nyora peppers are authentic to making true Catalan romesco sauce. If they're not available, substitute additional large red peppers such as dried ancho chiles. Barb and Vitaly love the idea of using hazelnuts instead of almonds, which are more common in this sauce. Use spot prawn instead of extra-large shrimp when available at your local fish market.

SERVES 4

8 Nyora chiles
2 large red bell peppers
¾ cup extra-virgin olive oil plus
   2 tablespoons
½ cup raw hazelnuts

2 tablespoons fine breadcrumbs
2 cloves garlic, coarsely chopped
1 medium tomato, peeled and seeded
2 tablespoons sherry vinegar
Coarse salt and freshly ground
   black pepper

16 extra-large shrimp, shelled,
   deveined, and rinsed
¼ cup fresh flat-leaf parsley, finely
   chopped, for garnish

1. Snap the stems from the Nyora peppers. Shake out and discard the seeds. Put the Nyoras in a heatproof bowl and cover with 2 cups boiling water. Set a small plate on top to keep the peppers submerged and let sit until softened, about 20 minutes. Discard the soaking liquid. Set the peppers aside.

2. Roast the red bell peppers: On the stovetop, hold the peppers with tongs over an open burner, turning them until they're blackened uniformly, about 3 to 5 minutes. (Alternatively, put the peppers on a baking sheet and roast in the oven at 450°F until the skins become brown and loosen, about 30 minutes.) Transfer to a bowl and cover tightly with plastic wrap for 15 minutes, allowing them to steam and cool slightly. Peel the skins from the peppers, remove the seeds, and set the peppers aside.

3. Heat 2 tablespoons of the olive oil in a small skillet over medium heat, then add the hazelnuts and cook, shaking the pan a few times, until lightly browned, about 4 minutes. Drain the hazelnuts and let cool slightly. Remove as much paper coating on the nuts as possible. Discard the oil.

4. Make the romesco sauce: Combine the Nyoras, roasted red bell peppers, hazelnuts, breadcrumbs, garlic, tomatoes, sherry vinegar, and ½ cup olive oil in the bowl of a food processor. Season generously with salt and pepper and pulse until completely puréed. Transfer to a small plastic container, cover, and refrigerate until needed. The romesco can be made a day ahead and kept covered in the refrigerator.

5. Heat the remaining ¼ cup olive oil in a large straight-sided skillet over high heat. Add the shrimp, season with salt and pepper, and cook until the shrimp turn pink and become firm, about 1 to 2 minutes per side.

6. Warm the cold romesco sauce. Transfer the shrimp to a serving platter and serve the romesco sauce on the side. Garnish with the chopped parsley and serve immediately.

LAURENT GRAS, *L2O,* Chicago, Illinois

PETER KLEIN, *Seedling Farm,* South Haven, Michigan (strawberries)

Shrimp with Tomatoes, Strawberries, and Lemon Vinegar

Murray salt—apricot-colored, flaky Australian salt from the Murray Darling basin—is mild and used for finishing when Laurent makes this salad at the restaurant. Basil seeds are sold under various names; look for tukmaria seeds, which are sold in specialty food stores. Start this recipe a day in advance because the seeds need to soak for at least 12 hours. Santa Barbara shrimp are spot prawns at their peak in the summer season and are prized for their firm texture and sweet, almost nutty flavor.

SERVES 4

1 ounce basil seeds
12 Santa Barbara shrimp or jumbo
  shrimp, deveined and tails left intact
2 tablespoons coarse salt;
  plus more for seasoning
¼ cup rice vinegar

2 large lemons
6 tablespoons extra-virgin olive oil
Freshly ground black pepper
1 pound ripe tomatoes (about 2 large
  tomatoes), scored with an X through
  the bottom skin

1 pound fresh strawberries (about
  2 pints or 20 large berries)
30 small fresh basil leaves

1. To rehydrate the basil seeds, combine them with ⅔ cup water and refrigerate overnight, preferably for 12 hours. Put the shrimp in a medium bowl. In a small saucepan, bring 2 cups water and the salt to a simmer until the salt is dissolved. Let cool completely and pour the salt water brine over the shrimp; cover and refrigerate for 45 minutes.

2. In a small saucepan, bring the vinegar to a simmer and remove from the heat. Using a vegetable peeler, remove the lemon zest in strips. Add to the pan with the vinegar and let cool. Transfer to a container and let steep, covered, for at least 1 hour and preferably for 3 hours. In a medium bowl, whisk 4 tablespoons of olive oil into the lemon vinegar and season to taste with salt and pepper. Set aside. Drain the rehydrated basil seeds and toss with 1 tablespoon oil in a small bowl. Set aside.

3. Prepare a large bowl of ice and water. Heat a large saucepan of water to boiling and cook the tomatoes for 30 seconds. Remove with a slotted spoon and place in the bowl of ice water to cool completely. Remove the skins and seeds from the tomatoes, then cut them into ¼-inch dice. Transfer to a medium bowl and set aside. Rinse and hull the strawberries and cut the strawberries into ¼-inch dice. Add them to the bowl of tomatoes.

4. To cook the shrimp, remove them from the brine, rinse under cold water, and pat dry. Place them in a steamer and cook until medium rare, 3 to 4 minutes. Cool completely.

5. To serve the salad, mix the tomatoes and strawberries with the vinaigrette, check the seasoning, and then portion onto four plates, mounding the mixture in the center of each plate. Scatter the basil leaves over each salad, then top with 3 shrimp per plate. Drizzle the remaining 1 tablespoon olive oil over the shrimp and sprinkle them with salt and pepper. Spoon the basil seeds around the salad.

A TIME TO STOP MAKING SENSE

Peter Klein was very comfortable navigating his way through Chicago's best restaurants after spending five years as a restaurant marketing guy. But when his love of food became an obsession, he decided it was time to do more.

His favorite fruit grower was retiring, so Peter thought this was the sign to jump into a new endeavor and become the producer he had wanted to be. The farm was an 81-acre swath of orchards in southern Michigan and boasted 70 varieties of apples, peaches, plums, pears, apricots, raspberries, strawberries, and blueberries. But there was the matter of a business plan. After drawing up the plan, Peter

and his wife thought this was a bad idea: The economics just didn't make sense. Some time went by, and Peter looked again at the plan, and "it still seemed like a really, really bad idea." Finally passion won out, and Peter quit his job, took out a loan for the land, bought the farm, and set about making it work.

Like most small farmers, Peter has found a way to cobble together a few revenue streams to make the farm a winning proposition. He now sells directly to about 100 Chicago-area restaurants, makes sorbets and smoothies at farmers' markets, and puts the "ugly apples" into the cider

mill for perfectly sweet cider. Peter is also the only apple supplier to the famous Zingerman's fancy food mail-order catalog. Zingerman's made Peter the first and only trusted direct shipper because of his insistence on picking apples only at the height of sweetness. Peter calls this "the science of sweetness."

Peter intends to keep the orchard growing as he tests multiple varieties of melons, fig trees, lingonberries, and pawpaws (a poor man's banana). And after five years, it's all starting to make sense.

Peter Klein and Laurent Gras

CHARLES PHAN, *The Slanted Door,* San Francisco, California

ANDY GRIFFIN, *Mariquita Farm,* Watsonville, California (fava shoots)

Stir-Fried Fava Shoots with Shrimp and Caramelized Shallots

Fava shoots usually appear with the first sign of spring and are similar to pea shoots. Although fava shoots are not a traditional Asian ingredient, their texture is perfect for fast-cooking methods, like their close cousin, the pea shoot, which is widely used in Chinese cooking. Shrimp is an ideal light pairing for the delicately flavored shoot.

SERVES 2

4 tablespoons canola oil
2 large shallots, thinly sliced
16 large shrimp, preferably gulf
  (about 1 pound), shelled, cleaned,
  and split in half

1 large clove garlic, minced
1 pound fava bean shoots, string
  pulled off along the side
3 tablespoons rice vinegar
2 tablespoons chicken stock

1 tablespoon fish sauce
¼ cup fresh cilantro leaves,
  for garnish (optional)

A MAN OF MANY SPOTS

Andy Griffin doesn't like to multitask. He likes to write. And he's honest—he admits that he can't accomplish more than one thing at a time. Thankfully, Andy's farm, Mariquita Farm (mariquita is Spanish for ladybug), multitasks for him, leaving time for him to do some of the things he enjoys most.

Andy has been writing the weekly newsletter for the CSA that he and fellow farmer Jeanne Byrne started in 1997. What started with 100 clients has grown to include 1,600 who populate the central California coast from Monterey to San Francisco. Even though the boxes of produce don't change much between weeks at times, Andy has worked hard to keep his produce feeling varied. Take tomatoes. To keep the monotony of tomatoes from settling in, Andy changes up the herbs that ship every week and includes an

extensive recipe library on his Two Small Farms website.

Creating a multitasking farm was a smart business strategy and not just because it allows Andy time to focus on growing his CSA business and writing. He is able to extend the harvest of most of his plants, selling not only weeds (young nettles, lamb's quarters, and purslane that are tasty when young and tender) but also young thinnings

1. Heat 1 tablespoon of the oil in a large sauté pan or wok over medium-high heat. Add the shallots, reduce the heat to medium, and cook the shallots until golden brown, about 5 minutes. Transfer to a plate.

2. Heat the remaining 3 tablespoons oil in the same skillet or wok over moderately high heat for 1 minute, or until the pan just begins to smoke. Add the shrimp and cook for about 30 seconds, or until they begin to turn opaque. Using a slotted spoon, transfer the shrimp from the wok to the plate with the shallots.

3. Add the garlic and cook for 30 seconds, then add the fava shoots. Immediately add ⅓ cup water and cook until the shoots are bright green and the water has evaporated, 1 to 2 minutes.

4. In a small bowl, combine the rice vinegar, chicken stock, and fish sauce. Add the shrimp and shallots along with the rice vinegar mixture to the pan and cook, stirring frequently, until the shrimp is cooked through, about 1 minute.

5. Remove from the heat and serve immediately. Garnish with fresh cilantro leaves, if using, and serve with steamed rice, if desired.

that make a perfect braising mix. He also plants crops that yield over long periods of time. Squash is a great example. He'll sell the "fiorelli"—unopened male flower buds—then the small and large sizes, and finally the overgrown versions that get bought for holiday decorations.

Andy's restaurant clients buy a lot of the farm's produce as well. Like other farmers, Andy is happy to work with his chef clients to grow what they like; as he walks through his fields, he points to the friarelli peppers he grows at the request of A16. Though Chef Charles Phan of The Slanted Door has not put in a special request, he has been a loyal supporter and regular customer since the days when Andy was working the farmers' market at San Francisco's Ferry Building.

Soy Butter–Poached Oysters with Radishes and Kimchi Juice

Rappahannock River Oysters have a sweet, full-bodied, slightly salty taste with a distinguishing light finish. Kimchi, a mix of vegetables in pickling juice and Korea's national dish, has a potent chile and garlic flavor, and burdock root has a mild radish-like taste. Both are often sold in Asian markets and specialty grocery stores. Use a mixture of radishes for a nice color contrast.

SERVES 6

2 teaspoons fennel seeds
2 teaspoons coriander seeds
½ cup soy sauce, preferably aged
½ cup red-wine vinegar
2 shallots, finely chopped
½ teaspoon freshly ground
   black pepper

1 stalk burdock root, peeled, cut
   into paper-thin rounds using a
   mandoline, and cut into half moons
4 sticks (1 pound) unsalted butter
   cut into small pieces
6 tablespoons Kimchi Juice
   (recipe follows)

3 tablespoons extra-virgin olive oil
3 radishes, preferably a mix of black,
   watermelon, and breakfast varieties,
   sliced thin, preferably with
   a mandoline, and julienned into
   match sticks (¾ cup)
36 oysters, shucked

1. Make the pickled burdock root: Toast the fennel and coriander seeds. Heat a small skillet and add the seeds. Cook for 1 to 2 minutes until fragrant. In a medium saucepan combine ¼ cup soy sauce, the vinegar, half the shallots, 1 teaspoon each of the coriander and fennel seeds, and ½ teaspoon pepper and bring to a just a boil. Let infuse for 5 minutes, then bring to a simmer. Place the burdock root in small glass bowl or jar. Pour the pickling liquid over the burdock root and let sit for at least 30 minutes (and up to 3 weeks).

2. Make the soy butter: In small saucepan, combine the remaining ¼ cup soy sauce, the rest of the shallots, and 1 teaspoon each of the coriander and fennel seeds. Cook over medium heat to reduce by half, about 3 minutes, then whisk in the butter, piece by piece. Strain, return to the saucepan, and keep warm.

3. In a medium bowl, whisk together the kimchi juice and olive oil. Add the radishes to the kimchi vinaigrette and mix well.

4. In a medium saucepan over medium-low heat, poach the oysters in the soy butter until barely warmed through, about a minute.

5. To serve, evenly divide the pickled burdock among 6 bowls and top with 6 oysters; drizzle with the soy butter and top with radishes.

Kimchi Juice

MAKES 6 TABLESPOONS

3 cloves garlic, chopped
1 (6-inch) piece fresh ginger, chopped

1½ teaspoons fish sauce or anchovy paste
1 tablespoon finely chopped onions (about ¼ small onion or 1 small shallot)

1 tablespoon coarsely chopped mild dried chile pepper, or 1½ teaspoons each paprika and cayenne

Place all ingredients in a food processor and add ½ cup water. Process until a smooth paste is achieved. Allow the garlic chile paste to sit for at least an hour. Strain through a fine-mesh strainer, pressing out all the liquid; alternately, you can use cheesecloth to squeeze out all juice.

continued

REBUILDING THE CHESAPEAKE WITH OYSTERS

The long history of the Chesapeake Bay oyster was too strong a pull to keep cousins Ryan and Travis Croxton out of the business their great-great-grandfather had started in 1899, when oyster "farming" was basically hunting and gathering the bivalves that were a natural part of the Bay. Oysters were a supplement to farming and were "free," as land leases had yet to be implemented. The cousins' fathers tried to discourage them from oyster farming—they had watched their fleets of boats destroyed by multiple hurricanes and the Bay become "polluted" from overfarming and lack of planning by local oystermen. The pollution of the Bay is different than we would think. "It's not a point source pollution like a factory, but the runoff of nitrogen and phosphorous that would normally be processed by oysters," says Ryan. And with the oyster population dwindling, this is "allowing other life to take over the Bay." While the oyster population of Chesapeake Bay is about 4 percent of what it was in 1900, Ryan and Travis believe that through their style of aquaculture, the Bay will not only become cleaner but also a better place to grow their oysters.

"The Chesapeake Bay is like the Napa Valley of oysters," says Ryan. The brackish waters vary from location to location and help create a wide variety of taste profiles from low-salinity Rappahannock River Oysters to brinier Olde Salts oysters from Chincoteague. To keep the bay safe for boats, good looking for local residents, and, most important, a constant food supply for their oysters, the Croxtons moved their business into "off bottom" farming. The oysters are grown in cages in the bay with only buoys to mark their location. The harvest consists of pulling the cages rather than dredging the bottom of the bay and killing much-needed grasses that provide nutrients to the oysters.

The Croxtons' model of sustainable aquaculture and great-tasting oysters has led them to be a favorite of chefs like Tom Colicchio of Craft and Eric Ripert of La Bernardin. "At first we couldn't have been more ignorant about how to sell, price, and ship our product to these great chefs, but their help got us on track." It also won the cousins a *Food & Wine* magazine award as one of its Best Young Taste Makers. Not bad for two guys told to stay out of the family business.

Travis Croxton, Tom Colicchio, and Ryan Croxton

NAOMI POMEROY, *Beast,* Portland, Oregon

DAVE HOYLE, *Creative Growers,* Noti, Oregon (tomatoes)

Crème Fraîche Galette with Heirloom Tomatoes

Many varieties of summer's best heirloom tomatoes should be used for this rustic, French country-style tart. It can be served with various soft cheeses mixed with practically any herb that is abundant and in season.

YIELDS ONE 12-INCH TART; SERVES 4 TO 6

FOR THE GALETTE

1 cup all-purpose flour; plus more for the work surface

½ teaspoon coarse salt; plus more for the tomatoes

1 teaspoon baking powder

1 stick (¼ pound) unsalted butter, chilled and cut into ½-inch pieces

½ cup crème fraîche, chilled

1 pint tomatoes, a combination of heirloom cherry tomatoes and other tomatoes, cut in half or sliced if large

⅓ pound semi-hard sheep's milk cheese, such as manchego

FOR THE GARNISH (OPTIONAL)

1 bunch microradishes or baby radishes, washed and trimmed

1 cup microgreens

Extra-virgin olive oil

Red-wine vinegar

Coarse salt

1. Make the dough: Combine the flour, salt, baking powder, and butter pieces in the bowl of a food processor or in a medium bowl if blending by hand. Blend just until the butter is incorporated into the dry ingredients, making sure not to overmix (some butter the size of peas is fine). Mix in the crème fraîche, again making sure not to overmix. Turn the entire mix out onto a cutting board and gently push it together into a pile. Wrap tightly with plastic wrap and refrigerate for 2 hours.

2. Make the filling: Put the tomatoes in a colander and sprinkle generously with coarse salt. Lay the tomatoes on several sheets of paper towel to drain (dried tomatoes will make a crisp tart).

3. In the meantime, heat the oven to 425°F. Dust a work surface well with flour and roll the dough into a 12-inch round about ⅛ inch thick. Dust flour under the dough if it starts to stick.

4. Carefully slide a rimless baking sheet under the dough. Leaving a 3-inch boarder, scatter the cheese on top of the dough, then arrange the tomatoes evenly over the cheese. Fold the edges of the dough over the tomatoes, making pleats as you fold and leaving the center of the tart open.

5. Bake the galette until golden brown, 30 to 40 minutes. Let cool on a rack.

6. While the galette cools, lightly dress the microradishes and microgreens with a bit of olive oil, some vinegar, and coarse salt. Drizzle the top of the galette with a touch of olive oil and a sprinkle of coarse salt. Slice the galette and serve with a few dressed microradishes and greens, if desired.

MICHEL RICHARD, *Central Michel Richard,* Washington, D.C.

MARK FURSTENBERG, Washington, D.C. (bread)

Cremini-Filled Grilled Cheese Sandwiches

Brioche, a bread rich in butter and eggs, is the perfect partner for Michel's super-rich grilled cheese sandwich. Accompanied with a mushroom juice, the pure mushroom essence is simple, satisfying, and nourishing. This sandwich does require time and effort, but the result is a very special dish.

SERVES 4

4 pounds fresh cremini mushrooms

1 cup heavy cream

2 shallots, minced

1 large clove garlic

Coarse salt and freshly ground
  black pepper

1 teaspoon soy sauce

Eight ¼-inch slices brioche

8 thin slices Gruyère cheese

2 tablespoons unsalted butter

1. Prepare the mushroom purée and juice: Process the mushrooms in small batches in a food processor until finely chopped, then transfer them to a medium saucepan. Cover and cook over medium-high heat, stirring often, until the juices are released from the mushrooms. Bring the liquid to a boil, then reduce the heat and simmer for 10 to 15 minutes, stirring occasionally, until the mushrooms are tender.

2. Line a fine-mesh strainer with a double layer of dampened cheesecloth and place it over a large bowl. Transfer the mushrooms and their liquid to the strainer to drain. Let cool slightly, then lift the cloth with the mushrooms over the strainer and wring out all the liquid from the mushrooms. You will have about 2 cups mushroom purée in the cheesecloth and 5 cups mushroom juice. You'll only need about 1 cup of purée; cover and refrigerate the rest for up to 2 days or freeze for up to 2 months.

3. To make the sandwich filling, combine 1 cup of the mushroom juice, ¾ cup of the heavy cream, and the shallots in a medium saucepan. Using a grater, grate the garlic directly into the pan (or mince and add it). Bring the mixture to a simmer and cook, stirring occasionally, until the liquid is reduced by about half to slightly more than 1 cup, about 5 minutes. Remove the pan from the heat. Put ¾ cup of mushroom purée in a small bowl. One tablespoon at a time, stir 6 tablespoons of the reduced juice mixture into the purée. Season to taste with salt and pepper.

4. To prepare the dipping sauce for the sandwiches, bring the remaining mushroom juice to a simmer in a medium saucepan. Skim off any foam that rises to the surface. Simmer for 15 minutes, until the juice is reduced by half, then add the remaining ¼ cup heavy cream and the soy sauce. Simmer for another 5 minutes, then reduce the heat to very low and keep warm for serving.

5. To construct the sandwiches, lay 4 slices of brioche on your work surface. Trim the slices of cheese to fit the bread and place 1 slice of cheese on each of the 4 slices of bread. Spread the sandwich filling on top of the cheese. Place another slice of cheese over the filling and cover with another slice of bread.

6. Melt the butter in a small saucepan and brush it on both sides of the sandwiches. Heat a large nonstick skillet or griddle over medium heat. When the pan is hot, add the sandwiches and brown on both sides, working in batches if necessary.

7. Pour the warm dipping sauce into 4 small bowls. Cut each sandwich in half and serve with the dipping sauce on the side.

CAREER CHANGER

"I realized that making something was very important to me," says master breadmaker Mark Furstenberg. After an early career fighting the war on poverty and other social issues for the Kennedy Administration, Mark pursued many entrepreneurial opportunities, but he realized that making something by hand was what he wanted to do.

After the opening of his first bakery in 1990, he knew quickly that he had found his calling. After glowing reviews of his bread in the *The Washington Post* and *The New York Times,* Mark was inundated with orders and calls to "save two loaves for Dr. So and So's dinner party." After one particularly positive review, the line out the door was 200 customers long, creating the need to limit each customer to two loaves. Mark admits to being totally unprepared for the craziness of the fad he created.

Although the phone rang pretty constantly, there's one call Mark won't forget. The voice on the other end of the phone was smoky and had a thick French accent. Jean-Louis Palladin, the king of Washington, D.C., chefs and chef/owner of Palladin, was calling for bread. Mark thought a friend was playing a joke on him and put the phone down. Eventually, Mark and Jean-Louis became close friends and Palladin introduced Mark to Michel Richard.

The first meeting with Richard was at his highly acclaimed Los Angeles restaurant Citrus. Mark walked into a kitchen strewn with champagne bottles that Michel and Jean-Louis had been "sampling" all afternoon. When Michel threw a loaf of bread on a table and challenged Mark to make one like it, Mark knew he was in over his head. Luckily, his friend helped him achieve the loaf that Michel asked for, which Mark named "Palladin Bread."

Mark has been at the forefront of artisanal baking for over 20 years and has worked with some of the best chefs from around the country, like Thomas Keller and Nancy Silverton. He also helped developed the baking program at The Culinary Institute of America® at Greystone. He packages his life-changing career move this way: "I knew bread, so I did it."

MARK GAIER & CLARK FRASIER, *Arrows,* Ogunquit, Maine

TED JOHNSON, Ogunquit, Maine (lobster)

Lobster Mac and Cheese

The best place to buy lobster is right off the boat, and Arrows has a direct source. The father of their sommelier, Danielle Johnson Walker, is their lobsterman. Arrows serves this classic entrée with the lobster in the shell placed on top of the macaroni and cheese. Here, however, the large pieces are baked within the pasta and creamy cheese sauce, making it a rich main course; you'll only need a simple salad or sautéed greens as a side.

SERVES 4

7 tablespoons unsalted butter; more for the baking dish
1 cup breadcrumbs, preferably fresh, or 2 slices stale white bread
Coarse salt and freshly ground black pepper

⅓ cup all-purpose flour
4 cups milk
2 cups grated sharp Cheddar
1 teaspoon grated nutmeg
1 teaspoon dry mustard
1 pound elbow pasta

Two 3-pound lobsters, steamed, shelled, and meat cut into 2-inch pieces
2 tablespoons finely chopped flat-leaf parsley, for garnish

1. Heat the oven to 425°F. Lightly butter a 3-quart ovenproof dish and set aside.

2. If using stale bread, tear it into 1-inch pieces and pulse them in a food processor until smooth. Melt 2 tablespoons of the butter in a skillet over medium heat, add the breadcrumbs, and swirl to coat with butter. Cook the breadcrumbs for 2 minutes, or until browned. Season with salt and pepper and set aside.

3. In a large saucepan, melt the remaining 5 tablespoons butter over medium-low heat. Whisk in the flour and cook, whisking constantly, for 2 minutes to make a roux.

Whisk in the milk in a slow, steady stream, whisking constantly for about 3 minutes. When it comes to a simmer, stir in the cheese, nutmeg, and mustard; season with salt and pepper to taste. Remove from the heat and cover.

4. Boil a large pot of water, season with salt, and cook the pasta as directed on the package instructions. Drain the pasta and pour into a large bowl. Add the cheese sauce and lobster meat; mix well. Transfer to the prepared dish. Sprinkle the breadcrumb topping evenly over the macaroni. Bake, uncovered, for 20 to 30 minutes, or until golden brown. Let cool for 5 minutes before serving. Garnish with the parsley and serve.

LINTON HOPKINS, *Restaurant Eugene,* Atlanta, Georgia

ALLAN BENTON, *Benton's Smoky Mountain Country Hams,* Madisonville, Tennessee (ham)

Gratin of Bay Scallops with Jerusalem Artichoke Purée and Crisp Country Ham

This is a very simple, rich dish with a terrific smoky crisp ham garnish on top. Linton says he uses Allan's prosciutto for a variation. Any bay scallops will do, but Nantucket are naturally sweet and very delicate; they're also seasonal, so look for them in the late fall and early winter months.

SERVES 4

8 very thin slices country ham (about ⅛ pound)
1 pound Jerusalem artichokes, peeled (about 10)

1 cup heavy cream
Coarse salt and freshly ground black pepper
1 pound bay scallops, preferably Nantucket

2 tablespoons unsalted butter
1 tablespoon extra-virgin olive oil
2 tablespoons chopped fresh chives, for garnish

1. Heat the oven to 325°F. Put the ham slices on Silpat® baking mats or a nonstick baking sheet and bake until golden brown and crisp like a cracker, about 15 minutes. Break into medium-size shards and set aside.

2. In a medium saucepan, simmer the artichokes with water to cover over medium heat for 25 minutes until soft. Transfer the artichokes to a blender and purée. Strain through a fine-mesh strainer (discard the liquid), then mix with the cream, and adjust the seasoning with salt to taste. Set aside.

3. Season the scallops with salt and pepper. Melt the butter and olive oil in a large nonstick skillet over high heat (but don't let it get so hot that it smokes), then add the scallops and cook on one side for 2 minutes, until light golden brown (only cook on one side). You may need to do this in batches.

4. With a slotted spoon, transfer the scallops, seared side up, to an 8 × 8-inch baking dish and cover with the artichoke purée. Position a rack 3 inches from the heating element and turn on the broiler. Broil the gratin until golden brown and heated through, about 1 minute. Sprinkle the crumbled ham on top, garnish with the chives, and serve.

ERIC WARNSTEDT, *Hen of the Wood,* Waterbury, Vermont

MATEO & ANDY KEHLER, *Jasper Hill Farm,* Greensboro, Vermont (cheese)

Sweet Potato Gnocchi with Braised Plums and Crumbly Blue Cheese

Sweet potatoes have more moisture than russet potatoes, so additional flour is needed to help keep them together. The plums add acidity to the sweetness of the potatoes and balance the sharpness of the rich blue cheese.

SERVES 4

3 medium sweet potatoes or yams
  (about 2½ pounds)
1 large egg
½ teaspoon coarse salt
3 cups all-purpose flour
1 cup cider vinegar

¾ cup sugar
1 shallot, finely chopped
1 tablespoon minced fresh ginger
1 teaspoon red pepper flakes
1 pint fresh small plums, pitted
  and quartered

4 teaspoons unsalted butter
2 tablespoons fresh lemon juice
4 ounces blue cheese, preferably
  Bayley Hazen Blue, or
  Stilton, crumbled

1. Heat the oven to 400°F. Clean and dry the sweet potatoes and pierce all over with a fork. Wrap them separately in aluminum foil and bake until tender, 40 to 50 minutes. Remove from the oven, unwrap, and let cool.

2. When the potatoes are cool enough to handle, peel off their skins, cut them into large chunks, and push them through a ricer into a large bowl. Measure 2 cups of potato purée. Allow to cool completely and if possible refrigerate for a few hours or overnight to allow the potatoes to "dry." Gently mix in the egg and salt, then add the flour, ½ cup at a time, to form a soft dough that holds together. (It's fine if you don't use all of the flour and the dough is a bit wet.) Be careful not to overmix the dough. Portion the dough into 10 to 12 small pieces.

3. On a lightly floured work surface, roll out one piece of dough (keep a kitchen towel over the remaining pieces to keep them from drying out) into an 8-inch-long rope about ½ inch thick. Cut into 1-inch pieces. Using a spatula, transfer the gnocchi to a lightly floured baking sheet and cover with plastic wrap or place the sheet in the freezer until the gnocchi harden then place in zip-top

bags until ready to use. Continue until all dough is rolled out and cut.

4. In a medium saucepan, combine the vinegar, sugar, shallots, ginger, and red pepper flakes. Bring the mixture to a boil, lower the heat, and simmer until reduced to a thick syrup. Gently fold in the plums, making sure they're well glazed with the sauce, and remove from the heat. Cover with plastic wrap and let the steam soften the plums; they will release a fair amount of liquid.

5. When ready to serve, bring a large pot of water to a boil, salt it generously, and add the gnocchi. Reduce the heat to a simmer and gently boil the gnocchi until they rise to the surface, about 30 seconds. Transfer to a sauté pan with a slotted spoon. Add 1 heaping tablespoon of the plum mixture and juice with 1 teaspoon butter per serving and heat over medium-low heat, gently tossing the gnocchi to coat with the sauce. Finish the sauce with lemon juice to taste.

6. Portion the gnocchi into 4 shallow bowls and sprinkle the crumbled blue cheese over the top.

continued

AGENT K'S CHEESE LAB

If James Bond made and aged cheese, Jasper Hill Farm would be his operation. Drive up in your car to the farm in Greensboro, Vermont, and you'll see what looks like any small-production farm, with 40 cows, a farmhouse, a barn, and facilities to process milk into flavorful cheeses. But around the corner from the farmstead, the picturesque farmland changes into ultramodern "cave," thanks to a 22,000-square-foot cellar nestled into the bedrock hillside across from the barn.

Once inside the building, the idea of a simple Vermont dairy farm is gone and the serious business of growing the farm economy of Vermont is very clear. Brothers Andy and Mateo Kehler with their wives Victoria and Angela developed the idea to help keep Vermont farmers in business and even to get new farmers to take the risk of cheesemaking. Presently, the cheese caves hold the hopes and profits of ten local dairy farms working on everything from Vermont Cheddar to bloomy rind cheeses from goats and sheep. The building houses five caves of varying sizes, with the temperature and humidity of each closely controlled for the types of cheese they hold.

While caves like this are common in Europe, the one at Jasper Hill is the first of its kind in the United States. On a walk through the cave, you'll find workers turning cheeses to age evenly, and painting on solutions of wine and salts to give the cheeses their flavor. But you'll also see something you wouldn't expect—an electric lift moving Cheddar cheese 30 feet off the floor, with workers dusting and vacuuming off the enormous wheels to keep the rinds free of cheese mites.

In addition to supporting farmers throughout New England with their cheese-aging cave, the family continues to make its own cheeses, from Constant Bliss (a slow-ripened lactic curd based on a Chaource) to Bayley Hazen Blue (a naturally rinded, lower-fat blue) and Aspenhurst (a 12-month aged variation on English Leicester). The farm produces about 75,000 pounds of cheese a year, while the caves age about 2 million pounds a year. By aging and marketing the cheese of local farmers and even some large producers like Cabot®, the Kehlers have designed a new model to keep farmers doing what they do best.

Andy Kehler and Eric Warnstedt

09.06.24

LEE CHIZMAR, *Bolete Restaurant & Inn,* Bethlehem, Pennsylvania

SKIP BENNETT, *Island Creek Oysters,* Duxbury, Massachusetts (oysters)

Angel Hair Pasta with Oyster Butter Cream Sauce and Caviar

Island Creek Oysters are legendary for their sweet, briny taste. The use of stellar ingredients like bacon, oysters, caviar, and cream create a luxurious yet simple recipe. At Bolete, Lee serves this dish with squid ink pasta.

SERVES 4

FOR THE OYSTER BUTTER
8 tablespoons (1 stick) unsalted butter
1 shallot, thinly sliced
1 teaspoon fresh thyme leaves
3 oysters, freshly shucked, with their liquor (juices)
½ teaspoon fresh lemon juice
Coarse salt and freshly ground black pepper

FOR THE CREAM SAUCE
1 tablespoon unsalted butter
2 shallots, finely sliced
1 clove garlic, minced
¼ pound fresh oyster mushrooms, wiped clean, trimmed, and sliced
3 slices bacon, cut into small dice
½ cup heavy cream
12 oysters, freshly shucked, with their liquor (juices)

1 teaspoon fresh lemon juice
1 tablespoon finely chopped fresh flat-leaf parsley
1 tablespoon finely chopped fresh chives
Coarse salt and freshly ground black pepper

TO SERVE
1 pound fresh or dried angel hair pasta
4 teaspoons domestic black caviar, for garnish

MAKE THE OYSTER BUTTER

1. In a heavy-bottomed saucepan, brown the butter over medium heat until golden and nutty. Remove from the heat and let cool slightly before slowly adding the shallots and thyme (if the butter is too hot, it may boil up when other ingredients are added). Allow to cool.

2. Put the oysters with their liquor, the lemon juice, and 2 to 3 tablespoons water in a blender or food processor and process until puréed. With the machine running, add the butter-shallot mixture in a thin stream until emulsified.

3. Season with salt and pepper to taste and cool. Cover and store for up to 4 days in the refrigerator.

MAKE THE CREAM SAUCE

1. Heat the butter in a medium sauté pan over medium heat. Add the shallots and garlic and cook for 5 minutes. Add the mushrooms and cook until they release their liquid, about 5 minutes. Add the bacon and continue to cook until crisp, about 5 minutes.

continued

2. In a medium saucepan, cook the cream over medium-high heat until reduced by half, about 8 minutes. Add the oysters with their liquor and simmer gently until the liquid and the cream begin to thicken, 2 minutes. Remove the pan from the heat. Add the mushroom-bacon mixture, then whisk in the oyster butter in small spoonsful at a time. Add the lemon juice and herbs and season to taste with salt and pepper.

1. Bring a large pot of salted water to a boil over high heat, and cook the pasta until tender, about 2 minutes if using fresh pasta or according to the package instructions if using dry. Drain.

2. To serve, portion the pasta into 4 serving bowls. Spoon the sauce over each portion, making sure each dish has 3 oysters. Garnish each with a teaspoonful of caviar.

MARC VETRI, *Vetri,* Philadelphia, Pennsylvania

TOM CULTON, *Culton Organics,* Silver Spring, Pennsylvania (ramps)

Ramp Ravioli with Lemon Zest

Italian producers label flour either 0 or 00 to describe the protein level. 00 is the finest and best for pasta since it's low in protein and gluten, making for a tender finished pasta. You can use half cake flour and half all-purpose flour as a substitute. Often ravioli is filled with a main ingredient and cheese, but in Vetri's version, Tom's ramps fill the ravioli entirely, and the ricotta serves as a sauce for the pasta to lie on top of. Ramps are a seasonal delicacy available mostly in May and June; an alternative would be a mixture of leeks, scallions, and a few garlic cloves.

YIELDS ABOUT 32 TO 40 RAVIOLI; SERVES 4

3 pounds ramps, bulbs and greens separated, roughly chopped; ¼ cup bulbs, minced, for garnish
5 tablespoons extra-virgin olive oil
3 tablespoons grape seed oil
1 large egg
1 cup breadcrumbs
½ cup grated Parmigiano-Reggiano; plus more for serving

Coarse salt and freshly ground black pepper
1 cup ricotta cheese

FOR THE PASTA
2 cups 00 flour (or 1 cup cake flour plus 1 cup all-purpose flour)
1 cup durum flour (or a mix of semolina and all-purpose flours)

3 large egg yolks, plus 1 large egg
Coarse salt
Cornmeal
4 tablespoons (½ stick) unsalted butter
2 teaspoons grated lemon zest

1. In a medium sauté pan, slowly cook the ramp greens in 3 tablespoons of the olive oil until tender, about 5 minutes. Remove the greens. In the same skillet, heat the grape seed oil over medium heat and cook the ramp bulbs for 3 minutes. Cool and purée the ramp greens and bulbs in a food processor. Add the egg, breadcrumbs, and Parmigiano and pulse until just combined. Season with salt and pepper. Set aside or refrigerate until ready to use.

2. In a medium bowl, whisk the ricotta with the remaining 2 tablespoons olive oil and season with salt and pepper. Set aside or refrigerate until ready to serve.

3. Make the pasta dough: Combine the flours, 3 egg yolks, and 3 to 4 tablespoons water in a food processor; season with salt and process until the mixture just be-

gins to form a ball, adding a bit more water if the dough seems dry, about 30 seconds. The dough should be firm and not sticky. Transfer to a lightly floured work surface and knead for 30 seconds. Transfer to a bowl, drape a towel over it, and let rest for 1 hour.

4. Cut the ball of dough into 6 pieces; cover and reserve the pieces you're not immediately using to prevent it from drying out. Dust the counter and 1 piece of dough with a little flour. Press the dough into a rectangle, flatten it with your hands, and roll it through a pasta machine set at the widest setting. Pull and stretch the sheet of dough with your hands as it comes off the machine's rollers. Continue putting the dough through the machine, reducing the setting each time until you

continued

get to the lowest setting, which is 1. Dust the sheets of dough with flour as needed. When you reach the lowest setting, pass the dough through 2 more times for a very thin and smooth sheet of pasta, if necessary. The dough should be paper-thin, about ⅛ inch thick, 36 inches long, and about 4 inches wide.

5. Beat the egg with 1 tablespoon water to make an egg wash. Dust the counter and one sheet of dough with flour, then brush the top surface of the dough sheet with the egg wash, which acts as a glue.

6. Drop 1-tablespoon mounds of the ramp filling on half of the pasta sheet, about 2 inches apart. Fold the other half over the filling like a blanket. Gently press out air pockets around each mound of filling. Use a sharp knife or a fluted pastry cutter to cut each pillow into squares; press the edges with the tines of a fork or your fingers to crimp them and make a tight seal. Dust the ravioli and a sheet pan with cornmeal to prevent the pasta from sticking and lay them out to dry slightly while assembling the rest of the dough sheets.

7. Bring a large pot of salted water to a boil. Reduce the heat to a gentle boil and cook the ravioli in batches if necessary, stirring gently to make sure the pasta doesn't stick. Cook for about 6 minutes, or until the pasta is tender. Transfer the ravioli to a large bowl with a large serving spoon.

8. In a small skillet, heat the butter over medium heat and cook until lightly browned, about 3 minutes.

9. To serve, put 1 tablespoon of ricotta across an individual serving plate. Arrange 8 ravioli on top, then spoon the brown butter over the pasta and sprinkle with lemon zest, the reserved minced ramps, and a bit of Parmesan.

BORN FOR IT

It takes a confident man to cook a pig stomach filled with sausage he had just made along with potatoes and celery pulled from his farm for Tom Colicchio and Mark Vetri. Add to the equation that this was the first time this man had made the dish and some would say the risk was too big. But for Tom Culton it was easy. Vetri is his best customer and a close friend, and Colicchio was someone he had just watched on *Top Chef* the night before. Tom Culton knew the Pennsylvania-German meal was a big hit when he heard the satisfied moans of his guests.

Tom is a very humble guy with a clear set of ideals who grows a wide variety of vegetables for his restaurant clients and farmers' market shoppers: "I want to be a good steward of the land and leave the soil in better condition than when I found it, and I want to make my farm, the woodlands around it, and the ponds on it safe for wildlife and the few animals I raise." This kind of succinct declaration is the norm rather than the rarity among farmers and artisans who grow on the same scale as Tom (27 acres under cultivation and 53 acres total).

Tom likes to grow heirloom vegetables (some of which he has gone to Europe and extracted the seed from plants himself) as well as crops like Lancaster Lad and Dent Corn that have been in the area for over 100 years. He will also sit down with his friend Mark Vetri to plan the season to Vetri's menu wishes. Sometimes this includes vegetables whose seeds are best brought home in the bottom of a boot to avoid any customs issues. This practice is very common with young farmers who are adventurous and love to try new crops.

Working the farm with his grandfather, girlfriend, and one intern "is a lot of work, but if you love what you do, it doesn't seem like work. This is what I was born to do."

DOUG KEANE, *Cyrus*, Healdsburg, California

LAEL FORD, *Lola's Garden*, Healdsburg, California (herbs)

Risotto with Fresh Peas and Pancetta

Chef Keane makes his risotto at Cyrus with an aromatic Parmesan broth and uses a hand-held mixer to make a foam before presenting his dish. Deliciously creamy with fresh pea flavors from two sources—peas and pea tendrils—this risotto is prepared with perfect vegetables and herbs from Lael's father's garden.

SERVES 6

2 cups fresh peas
4 sprigs fresh flat-leaf parsley,
  2 left whole and 2 chopped
  (2 tablespoons)
4 sprigs fresh thyme
2 bay leaves
1 teaspoon black peppercorns
1 teaspoon fennel seeds

4 cups vegetable broth
8 tablespoons (1 stick) unsalted butter
½ small yellow onion, finely chopped
1 clove garlic, minced
2 cups carnaroli or arborio rice
2 cups dry white wine
¼ pound pancetta or bacon
  (about 6 slices), diced

2 cups pea shoots or tendrils
1 tablespoon finely chopped
  fresh chives
Coarse salt and freshly
  ground black pepper

1. Bring a small saucepan of water to a boil. Add the peas and cook for 1 minute. Drain and cool. Transfer to a food processor or blender and purée; strain through a fine-mesh strainer and discard any solids. Set aside.

2. Wrap the whole parsley sprigs, thyme, bay leaves, peppercorns, and fennel seeds tightly in cheesecloth and tie with butcher's twine.

3. Heat the broth in a medium saucepan over medium heat to a simmer. Melt 4 tablespoons of the butter in a large saucepan over medium heat; add the bouquet of herbs, the onions, and garlic. Cook until the onions and garlic are softened, about 5 minutes. Add the rice and stir to coat evenly with the onion mixture. Add the wine, increase the heat to medium high, and cook, stirring constantly, until the wine is almost completely absorbed, about 15 minutes. Reduce the heat to medium, then add the warm broth 1 cup at a time, stirring the rice constantly until most of the liquid is absorbed before adding additional broth. Continue to add broth, stirring until the rice is almost cooked through, about 20 minutes.

4. Meanwhile, in a medium skillet over medium-high heat, cook the pancetta or bacon until crisp, 5 to 8 minutes. Drain on a paper towel–lined plate, then transfer to a small bowl and set aside. Wipe out the skillet and heat 1 tablespoon butter over medium heat; add the pea shoots and cook until just wilted, about 1 minute. Set aside.

5. When the rice is just cooked through, remove the bouquet of herbs, then add the remaining 3 tablespoons butter, the pea purée, chopped parsley, and chives. Season with salt and pepper to taste.

6. To serve, ladle the risotto into soup bowls. Top each bowl with the crisp pancetta or bacon and pea shoots.

continued

Risotto with Fresh Peas and Pancetta

A DOG AND A GARDEN

The relationship between farmer and chef may get no closer than the marriage of Lael Ford and her husband Chef Doug Keane. Doug and Lael met in the '90s, when he was a chef at Le Jardiniere in San Francisco but thinking about a place to call his own. Fast forward more than a decade—the two met again and were married in 2006.

By this time, Doug had been garnering awards at Cyrus in Healdsburg, California, for a few years and wanted to start a garden to grow produce to serve in the restaurant. He and Lael bought a house on 5 acres a few minutes from her family's 500-acre ranch but soon realized that the better soil, tractor, and expertise lay with her dad, Peter Newman.

Peter had been collecting ranch land and slowly converting 20 percent of it to vines for Bordeaux wines. His expertise in farming proved invaluable as Lael and Doug started Lola's Garden (in memory of Doug's beloved Labrador Retriever). Lael grows tomatoes, eggplant, lemon cucumbers, and radishes at the garden on her dad's land. She is also experimenting with a wide variety of melons. The poor soil of the couple's 5 acres proved to be a perfect spot for herbs that Doug and Lael cook with at home and at Cyrus.

Doug's stints in the kitchens of Lespinasse and The Four Seasons in New York as well as at Restaurant Gary Danko in San Francisco have led him and Cyrus to receive high acclaim for their consistent attention to detail, impeccable service, and use of only superior fresh products. Whether Doug is setting medallions of bluefin tuna on top of Lael's shaved lemon cucumbers or making his own style BLT with pork belly on top of the garden's heirloom tomatoes, the relationship between Doug Keane's cooking and Lael Ford's garden is ever-present.

RICK BAYLESS, *Frontera Grill*, Chicago, Illinois

MARTY & KRIS TRAVIS, *Spence Farm*, Fairbury, Illinois (lamb's quarters)

Tacos with Greens and Seared Onions

Thought of by many as a weed, lamb's quarters, known as quelites in Mexico, is a tasty and nutritious green. If you can't find it, feel free to substitute Swiss chard. Be sure to have all your ingredients ready before you warm the tortillas, as the cooking of the filling goes very quickly.

YIELDS A GENEROUS 2 CUPS OF FILLING, ENOUGH FOR 8 SOFT TACOS

8 to 10 corn tortillas; plus a few extra, in case some break

Coarse salt

9 cups (about 1 pound) loosely packed, stemmed lamb's quarters (quelites) or 6 cups loosely packed, sliced green or red chard leaves (slice them ½ inch thick; you'll need a 12-ounce bunch)

1 tablespoon olive or vegetable oil

½ pound fresh shiitake mushrooms, stems removed and thinly sliced

1 medium white onion, sliced ¼ inch thick

3 cloves garlic, peeled and finely chopped

¾ cup chicken or vegetable broth

½ cup finely crumbled goat cheese; plus more for garnish

¾ cup Chipotle Tomatillo Verde Salsa, for serving (recipe follows)

Sprigs fresh cilantro, for garnish

1. Warm the tortillas. Set up a steamer (a vegetable steamer in a large saucepan filled with ½ inch of water works well) and heat to a boil. Wrap the tortillas in a heavy kitchen towel, lay it in the steamer, and cover with a tight-fitting lid. Boil for 1 minute, turn off the heat, and let stand without opening the steamer for about 15 minutes.

2. While the tortillas are steaming, prepare the filling. Bring 3 quarts of salted water to a boil in a large pot. Add the greens and cook until barely tender, 1 to 2 minutes for the lambs' quarters, 1 to 2 minutes longer for the chard. Drain in a colander, then spread out on a large plate or baking sheet to cool. When cool enough to handle, roughly chop, if necessary, to fit into the taco.

3. Heat the oil in a large (10- to 12-inch) skillet over medium-high heat. Add the mushrooms and cook for 5 minutes, or until they release their liquid, then add the onions and cook, stirring frequently, until golden brown, about 5 minutes. Add the garlic and stir for 1 minute. Add the chopped greens and broth and season with salt. Cook for about 3 minutes over medium-high heat, or until most of the liquid has cooked out.

4. Remove the warm tortillas from the steamer and place in a cloth-lined basket. Transfer the greens into a deep, warm serving dish, sprinkle with the cheese, and serve at the table with the warm tortillas, a bowl of salsa, and a small plate of cilantro. Alternatively, you can spoon filling in the center of the tortillas and roll them up around the filling. Arrange two on each plate, then spoon the salsa in a strip across their middles, sprinkle with more cheese, and top with sprigs of cilantro.

Chipotle Tomatillo Verde Salsa

YIELDS ABOUT 1¼ CUPS

3 large cloves garlic, unpeeled
8 ounces (5 to 6 medium) tomatillos, husked and rinsed

3 to 6 canned chipotle chiles en adobo, stemmed and finely chopped

½ teaspoon coarse salt (optional)
¼ teaspoon sugar (optional)

1. In a heavy, ungreased skillet over medium heat, roast the unpeeled garlic, turning occasionally, until blackened in spots and soft, 10 to 15 minutes. Let cool, slip off the papery skins, then roughly chop.

2. Turn on the broiler to high. Put the tomatillos on a baking sheet and place about 4 inches below the element. Let the tomatillos blister, blacken, and soften on one side, about 5 minutes, then turn them over and roast the other side. Let cool completely on the baking sheet.

3. Scrape the tomatillos (and any juices that have accumulated around them) into a food processor or blender and add the garlic. Pulse until everything is coarsely puréed.

4. Transfer to a serving bowl and stir in the chipotle chiles along with enough water (about 3 to 4 tablespoons) to give the salsa a spoonable consistency. Taste and season with salt, plus a little sugar, if you want to soften the tangy edge.

continued

Sides

TONY MAWS, *Craigie on Main,* Cambridge, Massachusetts

KOFI INGERSOLL & ERIN KOH, *Bay End Farm,* Buzzards Bay, Massachusetts (tomatoes)

Vegetable Succotash with Spicy Yellow Tomato Coulis

Bay End Farm, originally founded in 1906, not only sells organic produce through their CSA and to top-notch restaurants, but also features an 8-room house, a 1930s swimming pool, tennis court, and dance hall for rent. Tony got married at the farm and spent the week at the Bay End retreat with his family and of course his friend Kofi. This succotash is usually served with steamed Wellfleet clams on top; allow about a dozen per person.

SERVES 4

FOR THE YELLOW TOMATO COULIS
2 pounds yellow tomatoes, roughly chopped
1 clove garlic
⅛ teaspoon cayenne or aji amarillo (yellow) chile paste
1 tablespoon extra-virgin olive oil
Coarse salt and freshly ground black pepper

FOR THE VEGETABLE SUCCOTASH
1 red bell pepper
3 tablespoons extra-virgin olive oil

2 tablespoons unsalted butter
½ cup small-diced new potatoes (3 to 4 small potatoes)
Coarse salt and freshly ground black pepper
½ cup small-diced baby zucchini (1 baby zucchini)
½ cup small-diced baby summer squash (1 baby squash)
½ cup fresh corn kernels (1 small ear corn)
8 okra, sliced into ¼-inch rounds
½ cup cooked beets, such as chiogga

½ cup (about ⅛ pound) sliced mixed green and yellow wax beans, cooked
¼ cup (about ⅛ pound) fresh fava beans, shelled, cooked, and peeled, if available, or fresh peas
2 tablespoons chopped sun-dried tomatoes
4 radishes, cleaned, trimmed, and thinly sliced
1 tablespoon chopped fresh herbs (any combination of thyme, marjoram, chives, parsley, and cilantro)

PREPARE THE COULIS

Combine all the ingredients except the salt and black pepper in a blender and blend on a low speed for 1 minute; don't pulse, as you don't want to incorporate any air into the coulis. Season to taste with salt and black pepper. Let the purée sit for 30 minutes, then strain through a fine-mesh strainer and set aside in a saucepan until ready to serve.

MAKE THE SUCCOTASH

1. Roast the pepper. Heat the oven to 400°F. Rub the pepper with 1 tablespoon of the olive oil and place on a baking sheet. Roast in the oven, turning a few times, until the pepper is lightly charred, 30 to 40 minutes. (Alternatively, you can char the pepper by holding it with tongs over the flame of a gas burner for 30 seconds, turning when skin is blistered, until all sides are charred.) Transfer to a bowl and cover tightly with plastic wrap for 15 minutes. When cool enough to handle, peel, seed, and finely chop. You should have about ½ cup.

continued

2. Heat the butter in a large sauté pan over low heat. Add the potatoes, season with salt and pepper, and cook until they're fork-tender, about 5 minutes. Add the remaining ingredients, except the radishes, herbs, and rest of the olive oil, and cover and cook over low heat until tender, about 5 minutes. Season to taste with salt and pepper. Mix in the radishes and herbs. Drizzle with the remaining 2 tablespoons olive oil, taste again for seasoning, and adjust as needed.

3. To serve, gently warm the tomato coulis and portion among 4 shallow bowls. Spoon the succotash into the center of each bowl. Serve immediately.

CHARLIE TROTTER, *Charlie Trotter's,* Chicago, Illinois

LEE JONES, *The Chef's Garden,* Huron, Ohio (pearl onions)

Pearl Onions and Fiddlehead Ferns with Vanilla Jelly and Onion Sorbet

In this exuberant dish, Chef Trotter uses onions in many ways, from a jelly to a sorbet of caramelized onions. The addition of vanilla flavor and crunch of the fresh fiddlehead ferns make this a palate pleaser with every bite. Farmer Lee's tiny pearl onions are one of his "boutique" vegetable crops, grown for sweetness and balance.

SERVES 4

15 red pearl onions, peeled
15 white pearl onions, peeled
2 sprigs fresh thyme
1 tablespoon red-wine vinegar
15 fiddlehead ferns
3 tablespoons vegetable oil
4 Spanish onions (about 4 pounds), peeled and sliced

1 vanilla bean, split in half
Coarse salt
1 tablespoon sherry vinegar
2½ teaspoons agar-agar or unflavored gelatin
½ cup sugar
2 teaspoons white-wine vinegar

¼ cup fresh flat-leaf parsley, finely chopped
1 tablespoon fresh lime juice
Watercress baby leaves for garnish (optional)

1. Put all the pearl onions in a medium saucepan with the thyme and red-wine vinegar. Cook the onions over a pot of simmering water until tender, about 20 minutes. Drain, discard the thyme, cool, and transfer to a medium bowl. Bring a medium pot of water to a boil, add the fiddlehead ferns, and cook for 3 minutes until crisp-tender. Drain, cool, and add to the bowl with the onions.

2. Heat the oil in a large sauté pan over medium heat, and cook the Spanish onions, stirring frequently, until they turn golden brown and start to caramelize, then lower the heat and cook until deeply carmelized and sweet, about 40 minutes. Add the vanilla bean when the onions are well browned and really cooked down (after about 20 minutes). Remove the pan from the heat and cool the mixture. When the vanilla bean is cool enough to handle, use a paring knife to slice it open lengthwise then scrape the inside of the bean into the onions; discard the bean pod. Add the onions to a blender and purée until smooth. Season to taste with salt and sherry vinegar.

3. Stir the agar-agar or gelatin into 2 cups water in a medium saucepan and bring to a simmer over medium heat. Add 2 cups of the onion-vanilla purée and stir until well mixed and just heated through. Remove from the heat, pour the mixture into a shallow container, cover, and refrigerate until firm.

4. Make a simple syrup by combining ¾ cup water with the sugar in a small saucepan; heat over medium-high heat for about 2 minutes, or until the sugar is dissolved. Remove from the heat and cool.

5. In a medium bowl, mix the remaining onion purée with the simple syrup and white-wine vinegar. Season to taste with salt. Put the onion mixture in an ice cream machine and follow the manufacturer's directions to make sorbet. Transfer the onion sorbet to a container and keep in the freezer until you're ready to serve.

continued

6. To serve, season the pearl onions and fiddleheads with salt, chopped parsley, and lime juice. Spoon the pearl onions and fiddleheads onto individual serving plates. Add a few small spoonfuls of chilled onion-vanilla jelly on top. Scoop a small amount of onion sorbet into the center of the plate, garnish with watercress leaves (if using), and serve immediately.

THE REAL DEAL

Farmer Lee Jones is a genius wrapped up in a TV-ready farmer archetype. His uniform is set: blue overalls, perfectly pressed short-sleeved button-down white shirt, and the capper, a shiny red bow tie. At first glance, you wonder if this farmer is for real. One look at the produce he brings to the table and you have your answer.

Three hundred different types of microgreens, 600 varieties of vegetables, herbs in seven different stages of growth, 87 varieties of heirloom tomatoes, root crops, and an ongoing experimental garden are the prelude to the full picture of Farmer Jones and his amazing business, The Chef's Garden®.

The business almost came to a crashing halt after a hail storm killed the crops and forced the family to give up three-quarters of their 1,200 acres in Huron, Ohio. The family, led by Lee's father, Bob, made it clear that the new path for the farm was to sell to chefs of the highest caliber. The farm would go from growing quantity to growing the highest-quality produce, doing it all with sustainability and the utmost respect for the soil as its mission. When chefs like Charlie Trotter, Alain Ducasse, and Daniel Boulud came to the farm with requests for special produce, the family knew they had made the right move.

Safety, accountability, quality, and nutrition are for some simply buzzwords, but The Chef's Garden has made them its mantra. Lee explains, "If a chef wants to know when his produce was picked, who picked it, and when it was shipped, we have the ability to give them that information immediately. If there were ever a problem with our produce, we could alert all other restaurants that received orders from us within minutes." The ability to use modern shipping techniques has been fully exploited by the Joneses: "We are able to pick an order in the morning and have it to the chef in less than 24 hours. We are as local as anyone else." Of course none of this would matter without flavor and nutrition. The Chef's Garden's attention to the soil and the replenishing of it allows the business to grow for maximum flavor, high nutrient content, and extended shelf life for chefs.

The farm is also the spawning ground for Lee's favorite project, Veggie U. Veggie U is a nonprofit program for fourth graders to get hands-on instruction about soil, seed, growing, and harvesting. The goal of Veggie U is for students to grow up with a love for healthy food, grown responsibly, and to combat the messages of processed food. Lee says "There's no such thing as junk food. It's either food or it's junk." Pretty straight shootin' from a great farmer.

Lee Jones and Charlie Trotter

Lee Jones and Charlie Trotter

BARBARA LYNCH, *No. 9 Park,* Boston, Massachusetts

CHRIS KURTH, *Siena Farms,* Sudbury, Massachusetts (fairytale eggplant)

Roasted Fairytale Eggplant in Chèvre Cream

Young, light purple, teardrop-shaped eggplant with white stripes are known for their creaminess. Barbara uses the sweetness of currants and the tartness of chèvre to enhance the natural nuttiness of this eggplant. Roasting brings out its smoky flavor and helps it keep its shape.

SERVES 6

1 pound tiny fairytale eggplant, left whole, or purple Japanese eggplant, cut into 2-inch slices
¾ cup extra-virgin olive oil
Coarse salt and freshly ground black pepper

½ cup currants
½ cup heavy cream
6 ounces chèvre cheese, crumbled
½ cup pistachios
1 shallot, finely chopped

1 clove garlic, finely chopped
1 anchovy fillet, rinsed, patted dry, and finely chopped
2 tablespoons aged sherry vinegar
Sea salt

1. Heat the oven to 350°F. Toss the eggplant with 3 tablespoons of the olive oil, season with salt, spread on a baking sheet, and roast until just tender but still holding their shape, about 25 minutes (though time will vary depending on the size of the eggplant).

2. Meanwhile, plump the currants: Put the currants in a small bowl, cover with hot water and let sit until soft, 5 to 10 minutes.

3. In a small saucepan, bring the cream to a simmer. Whisk in the cheese and cook gently, stirring, until there are no lumps, about 6 minutes. (For a completely smooth dressing, pass it through a fine-mesh strainer.) Season to taste with salt and pepper and keep warm.

4. In a medium nonstick skillet over medium heat, toast the pistachios for 2 to 3 minutes until just fragrant and lightly toasted.

5. Heat 1 tablespoon olive oil in a small sauté pan over medium heat. Add the shallots, garlic, and anchovies, and cook, stirring, until the shallots are tender, about 5 minutes. Transfer to a small bowl and set aside. Drain the currants and add them to the anchovy mixture. Add the pistachios and the vinegar and whisk in the remaining ½ cup olive oil. Season to taste with salt and pepper.

6. Portion the chèvre cream among 6 plates, spooning it in the center. Stand the whole eggplants up in the cream (you may need to slice a little off the bottom to get them to stand) or lay slices on top of it. Drizzle a couple of spoonfuls of the anchovy vinaigrette over the top and sprinkle with a little sea salt.

MICHAEL ANTHONY, *Gramercy Tavern*, New York City

ZAID KURDIEH, *Norwich Meadows Farm*, Norwich, New York (swiss chard)

Curried English Peas and Pickled Swiss Chard

Crisp fresh peas seasoned with aromatic curry powder and a hint of acidity from traditional pickling spices combine familiar flavors in an unusual side dish. This is delicious with any grilled meat, white fish, or poultry.

SERVES 4

FOR THE PICKLED CHARD STALKS
1½ cups sugar
4 cups rice vinegar
¼ cup coarse salt
¼ teaspoon mustard seeds
¼ teaspoon black peppercorns
¼ teaspoon fennel seeds
¼ teaspoon coriander seeds
1 small red beet, peeled and
    roughly chopped
3 cups Swiss chard stalks,
    cut into 2-inch pieces

FOR THE CURRIED PEAS
2 tablespoons extra-virgin olive oil
2 large scallions (white and green
    parts), finely minced
1 clove garlic, minced
1 teaspoon curry powder, preferably
    Imperial
1 cup milk
8 Swiss chard leaves,
    cut into narrow ribbons
2 cups fresh English peas
    (or 2 pounds fresh peas, shelled)

1 cup vegetable stock or water
1 teaspoon fresh lemon juice
1 tablespoon fresh flat-leaf parsley,
    finely chopped
Coarse salt and freshly ground
    black pepper

A BLEND OF TRADITIONAL AND MODERN

Farmers have to be the most resourceful, creative, and resolute businessmen and women on the planet. Zaid and Haifa Kurdieh of Norwich Meadows Farm certainly are. Zaid and Haifa are Muslims who farm in upstate New York. Zaid grew up in Wyoming, while Haifa was raised in Jordan. They both have farming in their family histories and bring their belief that they should be good stewards of the land and their animals.

The Kurdiehs follow the Halal (Arabic for lawful) method of raising and processing chickens and because of it have a growing following at farmers' markets and with New York chefs. Practicing Halal produces animals that are raised to a proper age on pure foods and pasture and that are then treated respectfully at the time of slaughter.

Their farm in upstate New York has been adapted with "high tunnels" to

withstand the winter climate and keep the farm alive. The tunnels block out the cold wind and snow, allowing the animals to continue growing even as the weather outside goes deep into winter. This year-round benefit can increase yield by 300 percent. Surprisingly, the Kurdiehs learned about the tunnels from farmers in Egypt who have to face cold winters in the desert.

1. In a large pot, combine the sugar, 1½ cups water, the vinegar, salt, spices, and beets, and bring to a boil. Remove from the heat, strain through a fine-mesh strainer into a medium bowl (discard any solids), and let cool. Add the chard pieces to the pickling liquid, cover, and refrigerate for 2 hours or overnight.

2. Just before serving, heat the oil in a large skillet over medium heat and cook the scallions and garlic until softened, about 3 minutes. Add the curry powder and milk and bring just to a boil. Add the Swiss chard leaves, peas, and vegetable stock and simmer until the peas are tender, about 2 minutes. Add the lemon juice and parsley, and season with salt and pepper.

3. To serve, spoon the curried pea mixture on plates and top with a bit of pickled chard stalks. Alternatively, transfer the pea mixture and pickled Swiss chard to separate serving bowls and have everyone serve themselves at the table.

BILL TAIBE, *LeFarm,* Westport, Connecticut

ANNIE FARRELL & BETSY FINK, *Millstone Farm,* Wilton, Connecticut (beets)

Roasted Beets with Mint

Use a variety of beets for various colors and levels of sweetness. Reds have a stronger flavor than chioggias, which are also known as candy stripes because they have rings of red and white when cut. Roasting beets brings out their natural sweetness. A drizzle of honey and balsamic vinegar with fresh mint marries all the flavors together.

SERVES 4

12 to 16 assorted small beets, such as dark reds, chioggia, and golden (about 2 pounds)
5 tablespoons olive oil

Coarse salt and freshly ground black pepper
4 sprigs fresh thyme
2 teaspoons honey

2 tablespoons balsamic vinegar
2 tablespoons fresh small mint leaves, for garnish

1. Heat the oven to 400°F. Put the beets in an oven-proof pan. Drizzle with 2 tablespoons of olive oil, then sprinkle with salt, pepper, and sprigs of thyme; toss to coat. Cover with aluminum foil and roast for 25 minutes, or until a knife slides through the beets with ease.

2. When cool enough to handle, peel the beets and cut into medium-size wedges. Set aside in a medium serving bowl.

3. In a medium bowl, mix the honey, vinegar, the remaining 3 tablespoons olive oil, salt, and pepper; pour over the beets and toss to coat. Taste and adjust the seasoning. Garnish with the mint.

VINNY DOTOLO & JON SHOOK, *Animal,* Los Angeles, California

JAMES BIRCH, *Flora Bella Farm,* Three Rivers, California (bitter greens)

Grilled Broccoli Rabe and Radicchio with Pancetta Dressing Topped with a Soft-Cooked Egg

In 1991, Jim started selling all sorts of his seasonal vegetables and fruit to the most popular restaurants in Los Angeles. Jon and Vinny love the flavors and textures of this dish—the smokiness of grilled bitter greens cooled with a creamy soft-cooked egg and balanced with the sweet and salty pancetta dressing, finished with a crunchy breadcrumb topping. This makes a great supper in itself. Use escarole or kale if you can't find broccoli rabe.

SERVES 4

2 slices day-old country or
  rustic bread, crusts removed
Olive oil
Coarse salt
6 slices pancetta (about ¼ pound),
  cut into ¼-inch dice
½ cup white balsamic vinegar
1 tablespoon mustard seeds
1 teaspoon crushed red
  pepper flakes

2 tablespoons sugar
1 teaspoon fresh thyme leaves, roughly
  chopped
6 tablespoons (¾ stick) unsalted
  butter, melted
¼ cup finely chopped red onions
  (about ½ medium onion)
¼ cup finely chopped fennel
  (about ½ bulb)

1 pound young broccoli rabe, washed,
  dried, and leaves removed (keep for
  another use)
2 heads radicchio, cored
  and leaves separated
2 tablespoons blended olive oil
  and grape seed oil
2 teaspoons minced garlic
4 large eggs
20 shavings Parmigiano-Reggiano

1. Heat the oven to 325°F. Lightly oil and salt the day-old bread and bake until golden brown, about 10 minutes. Let cool, tear into pieces, and process in the food processor until finely ground; set aside.

2. In a medium skillet, heat the pancetta and cook over medium-high heat for 5 minutes until lightly golden brown. Drain on a paper towel–lined plate. In a medium bowl, mix the vinegar, mustard seeds, red pepper flakes, sugar, and thyme. Whisk in the melted butter and add the red onions, fennel, and pancetta. Set the pancetta vinaigrette aside.

3. In a large bowl, toss the broccoli rabe with the radicchio leaves, oil, and garlic; add salt to taste. Heat a grill or grill pan until hot but not smoking. Put the greens (in batches) on the grill for 30 seconds, turning them over frequently until just wilted; transfer to a large bowl. Continue until all of the broccoli rabe and radicchio are grilled and toss them with 4 tablespoons of the pancetta vinaigrette.

4. Bring a medium pot of water to a boil over medium-high heat and use a slotted spoon to lower the eggs into the water. Adjust the heat to maintain a simmer and cook the eggs for 5 minutes. Fill a medium bowl with ice and water, then remove the cooked eggs from the pan into the ice water bath. When the eggs are cool enough to handle, gently crack the shell all over, start to peel, and intermittently submerge in the ice bath (if they're a bit too hot) and continue to peel.

5. To serve, portion the grilled broccoli rabe and radicchio onto 4 serving plates, mounding it in the center of each plate. Put 5 Parmigiano shavings on top of the greens, then set one whole soft-cooked egg on top. Drizzle the remaining vinaigrette on top of the egg and around the plate and top generously with the breadcrumbs.

continued

LAND, WATER, AND SKY CONVERGE

Sitting at 1,500 feet above sea level with a view of the Sierra Nevada peaks that reach 13,000 feet is James and Dawn Birch's Flora Bella Farm. The farm is located in the small town of Three Rivers, California (named for the forks of the Kaweah River—the middle, north, and south—which feed James his fresh, untouched, snow-melted water), just outside of Sequoia National Forest. The rivers, soil, and cool evenings make for what chefs Jon Shook and Vinny Dotolo at Animal in Los Angeles call "the best arugula anywhere" as well as great kale, collard greens, and about 60 other varieties of fruits and vegetables.

The land is also home to wild greens like lamb's quarters, purslane, and stinging nettles, which Nancy Silverton of Osteria Mozza loves for her pizzas. James also has a strong following at the Santa Monica and Hollywood farmers' markets, two of the most well-stocked in the country. He makes the 450-mile round trip twice a week to get his produce to his chef clients and to his farmers' market regulars. "On the days I think I don't want to do this again, I go to the market and get so energized by my customers that I leave thinking 'what do I want to plant next?'."

The energy that James receives goes back into the community when he and Dawn take their farm to inner-city classrooms in Los Angeles to educate children about nutrition and the resources that goes into the food they grow. The Birches also work with Sustainable Economic Enterprises of Los Angeles (SEE-LA), which has built The Farmer's Kitchen, a community teaching and retail kitchen that also delivers farm-fresh products to the community.

One conversation with James Birch will have us all eating out of his hand.

Jon Shook, James Birch, and Vinny Dotolo

LACHLAN MACKINNON-PATTERSON, *Frasca Food & Wine*, Boulder, Colorado

BOB & MIKE MUNSON, *Munson Farms*, Boulder, Colorado (sweet corn)

Sweet Corn Sformato

Sformato is a type of Italian soufflé but not quite as airy and not nearly as time-consuming to make. The flavor of the sweet corn isn't lost in the eggs or overwhelmed by the cheese. This baked custard dish is a great alternative for brunch or as part of a light meal with a salad.

SERVES 4

5 tablespoons unsalted butter; plus more for the ramekins
½ medium onion, minced (about ¼ cup)
2 cups fresh corn kernels (about 2 ears of corn)

½ cup heavy cream
3 large eggs
1 small shallot, minced
½ cup grated Montasio or Asiago cheese

Coarse salt and freshly ground black pepper
¼ cup chopped fresh chives, for garnish

1. Heat 4 tablespoons of the butter in a medium skillet over medium heat, add the onions and cook until almost tender, about 3 minutes. Add the corn and cook for another 2 to 3 minutes. Add 1½ cups water, increase the heat until just simmering, and cook for 10 minutes, or until the water is mostly cooked out. Add ¼ cup of the cream and bring back to a simmer, then remove from the heat.

2. Heat the oven to 300°F. Transfer the corn mixture to the bowl of a food processor or blender and purée until completely smooth. You might need to add a bit more water, a tablespoon at a time, to get a smooth consistency. In a medium bowl, whisk the eggs, then slowly add the hot corn mixture, stirring constantly, so the eggs don't start to cook.

3. Grease four 4-ounce ramekins with butter and place in a small baking pan with at least 3-inch sides. Fill the ramekins to the top with the corn mixture, place the baking pan in the oven, and add hot water halfway up the sides of the ramekins; bake for 30 minutes, or until set. Remove from the oven and set aside to cool.

4. Make a cheese sauce by heating the remaining 1 tablespoon butter in a small skillet over medium heat and cooking the shallots for 3 minutes. Add the remaining ¼ cup cream, then bring back to a simmer and stir in the cheese until completely melted. Season with salt and pepper. Keep warm until ready to serve.

5. To serve, unmold the ramekins when they are cool enough to handle, invert onto serving plates, and spoon the sauce around the custard. Garnish with the chives.

LINTON HOPKINS, *Restaurant Eugene,* Atlanta, Georgia

ALLAN BENTON, *Benton's Smoky Mountain Country Hams,* Madisonville, Tennessee (bacon)

Butter Bean and Corn Succotash with Candied Bacon

Benton's bacon has a strong hickory flavor that is assertive enough to be "candied" without losing its smokiness. At Restaurant Eugene, Linton uses the candied bacon as a garnish on a salad or as a bar snack. Butter beans, also known as lima beans, are essential to an authentic succotash. While the Native American dish has dozens of variations, most contain the essential ingredients of corn and beans. Peak season for pod beans as well as corn is August to September.

SERVES 6

½ cup brown sugar
1 teaspoon cayenne
½ pound smoked bacon
   (16 thin slices)
Coarse salt and freshly ground
   black pepper

2 cups fresh butter beans or lima
   beans, shelled (about 2 pounds
   fresh lima pods)
2 tablespoons unsalted butter
1 tablespoon olive oil
1 small Vidalia onion, finely chopped

1 clove garlic, minced
2 cups fresh corn kernels
   (2 medium ears of corn)
½ cup chicken stock
½ cup heavy cream
¼ cup fresh flat-leaf parsley,
   finely chopped

1. Heat the oven to 325°F. In a small bowl, mix the brown sugar and cayenne. Put the bacon in a medium bowl and add the brown sugar mixture. Use your hands to coat the bacon with the mixture and then arrange the slices on a baking sheet. Set another baking sheet on top of the pan with the bacon (with a sheet of parchment in between) to keep it from rippling and place in the oven. Bake for 10 minutes and then raise the heat to 375°F and continue to cook until the bacon is crisp and shiny from the melted sugar. When cool enough to handle, crumble into 1-inch pieces and set aside.

2. In the meantime, bring a medium saucepan of salted water to a boil. Add the beans and cook until tender, about 3 minutes. Prepare a medium bowl of ice water. Drain the cooked beans and cool in the ice water to stop the cooking immediately. Drain and reserve.

3. Heat the butter and olive oil in a medium skillet over medium-low heat; add the onions and cook until soft, about 10 minutes. Add the garlic and cook for 30 seconds, then add the corn and chicken stock. Bring to a simmer and cook for 15 minutes, until the chicken stock is reduced to a glaze or very little liquid is left in the skillet. Add the beans and cream and cook for 10 minutes to reduce the cream by about three-quarters. Adjust the seasoning with salt and black pepper. Transfer to a serving dish, sprinkle with the parsley, and top with the candied bacon.

YEARS IN THE MAKING

"I just want to produce something as good as our European cousins," says Allan Benton in his sweet Virginia drawl. From his self-described "thoroughbred hillbilly operation" in Madisonville, Tennessee, Benton ships aged hams (12 to 28 months), smoked country bacon, and his own prosciutto around the country to chefs and private customers who crave his product. Allan says, "There is nothing fancy or scientific or modern about what we do. We are just patient and we stayed with our own game of aging hams for longer than anyone else."

Allan grew up in rural Scott County, Virginia, "20 miles from a town and so deep in the country that you had to look straight up to see sunlight," with his grandparents close by. His grandparents smoked ham in their log smokehouse, and it was watching them get showered with so much love and respect from friends and neighbors who ate their ham that made Allan want to continue the tradition. Since they lived on such hilly ground that grain did not grow well, the pigs foraged for acorns that gave them their superior flavor. Allan says, "I feel so fortunate that my grandparents took so much pride in their product and passed that on to me."

Allan says he owes a deep debt of gratitude to local chef John Fleer and proprietor Sam Bell of Blackberry Farm in the Smoky Mountains for sharing his products with chefs across America. This has led to great relationships with chefs and restaurateurs throughout the country, including Linton Hopkins, Frank Stitt, David Chang, and many others.

His other great supporters have been his own children. Allan had heard of prosciutto but had no idea what it was. After buying some at a local market and doing a taste-test comparison against his own hams sliced to the same paper thinness, he knew he had his next product. As the kids went off to college with Baggies of dad's prosciutto, the calls came home to start marketing the product. Thanks to their goodie bags, the kids were the most popular in the dorm.

Whenever Allan thinks about his good fortune he can't help but voice it: "I enjoy what I do and I feel so blessed to be able to do it." It's as if the thought is always ruminating at the front of his mind.

BRIAN LEWIS, *The Farmhouse at Bedford Post*, Bedford, New York

JOHN UBALDO, *John Boy's Farm*, Cambridge, New York (bacon)

Brussels Sprouts with Brown Butter, Bacon, and Sage

Brown butter brings out the Brussels sprouts' natural nutty sweet flavor. If you use tiny Brussels sprouts, you won't need to cut them in half. Slab bacon is sold unsliced; alternatively, you can use thickly sliced bacon in this recipe.

SERVES 4

¼ pound smoked slab bacon,
   cut into ½-inch dice (about 1 cup)
2 cups Brussels sprouts,
   trimmed and cut in half

Coarse salt and freshly ground
   black pepper
2 tablespoons unsalted butter
6 fresh sage leaves, thinly sliced

1. Heat a medium skillet over medium-low heat, and cook the bacon for 10 minutes until crisp and browned. Use a slotted spoon to remove the bacon; drain on a paper towel–lined plate. Drain all but 2 tablespoons of bacon fat from the pan.

2. Heat the reserved bacon fat in the same pan over medium heat and add the Brussels sprouts. Reduce the heat to medium low and cook until the Brussels sprouts are deep brown, about 15 minutes; season with salt and pepper. Add the butter and sage and continue to cook for 5 minutes, until the sage has become a bit crisp and the butter has browned. Add the bacon and toss with the Brussels sprouts.

BILL TAIBE, *LeFarm,* Westport, Connecticut

ANNIE FARRELL & BETSY FINK, *Millstone Farm,* Wilton, Connecticut (tomatoes)

Roasted Stuffed Tomatoes with Farro

Annie and Bill love the smoky flavor from the charred roasted tomatoes balanced with the natural sweetness of the fresh beans. Farro is related to spelt and has a nutty taste and gratifying chewiness; it makes a terrific filling for tomatoes at their peak.

SERVES 4

4 Brown Jewel, Ox Heart, heirloom, or other large tomatoes
6 tablespoons extra-virgin olive oil
1 cup farro
1 cup port wine

2 tablespoons red-wine vinegar
1 teaspoon honey
1 cup shelled fresh beans, such as cranberry, borlotti, or fava

Coarse salt and freshly ground black pepper
¼ cup fresh sunflower seeds
Fennel fronds, fresh basil leaves, and sunflower petals, for garnish

1. Heat the oven to 450°F. Core and hollow out the tomatoes, making sure not to pierce the flesh. Arrange on a roasting pan and brush with 2 tablespoons of the olive oil. Roast for 10 minutes, or until the skin is charred and slightly blackened.

2. Bring a medium saucepan of water to a boil, then stir in the farro. Cover, reduce the heat to low, and simmer until the farro is tender, 25 to 35 minutes. Drain well, let cool, and transfer to a large bowl.

3. To make the sweet-and-sour sauce, combine the port wine and red-wine vinegar in a small saucepan and cook over medium-high heat until reduced by three-quarters, about 15 minutes. Stir in the honey and set aside.

4. In a small saucepan, cook the beans in boiling salted water until tender, 2 to 3 minutes. Drain and cool; add to the bowl of farro.

5. Add the sweet-and-sour sauce, the remaining 4 tablespoons olive oil, the sunflower seeds, and salt and pepper to taste to the farro-bean mixture. Mix well.

6. Spoon the mixture into the tomatoes. Garnish with fennel fronds, basil leaves, and sunflower petals around the plate. Serve warm or at room temperature.

continued

MORE THAN
GENTLELADY FARMERS

The affluent suburb of Wilton, Connecticut, seems like an unusual place for a 75-acre farm, but farmers Annie Farrell and Betsy Fink have established a sustainable model that feeds beautiful tomatoes, corn, and beans to restaurants like LeFarm of Westport, Connecticut, and grass-fed beef with a fat content as high as any grain-finished animal to The Dressing Room of Westport, Connecticut.

Annie came to Millstone as a "farmer for hire" and set about building a system that would be highly productive, extremely efficient, and environmentally low impact. A perfect example is her chicken "Coupe de Villes" (mobile chicken houses with white walls and a Cadillac® emblem). The houses are moved around the farm to follow the grazing cows and pigs. As the chickens (Buff Orpingtons, Domin-iques, Barred Rocks, Ameraucanas, and a few Wynandottes) eat their grass/organic feed/flax diet along with insects from the livestock droppings, the insect population is kept in check and the chickens produce eggs high in healthy Omega-3 fatty acids. Annie is also well known for steward-ship of Devon cattle, the breed that is perfectly suited for grass feeding and shines brightest when used for ham-burgers. She takes complete control of the animals from breeding through slaughter, making sure one of her staff is present for slaughter and packaging. This attention to detail is what makes her so special.

Annie and Betsy have strong beliefs in a model of farming that not only promotes local production but also interacts with schools, chefs, and even other farmers to produce a heightened awareness of healthy food and sound environ-mental practices. Whether they are giving a tour of the farm, which includes wetlands with a raised path built by Annie's son that seemingly transports visitors to the Amazon, or are spending the morning with Chef Bill Taibe picking tomatoes and basil for his beautiful salads, the farmers are always conscious of letting guests know about the model they have created to lower carbon emissions and feed the community safe, healthy food.

Bill Taibe and Annie Farrell

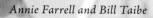
Annie Farrell and Bill Taibe

MATTHEW GENNUSO, *Chez Pascal,* Providence, Rhode Island

KARL SANTOS, *Shy Brothers Farm,* Westport Point, Massachusetts (cheese)

Savory Bread Pudding with Bacon and Farmstead Cheese with Tomato Jam

Hannahbells are the Santos brothers' version of tiny handmade cow's milk cheeses known in France as *button de culotte,* or "trouser buttons." The "shy" Santos brothers named their cheese after their mother. Matt uses these versatile cheeses in a variety of ways, either in baked dishes or on top of a hearty salad of mixed greens.

SERVES 8

One 1-pound loaf Italian or French country-style bread, crusts trimmed and cut into large cubes

4 tablespoons (½ stick) unsalted butter, melted

¼ pound sliced smoked bacon (about 8 slices), cooked and crumbled; rendered fat reserved

1 cup heavy cream

3 cups milk

3 large eggs

2 egg yolks

2 tablespoons chopped fresh thyme

¼ teaspoon coarse salt

⅛ teaspoon freshly ground black pepper

4 large ripe red or yellow tomatoes, quartered

¾ cup brown sugar

¾ cup granulated sugar

1 lemon, very thinly sliced

½ pound Hannahbell cheese or soft-ripened cow's milk cheese

1. Put the cubed bread in a large bowl, then pour the butter and 1 tablespoon of the rendered bacon fat over the bread and mix to coat evenly. In another large bowl, combine the cream, milk, eggs, egg yolks, thyme, ¼ teaspoon salt, and ⅛ teaspoon pepper. Pour the mixture over the bread and allow to sit for at least 2 hours and up to 4 hours.

2. To make the tomato jam, combine the tomatoes, both sugars, ½ cup water, and the lemon slices in a medium, heavy-bottomed pot. Bring to a simmer and cook for 2 hours over low heat, stirring occasionally and making sure the mixture doesn't stick to the bottom of the pan. The jam will be done when most of the liquid is reduced and the mixture becomes very thick. Let cool. If not using right away, let cool completely, cover, and refrigerate for up to a week.

3. Heat the oven to 350°F and lightly grease the bottom of a 9 × 5-inch loaf pan. With a slotted spoon, arrange a third of the bread evenly in the bottom of the dish. Add a layer of crumbled bacon over the bread and then a layer of cheese (you can break off small pieces) on top of the bacon. Repeat the layers, reserving a quarter of the cheese to cover the final layer. Place the baking dish in a roasting pan, pour boiling water into the pan to come halfway up the sides of the baking dish, and place in the oven. Cook for about 1 hour 45 minutes, or until a knife inserted into the center of the bread pudding comes out clean. Let cool completely.

4. When ready to serve, heat the tomato jam over low heat, adding a bit of water, a tablespoon at a time, if it's a bit thick. Remove the bread pudding from the loaf pan by unmolding onto a large plate. Cut into ½-inch slices. Heat a large skillet over medium heat and brown the slices for 1 minute per side, or until lightly golden. Serve warm, with the warm tomato jam on the side.

NANCY SILVERTON, *Osteria Mozza,* Los Angeles, California

MIMMO BRUNO, *DiStefano Cheese,* Baldwin Park, California (burrata)

Crostini with Burrata, Marinated Escarole, and Caramelized Shallots

Cheesemaker Mimmo Bruno started making cheese in Puglia, Italy, as a kid. He is well known in the food community as the first to introduce burrata cheese to the United States. Nancy mixes sweet onions, bitter escarole, and salty bacon with Mimmo's creamy burrata cheese for incredibly balanced flavor.

SERVES 4

FOR THE MARINATED ESCAROLE
3 medium shallots, peeled,
  2 left whole and 1 finely
  chopped (1 tablespoon)
4 cloves garlic, peeled, 2 left whole
  and 2 finely chopped
  (about 1½ teaspoons)
¾ cup extra-virgin olive oil
1½ teaspoons coarse salt
1 medium head escarole, cut in half
  lengthwise and washed thoroughly
1 tablespoon plus 1 teaspoon
  Champagne vinegar
Freshly ground black pepper

FOR THE CARAMELIZED SHALLOTS
2 tablespoons extra-virgin olive oil
6 large shallots, sliced lengthwise
  into ¼-inch-wide strips
Coarse salt and freshly ground
  black pepper
½ cup balsamic vinegar
1 tablespoon honey

Two ¼-inch-thick slices bacon,
  preferably applewood-smoked,
  cut diagonally into ¼-inch pieces

Four ½-inch-thick slices bâtard
  (or 8 slices baguette or 2 large slices
  rustic white bread)
½ cup olive oil; plus more for drizzling
1 clove garlic, sliced in half
8 ounces burrata cheese
  (divided into 4 pieces)
Freshly ground black pepper

MAKE THE MARINATED ESCAROLE
1. In a blender or food processor fitted with a metal blade, purée the 2 whole shallots and the 2 whole cloves garlic with ½ cup of the olive oil and 1 teaspoon of the salt. In a medium bowl, mix the escarole with the puréed mixture.

2. Heat a grill or a large, heavy-bottomed skillet over high heat and char the escarole for 7 to 8 minutes on each side, until tender. Remove from the skillet or grill and discard any pieces that are too blackened. Put the escarole in a bowl and cover with plastic wrap until cool. Cut off the root and discard it, then coarsely chop the escarole into 1-inch pieces.

3. In a large bowl, combine the Champagne vinegar, chopped shallots, chopped garlic, the remaining ½ teaspoon salt, and pepper to taste. Add the escarole and toss. Add the remaining ¼ cup olive oil, toss again, and set aside. Let the escarole marinate for at least 15 to 30 minutes before serving.

MAKE THE SHALLOTS
In a small skillet, combine the olive oil, shallots, and salt and pepper to taste. Over high heat, brown the shallots on one side for about 2 minutes then flip them to brown the other side, being careful not to stir the shallots too often or they will soften. Add the balsamic vinegar and cook over high heat until it's reduced to a syrupy consistency; add the honey and stir to combine.

1. In a small skillet over medium heat, cook the bacon until cooked all the way through but not too crisp. Drain on a paper towel–lined plate.

2. Heat the oven to 325°F. Arrange the bread slices on a baking sheet, brush the tops with olive oil, and bake for 15 to 20 minutes, or until they're lightly toasted and golden brown. (You can also toast the bread in a toaster but without the oil. Then brush the toast with oil after they're done.) Rub the oiled side of the crostini with the garlic.

3. To serve, arrange the crostini, oiled side up, on a serving platter. Pile an uneven layer of escarole over each crostini and sprinkle the bacon over it. Put 1 piece of burrata on top of the bacon, leaving a 1-inch border of escarole, and top with 1 teaspoon of the caramelized shallots. Drizzle with olive oil and freshly ground black pepper.

continued

MOZZARELLA'S SWEET COUSIN

Since the age of 12, Mimmo Bruno has had one focus and one goal—to make the burrata cheese of his hometown, Bari, in the Puglia region of Italy, as popular in the United States as it is back home. From the outside, his burrata looks like a nice ball of mozzarella, but slice into it and put a piece in your mouth and the experience is new and astounding. Mimmo stretches the curd into a thin sheet, then fills it with a mix of sweet cream (from Italy) and shreds of the mozzarella called stracciatelle ("rags") and ties it all up like a hobo bag.

Mimmo came to Los Angeles in 1993 to set up shop and make the cheeses he loved in his hometown. The mozzarella and ricotta were an easy sell, but as they became commodity cheeses the business lost its luster. Mimmo started making his favorite cheese—burrata—but creating a successful business was slow-going. For years the only person Mimmo could find that believed in his burrata was Osteria Mozza owner Nancy Silverton (then at Campanile and La Brea Bakery). Nancy continued to support Mimmo when she opened Osteria Mozza, which helped spread the word about his rich, sweet cheese.

Mimmo wants to focus on making his burrata. He sees the popularity of the cheese exploding and relishes the thought that the world has come around to his vision of a great cheese.

Mimmo Bruno and Nancy Silverton

RICK BAYLESS, *Frontera Grill,* Chicago, Illinois

MARTY & KRIS TRAVIS, *Spence Farm,* Fairbury, Illinois (corn)

Sweet Potatoes with Corn, Swiss Chard, and Caramelized Onions

The natural mild spice flavor of sweet potatoes along with the sweetness of the corn and caramelized onions add complexity to Swiss chard's simple flavor. Rick uses sherry vinegar for its richness, but you could use balsamic vinegar to add sweetness or white-wine or Champagne vinegar for its lightness.

SERVES 8 TO 10

⅓ cup vegetable oil, olive oil, or a mixture of the two

2 medium dried guajillo (New Mexico) chiles (½ ounce total), stemmed and seeded

2 cloves garlic, peeled and cut into quarters

¼ cup sherry vinegar

Coarse salt

1 large red onion, cut into ½-inch dice

3 medium sweet potatoes (about 2 pounds total), peeled and cut into ½-inch dice

6 cups Swiss chard, thick lower stems cut off, leaves sliced crosswise into ½-inch strips

3 medium ears fresh corn, kernels removed

1. Heat the oil in a large (12-inch) skillet with a tight-fitting lid over medium heat, then add the chiles and garlic. Stir the chiles until toasty smelling, about 30 seconds (if the oil isn't too hot). Remove from the heat and transfer the chiles, oil, and garlic to a blender or food processor along with the vinegar and a scant teaspoon salt. Blend until smooth.

2. Return the skillet (it will have a light coating of oil) to medium heat and add the onions. Cook, stirring frequently, until richly browned, about 10 minutes. Add the sweet potatoes, the chile mixture, and salt to taste. Stir well, then cover and simmer (check to see if the potatoes are steaming and if so add ¼ cup water) until the sweet potatoes are fork-tender, 15 to 20 minutes.

3. Add the Swiss chard and corn kernels, then continue cooking, covered, for another 4 to 5 minutes, or until the chard has wilted and the corn is warmed through. (If it doesn't all fit, add the chard and when the chard has wilted and made space in the skillet, add the corn.) Stir to combine. Taste and season with additional salt if needed.

FOREVER EXPERIMENTING

Marty Travis had been happy making historic reproduction Shaker furniture for 30 years, but when he met and married Kris, things went in a new direction. Kris came from Florida and wanted to get back to the land. Luckily, Marty's family owned the oldest family farm in Livingston County, Illinois. Starting from scratch in 2003, they harvested wild ramps and nettles and quickly moved on to squash blossoms and heirloom tomatoes, all on a stretch of land surrounded by industrial farms growing corn and soy beans.

After talking to chefs in Chicago who always asked, "So what else do you have?" their response was, "What do you want us to grow?" From a conversation like that with Rick Bayless, they decided to start working on rare breeds of corn. Iroquois White Corn was on Bayless's wish list after his supplier, The Iroquois Nation, stopped producing the corn. Marty and Chris found a small supply of very expensive seeds in Canada and managed to grow eight rows their first year. The following year, those eight rows produced 9 pounds of seed and combined with the last 5 pounds they could find grew to an acre of heirloom corn. Keeping these heirloom varieties alive is important to Marty and Kris as a way of teaching young farmers new ways to grow a small farm and visiting school kids the history of our country through its food.

The farm is an ongoing place for experimentation and growth. Marty and Kris, along with Marty's son Will, continue to expand their farm with plans to raise heritage breeds of hogs, cows, sheep, turkeys, and ducks.

Marty Travis, Kris Travis, and Rick Bayless

PAUL VIRANT, *Vie*, Western Springs, Illinois

WILL ALLEN, *Growing Power*, Milwaukee, Wisconsin (potatoes)

Braised New Potatoes with Mustard and Leeks

At Vie, Paul serves this dish with wood-grilled fish and hearty mustard greens. Its simplicity enhances Growing Power's tender, round new red potatoes. New potatoes are commonly known as new reds, but the "new" applies to any potatoes harvested before they're mature.

SERVES 4

2 tablespoons unsalted butter
2 small leeks (white and light
  green parts), cut lengthwise,
  sliced, and washed

1 tablespoon fresh thyme leaves,
  roughly chopped
3 fresh bay leaves
1 pound new potatoes, washed
  and sliced ½ inch thick

1 cup chicken stock
2 tablespoons whole-grain mustard
⅓ cup heavy cream
Coarse salt and freshly ground
  black pepper

Heat the butter over medium heat in a large skillet. Add the leeks and thyme and cook for 2 minutes, then add the bay leaves, potatoes, and stock; stir in the mustard and bring to a boil. Reduce the heat to medium low and simmer until the potatoes are tender, about 10 minutes. Add the cream, bring to a simmer over medium heat, and cook for 5 minutes until just thickened and the liquid is reduced to about 1 cup. Remove the bay leaves and season with salt and pepper to taste.

FARMS WITHOUT FENCES

"We want to change the existing food system to work for everybody," says Will Allen of Milwaukee's Growing Power. His farm, education center, and "labs," as Growing Power has come to be known, grow vegetables, fruits, and fish in some of the most unlikely places. Abandoned lots in Milwaukee and Chicago are now teeming with staff and interns growing and educating local kids and adults in the beauty of creating healthy soil, raising aquaculture perch and tilapia, and cultivating fresh greens that look like they come from the sun-drenched farms of California. But the real goal here is to bring healthy, affordable, and safe foods to the parts of this country that have been mostly served by corner bodegas carrying only processed food.

And as Allen likes to say, "We don't build fences, we build communities."

At Growing Power there is no waste, and everything is connected. The aquaponic system is a prime example. Allen and his crews took 3 acres of urban wasteland and turned them into a fresh fish farm, with almost 10,000 perch and tilapia swimming in water that is filtered by the soil and pebbles. They grow greens that were started in compost that Growing Power uses to heat the hoops that cover the whole operation. Will's hope is to move initiatives like this into abandoned buildings in urban areas and thrive "off the grid" since his compost produces methane gas to keep everything humming.

Allen wants to see gardens and aquaponic systems sprout throughout the country as oil prices rise and as vacant lots blight the landscape and farmland is eaten up for suburban housing. He sees the future of farming not in the rural communities that "have been taken over by corporations" but in cities, with children growing their own food and experiencing the great taste and reward of producing what they eat. With such a strong point of view and the energy to implement his ideas, it's no wonder that Allen has received a $100,000 Ford Foundation leadership grant, and a $400,000 Kellogg Foundation grant to create urban agriculture jobs, and in 2008 was named a MacArthur Fellow. Pretty genius.

Will Allen and Paul Virant

GALE GAND, *Tru*, Chicago, Illinois

JUDY SCHAD, *Capriole Farm*, Greenville, Indiana (cheese)

Goat Cheese and Chive Hash Browns

These hash browns are a wonderful reduced-fat version since goat's milk cheese has all the taste of cow's milk cheese but much less fat. There are two ways to make hash browns: with cooked potatoes or raw ones. Gail and Judy prefer the interior texture as well as the crisp crust when starting with raw potatoes. The lemony flavor and underlying sweetness make these hash browns unusually light.

SERVES 4

3 large potatoes, preferably
   Yukon Gold, peeled

1 large egg, beaten

½ cup rice flour (or cake flour)

1 cup crumbled goat cheese

2 tablespoons chopped fresh chives

Coarse salt and freshly ground
   black pepper

2 tablespoons canola oil

1. Grate the potatoes in a food processor then rinse them in a colander until the water runs clear. Add the potatoes by the handful onto a clean kitchen towel, and then squeeze them dry (you'll need to work in batches). Put the potatoes in a large bowl and stir in the egg, flour, goat cheese, chives, and salt and pepper to taste.

2. Pour 2 tablespoons oil in a large nonstick skillet and heat it on medium-high heat. Scoop out about ½ cup of potato mixture and drop it gently into the hot oil, flattening it with the back of the cup slightly. Repeat, spacing the pancakes out but filling the pan as much as possible. Fry each pancake on one side until golden brown, about 2 minutes, then carefully flip and fry the other side, cooking for another 2 minutes.

3. Remove with a spatula, letting excess oil drain off, and transfer to a brown paper bag or paper towel–lined plate. Tent with foil to keep warm until all the pancakes are cooked. Serve immediately.

GOATS FROM A TO Z

The 500-plus goats residing at Capriole, Judy Schad's farm in Greenville, Indiana, have names like Aurora, Zena, and everything in between. Every year, the new kids on the farm are all given names starting with the same letter. 2009 was the year for X, and Judy didn't like Y, so she quickly moved to Z.

Judy spent her childhood summers on her grandparents' farm, so she was no stranger to the pleasure that came from working the land. When it came time to finish her Ph.D. thesis on Renaissance literature, she thought better and headed to the country. Judy knew she was city folk coming to the country and wanted to make sure she was not getting into something she would regret. After much research Judy decided that goats would be the best animals to spend a lot of time with. After all, they're smart, social, clean, and not so big they'll knock you over; the deciding factor for Judy: They have "nice poop."

Judy started what she calls "pretending to farm" on her 80 acres in 1978; since that time, Capriole has grown into a farmstead operation making over 1,000 pounds of goat cheese each week. The pride of Capriole is its aged raw-milk goat cheeses. As one of the first producers of its kind, Judy has been working to spread the word about this cheese that she says closely represents the natural biodiversity of her animals and her land. The rewards of cheese usually come in recognition from consumers, chefs, and the cheese cognoscenti. Capriole's O'Banon (named after the former governor of Indiana), an aged and marinated cheese wrapped in chestnut leaves that were soaked in bourbon, won first place at the American Cheese Society for the open category of goat's milk cheeses.

Capriole's ripened, aged, and raw-milk goat cheeses are distributed nationally, and Judy spends at least one day a week at Chicago's Green City Market. Judy's easy-going style, ability to connect with anyone, and love of sharing her great product have made Capriole's cheeses a favorite of chefs like Gale Gand.

Gale Gand and Judy Schad

SEAN BROCK, *McCrady's,* Charleston, South Carolina

GLENN ROBERTS, *Anson Mills,* Columbia, South Carolina (oats)

Savory Oats with Fig Chutney

When oats are harvested, they're so moist they must be toasted to be hulled. This process significantly reduces the cooking time. Anson Mills "stone cuts" their oats on an angle to duplicate the original coarse corn texture. At McCrady's, these oats are served with seared foie gras, but a simple sautéed pork chop or roasted chicken is a suitable main course.

SERVES 4

1 cup steel-cut or stone-cut oats
Coarse salt
1 cup dried figs, roughly chopped
1 cup sugar
1 cup dry white wine

2 tablespoons Chardonnay vinegar
  or white-wine vinegar
1 cup fresh figs, roughly chopped
1 apple, peeled and chopped
1 tablespoon yellow mustard seeds

1 tablespoon dried mustard
Freshly ground black pepper
12 small fresh mint leaves,
  for garnish

1. Rinse the oats and put them in a medium saucepan; add 2 cups water and a pinch of salt. Bring the oats to a simmer over high heat and cook, stirring frequently, for 3 to 4 minutes, or until the oats thicken. Remove the pan from the stove, cover, and let rest for 5 minutes.

2. Put the dried figs in a medium saucepan and just cover with water. Add the sugar, wine, and vinegar. Bring to a boil, then reduce the heat to medium low and simmer very gently for 15 minutes. Add the fresh figs, apples, mustard seeds, and dried mustard; continue simmering for 15 to 20 minutes, until most of the water is absorbed.

3. To serve, transfer the oats to a bowl, mix in the fig chutney, sprinkle with pepper, and garnish with small mint leaves. Alternatively, serve at the table with the fig chutney on the side.

GREG HIGGINS, *Higgins Restaurant & Bar,* Portland Oregon

CAROL & ANTHONY BOUTARD, *Ayers Creek Farm,* Gaston, Oregon (barley)

Forest Mushroom and Naked Barley Pilaf

Naked, or hull-less, barley is an ancient grain with super nutritional value. Pearl barley can be substituted in the pilaf, but you'll need to reduce the water by a quarter of the amount. Use a variety of seasonal mushrooms to really add depth to the dish. This is great served alongside seasonal game or as a stuffing for almost any poultry.

SERVES 8

¼ cup extra-virgin olive oil
1 small shallot, minced
1 pound fresh chanterelle, shiitake,
  lobster, or cremini mushrooms,
  or a mix, cleaned and thinly sliced

1 clove garlic, minced
1 tablespoon pimentón or paprika
2 sprigs fresh rosemary
Coarse salt and freshly ground
  black pepper

2 cups naked (hull-less) barley
1 cup grated Parmigiano-Reggiano
  or other hard grating cheese
3 tablespoons fresh flat-leaf parsley,
  finely chopped

1. Heat the oven to 375°F. Heat the olive oil in a large ovenproof pot over medium heat and sauté the shallots for 3 minutes. Add the mushrooms and cook for 5 to 8 minutes, or until the mushrooms are tender. Add the garlic and cook for 1 minute, then stir in the paprika, rosemary, and 8 cups water. Bring to a simmer, season with salt and pepper, and stir in the barley.

2. Cover the pot, place in the oven, and bake for 50 to 60 minutes, or until all the broth is absorbed and the barley is cooked but still firm. Remove from the oven and stir in the cheese and parsley.

STAGGERING DIVERSITY

A walk around Ayers Creek Farm will make your head spin, whether it's from Anthony Boutard's diverse variety of fruits, vegetables, and grains that grow on his 160-acre farm outside of Portland, Oregon, or his wife Carol's endless (and very funny) jokes. The Boutards' orchards of rare French plums are in sight of Old Flynt corn from New England, blackberries are ripening on vines next to the sweetest table grapes imaginable, and grains like barley wave next to fields ready for winter crops of radicchio and chicory. Carol loves to walk the farm and recite the sometimes cheesy names of the produce, including "sweet seduction" grapes that she assures will make anyone fertile after 20 minutes of eating a handful.

Anthony was brought to Oregon to work as a forester by 1000 Friends of Oregon, an organization founded in 1975 to preserve and protect Oregon's land, including farmland that was in threat of becoming developed for housing. Carol thought she and Anthony would buy a few acres of timber, tinker in the garden, and live off the sales of lumber. It didn't quite work out that way. Turns out, timberland was expensive and farmland was not. Anthony, being a Renaissance man, saw the opportunity to buy a farm that sat above wetlands (buy a pump and they'd be in business) and start to grow all the produce and grains that interested him. Carol, on the other hand, saw nothing but back-breaking work and tears. Luckily, Anthony's vision led the way.

So Anthony and Carol bought Ayers Creek Farm and turned it around, growing produce that has tremendous character and flavor, that stands on its own and isn't just a vehicle for other flavors. Shortly after, the farm was selling at local markets and then expanded to restaurants and grocery stores. Chefs like Greg Higgins love the corn that comes from the farm because it makes polenta that "hits the mouth and nose at the same time with a full flavor not usually experienced in polenta."

Greg Higgins, Carol Boutard, and Anthony Boutard

SEAN BROCK, *McCrady's,* Charleston, South Carolina

GLENN ROBERTS, *Anson Mills,* Columbia, South Carolina (rice)

Carolina Gold Rice with Ramps, Asparagus, and Morels

Glenn uses the Old World method of milling rice grains, which, after manual pounding, leaves part of the bran and germ intact, producing an excellent-flavored and -textured long-grain rice. Wild ramps resemble large scallions with a bit of purple on their stems and have a strong onion taste. Partnered with the other spring vegetables, they add color and flavor to the golden-hued rice. Sean uses asparagus juice as a "broth" to enhance the rice's delicate flavor.

SERVES 4

½ cup Carolina Gold Rice
Coarse salt and freshly ground
  white pepper
3 tablespoons unsalted butter
½ teaspoon coarse dried red pepper,
  such as piment d'Espelette

15 or 20 ramps, ends trimmed
  and washed
1 pound asparagus, trimmed and
  chopped into 1-inch pieces
1 tablespoon canola oil

½ pound fresh morels (or dried
  and soaked)
1 large clove garlic, sliced
3 sprigs fresh thyme, roughly chopped
1 tablespoon red-wine vinegar,
  preferably Banyuls

BRINGING FOOD BACK TO LIFE

"Glenn Roberts is a walking encyclopedia of food," says master ham maker Allan Benton. Roberts, of Anson Mills in Columbia, South Carolina, has made it his job to start with the cuisine of his mother's days and go back from there, as he looks to grow grains from an era when food was whole and full of texture, flavor, and even stories. Whether he hunts down white Carolina mill corn for grits that have a perfect

creamy mouth-feel or creates soba that gets shipped to Japan, Roberts is bringing back to life great flavors that were lost to mass production.

Anson Mills' land race seed (public domain seed improved only by farmers) is now grown all over the United States and has proven to grow well in Italy as well. Glenn's deep investment in The Carolina Gold Rice Foundation has led to his insuring farmers against

failure for new crops from his seed. Glenn's trial and error paid off and now he is working to expand the larder by helping others grow these sometimes slow, low-yield but ultimately rewarding rare crops.

"Chefs are the engine of what we do," says Glenn, who for years has been working with some of the best chefs from around the country (including Thomas Keller, Sean Brock, David

1. In a medium pot, bring 4 cups water, salted generously, to a boil. Add the rice and stir a couple of times. Bring the water back to a boil, then simmer on medium-low heat for 15 minutes. Drain the rice in a colander and rinse with cold water. Put the rice back in the pot and season to taste with salt and white pepper.

2. Melt 1 tablespoon of the butter in a small saucepan, add the red pepper, and cook until hot, then toss with the ramps in a medium bowl to coat with the butter. Heat a grill pan or a grill over medium-high heat and cook the ramps until they're just wilted, about 30 seconds.

3. Fill a medium saucepan with water, bring to a boil, and cook the asparagus for 2 minutes, until just tender, then cool under cold water. Put the asparagus in a food processor and purée until smooth. Put the purée in a fine-mesh strainer over a bowl and press out as much liquid from the asparagus as possible. Save the purée as side dish or for another use; reserve the liquid.

4. Heat the oil in a large skillet over medium-high heat, add the morels, and allow to brown on one side, about 1 minute, then turn and brown on all sides. Stir in the garlic and thyme. Cook for another 3 minutes. Remove from the heat, then add 1 tablespoon butter and the vinegar.

5. Add the asparagus juice to the rice, then heat over medium low until just heated. Stir in the remaining 1 tablespoon butter and, when melted, remove the pan from heat.

6. To serve, put a serving of rice on each plate or in one large serving dish and top with the morels and ramps.

Chang, and Jody Adams) as he grew Anson Mills into a force in the heirloom grain business. He has a special fondness for Sean Brock of McCrady's in Charleston, South Carolina: "He is like a lighthouse—he takes everything in and does amazing things with it. He even took my cereal grain a step further by cooling it with liquid nitrogen before milling it, locking in the flavor by keeping it so cold." Glenn works so closely with chefs that he will only take orders after an extensive conversation to make sure the chef is getting exactly what he or she wants and knows precisely how to handle Glenn's product. With a catalog of over 200 wholesale ingredients, this kind of service is a boon to chefs looking for something unique.

Desserts

JOHNNY IUZZINI, *Jean Georges,* New York City

RICK BISHOP, *Mountain Sweet Berry Farm,* Roscoe, New York (strawberries)

Strawberry Cheesecake with Balsamic-Roasted Strawberries

This is a no-bake cheesecake recipe without eggs. It's a bit lighter than other versions, and the puréed strawberries make this cake pink. Rick grows Tristar strawberries, which he says produces medium to small flavorful fruit, a favorite with pastry chefs desiring great dessert-quality berries. Johnny glazes them with balsamic vinegar, making this cheesecake intriguing.

SERVES 8

FOR THE CHEESECAKE
3 pints fresh strawberries,
    2 pints hulled and cut in half,
    and 1 pint left whole
1 cup sugar
2½ teaspoons unflavored gelatin
    or agar-agar
½ cup milk
½ cup heavy cream
Two 8-ounce blocks cream cheese,
    at room temperature

1½ teaspoons grated orange zest
    (from ½ orange)
1½ teaspoons grated lemon zest
    (from 1 lemon)
2 teaspoons fresh lemon juice
    (about ½ lemon)

FOR THE GRAHAM CRACKER CRUST
8 tablespoons (1 stick) unsalted
    butter, at room temperature

½ cup sugar
1 teaspoon grated lemon zest
Pinch of coarse salt
¼ cup all-purpose flour
1 teaspoon baking powder
2 cups graham cracker crumbs

FOR THE GARNISH
¼ cup sugar
1 tablespoon balsamic vinegar

MAKE THE CHEESECAKE

1. In a medium bowl, toss the 2 pints halved strawberries with ¼ cup of the sugar and let macerate (release their juices) for 10 minutes. Put the strawberries and their juice in a food processor and process until smooth.

2. In a medium saucepan, heat ¼ cup water over low heat and add the gelatin or agar-agar; cook for 1 to 2 minutes, stirring constantly, until the gelatin or agar-agar is dissolved. Add the milk, cream, the remaining ¾ cup sugar, and the cream cheese, whisking until smooth and slightly warmed, but not boiling hot. Remove from the heat and add the strawberry purée, zests, and lemon juice; let cool.

MAKE THE CRUST

1. In a large bowl, combine the butter, sugar, lemon zest, and salt. With an electric mixer, beat until creamy. Sift together the flour and baking powder and combine with the graham cracker crumbs. Add all at once to the butter-sugar mixture. Mix until it holds when pressed together.

2. Press the graham cracker mixture evenly into the bottom and up the sides to the top of a 9-inch springform pan. Refrigerate for 1 hour.

continued

3. Heat the oven to 350°F. Prick the bottom of the crust all over with a fork. Bake for 15 to 20 minutes, or until golden brown. Allow to cool completely, then pour the filling into the crust and chill, loosely covered with plastic wrap but not touching the cake, for 3 hours.

MAKE THE GARNISH
Just before serving, heat the oven to 450°F. Toss the remaining pint of strawberries with the sugar and balsamic vinegar. Spread on a baking sheet and roast in the oven for 5 to 10 minutes, or until the strawberries are slightly browned but not mushy. Transfer to a bowl, with their juices. Alternatively, you can heat a skillet over medium-high heat, add the sugar, and cook the strawberries, turning often to coat with the syrup from the juices they release, about 2 minutes.

TO SERVE
Release the sides of the springform pan. Cut the cheesecake into slices, top each slice with a few roasted strawberries and their juices, and serve.

CHARLIE TROTTER, *Charlie Trotter's,* Chicago, Illinois

LEE JONES, *The Chef's Garden,* Huron, Ohio (carrots)

Milk Chocolate Semifreddo with Star Anise Carrot Cake

A semifreddo is basically an ice cream cake, and Chef Trotter uses carrots, chocolate, and spices as unexpected partners in his version. Star anise enhances the sweetness in the carrots and adds a distinctive hint of licorice to the rich chocolate. There are no egg yolks in this recipe—it's the meringue that gives the semifreddo a smooth texture.

SERVES 6 TO 8

FOR THE MILK CHOCOLATE SEMIFREDDO
8 ounces milk chocolate, chopped
1 cup heavy cream
2 egg whites
1 cup sugar

FOR THE STAR ANISE CARROT CAKE
2 large eggs
2 tablespoons olive oil

½ cup plus 2 tablespoons sugar
¼ teaspoon coarse salt
¾ cup whole-wheat flour
1½ teaspoons ground star anise
⅛ teaspoon baking powder
½ teaspoon baking soda
2 cups shredded carrots, with greens
   reserved (for garnish, optional)

FOR THE CARROT SOUP
2 cups fresh carrot juice
2 tablespoons cornstarch
1 tablespoon sugar
Pinch coarse salt

MAKE THE SEMIFREDDO

1. Put the chocolate in a heatproof glass bowl and melt slowly in the microwave. Alternatively, you can set the bowl over a pan of simmering water (don't let the bowl touch the water) and stir until the chocolate is completely melted and just warm. Set aside.

2. Using a handheld electric mixer, whip the cream in a medium bowl until it forms soft peaks; set aside.

3. Combine the egg whites and sugar in a heatproof bowl and place over a pan of simmering water. Whisk continually until the whites are just hot, about 2 minutes. Remove from the heat and transfer to a large bowl. Beat the egg white-sugar mixture with a handheld electric mixer until stiff peaks form and the egg whites are shiny and glossy, 3 to 5 minutes.

4. Fold the cream into the melted chocolate, then carefully fold the meringue into the chocolate mixture. Pour the chocolate mixture into a 9 × 13-inch pan and put in the freezer until firm, at least 3 hours or overnight until frozen.

MAKE THE CAKE

1. Heat the oven to 350°F. Combine the eggs, oil, sugar, salt, flour, star anise, baking powder, and baking soda in a large bowl. Mix until just incorporated; add the carrots.

2. Line an 8 × 4-inch (or 4-cup) loaf pan with parchment or use a nonstick baking pan. Pour the cake batter into the pan and bake for 45 minutes, or until the center springs back when lightly touched.

continued

3. When cool enough to handle, unmold onto a baking rack (run a small knife around the edges if necessary to release the cake from the pan) and let cool. Cut into 2-inch slices then cut each slice in half and set aside.

MAKE THE SOUP

In a small saucepan, heat the carrot juice over medium heat, then add the cornstarch, and whisk until the carrot juice mixture thickens, about 2 minutes. Remove from the heat. Chill for 1 hour or until cold. Season with sugar and salt to taste.

TO SERVE

Ladle a small amount of carrot soup in a shallow bowl. Place 5 to 8 carrot cake pieces on top of the carrot soup. Place 3 to 4 small scoops of the chocolate semifreddo on top the carrot cake. Garnish with carrot greens, if desired.

MICHELLE BERNSTEIN, *Michy's,* Miami, Florida

GABRIELE MAREWSKI, *Paradise Farms,* Homestead, Florida (mangos)

Honey Mango Upside-Down Cake

This cake is a great twist on an old favorite, with the mangos enhanced with the subtle taste of honey instead of the more commonly used brown sugar. Avocado honey, made from the blossoms of avocado trees, is darker than regular honey and has a rich buttery taste. Traditionally this cake is baked in a well-seasoned cast-iron skillet, which heats evenly and retains the heat perfectly.

YIELDS ONE 10-INCH CAKE; SERVES 10

12 tablespoons unsalted butter
  (1½ sticks), softened
¼ cup avocado honey
3 medium to large mangos, ripe
  but still firm, peeled and cut
  into large chunks

½ cup milk
1 tablespoon white vinegar
1½ cups all-purpose flour
2 teaspoons baking powder
½ teaspoon table salt
¾ cup sugar

2 large eggs
2 tablespoons honey
1 teaspoon pure vanilla extract

1. Heat the oven to 350°F. Butter a 10-inch cake pan or a large cast-iron skillet.

2. Melt 4 tablespoons butter in a medium saucepan or a cast-iron skillet over medium heat; add the avocado honey and simmer until the mixture turns amber colored. Add the mangos to the pan, stir to coat them in the caramel, and then pour the mixture into the prepared cake pan or leave in the cast-iron pan.

3. Combine the milk and vinegar and set aside. In a separate bowl, sift together the flour, baking powder, and salt.

4. In a large bowl and using an electric mixer, beat the remaining 8 tablespoons butter with the sugar until light and fluffy. Add the eggs one at a time, mixing just to combine. Add the milk-vinegar mixture, the honey, and vanilla. With the mixer on low speed, add the dry ingredients into the butter-sugar mixture, alternating dry and wet three times, being careful not to overmix.

5. Slowly pour the batter over the caramelized mangos and bake for 45 minutes, or until the top of the cake is golden brown and the cake has pulled away from the sides of the pan. Let cool for 15 minutes in the cake pan or skillet, run a thin knife around the edge, then invert the cake (with oven mitts if necessary) onto a serving plate, making sure the cake pan or skillet and plate are pressed firmly together. Let sit for 15 minutes then serve. Leftover cake will keep for 2 days.

SUPERNATURAL FLAVORS

Miami chefs have noticed something unusual about Gabriele Marewski's produce. It practically vibrates with flavor. This supernatural intensity is what Paradise Farms, a 5-acre, certified organic farm in Homestead, Florida, is all about.

When Gabriele bought the abandoned avocado grove abutting her property in 1999, she plunged headfirst into creating an earthly paradise, clearing waist-high weeds, installing irrigation systems, and laying the circular planting beds that would hold her first crop of lettuces. She organized the farm, starting with those circular beds, around the principles of sacred geometry and feng shui, believing that the design of the farm would help channel nature's energy and produce spiritually energized food with richer flavor.

Paradise Farms is biodynamic and vegan, with everything done on the farm meant to promote a healthy and healing lifestyle. All of the planting, weeding, and harvesting is done by hand by Gabriele herself, one full-time employee, and a revolving cast of volunteers eager to learn about organic farming.

Since her first crop of lettuces, Gabriele has expanded to include microgreens, herbs, edible flowers, heirloom tomatoes, baby root vegetables, honey, and a large variety of tropical fruits that go beyond the farm's original avocados and mangos to include jackfruit, monstera deliciosa, and cotton candy fruit.

The love and care that Gabriele puts into every aspect of her product has paid off. She sells all of her farm's produce to just 20 of the top restaurants in Miami, preferring to keep her client base small so she can attend precisely to her clients' individual needs. She'll go out of her way to source a new tomato or flower for her chefs and grow it to their specifications. She cultivates her relationship with each one of her customers, delivering to their restaurants herself twice a week, talking with them about upcoming produce, and planning for the next growing season.

One of the most exciting results of her symbiotic relationship with her clients has been the Dinner in Paradise program, a series of farm to table dinners she founded in 2005 with Chef Michael Schwartz of Michael's Genuine Food & Drink. The dinners raise money for local charities and showcase the talents of local chefs, all customers of Paradise Farms. For the attendees, sitting under the stars in the middle of winter, surrounded by Gabriele's mango trees and fields of greens, paradise seems pretty close at hand.

DAN BARBER & ALEX GRUNERT, *Blue Hill,* New York City

RALPH ERENZO & BRIAN LEE, *Tuthilltown Spirits,* Gardiner, New York (apple vodka)

Poppy Seed Cake with Apple Vodka

There is a difference between vodka made with apples and vodka flavored with apples. Spirit of the Hudson Vodka is distilled with apples and doesn't have a particularly strong apple flavor, but at 80 proof, it packs in a lot of alcohol. This cake has extraordinary texture and flavor thanks to the unusual spirits and the mousse and cider gelée layers. You could make just the apple cake and serve it with simple sautéed apples with a bit of sugar and butter, if pressed for time. Be sure to use the freshest poppy seeds you can find.

SERVES 5

FOR THE CAKE
¼ pound (1 stick) unsalted butter, softened; plus more for the pan
All-purpose flour for the pan
¼ cup ground white poppy seeds
¾ cup honey
1 medium apple, preferably Honeycrisp, peeled and shredded
½ teaspoon ground cinnamon
½ teaspoon ground cloves
1 teaspoon orange zest

5 large eggs, separated (reserve 1 white for another use)
¾ cup almond flour
½ teaspoon fine salt
4 tablespoons apple vodka

FOR THE MOUSSE
¼ cup ground white poppy seeds
¼ cup port (optional)
1½ teaspoons unflavored powdered gelatin
2 tablespoons apple vodka
2 tablespoons plum jam

7 ounces white chocolate, melted (1¼ cups white chocolate chips)
2 large egg yolks
1 vanilla bean, split lengthwise and seeds scraped out with a small knife, or 1 teaspoon pure vanilla extract
1 cup heavy cream

FOR THE GELÉE
⅓ cup apple cider
½ teaspoon unflavored powdered gelatin

1. Heat the oven to 325°F. Butter and flour an 8-inch pan and set aside. In the bowl of a mixer, combine the softened butter, ground poppy seeds, half of the honey, the shredded apple, spices, and orange zest and beat with the paddle attachment until light and fluffy.

2. With the mixer running, add the egg yolks one at a time, beating until incorporated. Pour in the almond flour and blend until just combined, being careful not to overwork the batter.

3. In a separate and very clean mixing bowl, beat the 4 egg whites until frothy, then add the remaining honey and the salt and beat until the meringue forms stiff peaks and is glossy, about 8 minutes.

4. Using a rubber spatula, gently stir one-third of the meringue into the batter to lighten it. Fold in the remaining meringue and pour into the prepared pan. Bake in the center of the oven until the cake is golden (cover with foil if the top is getting too brown) and a toothpick inserted in the center comes out clean, about 50 to 60 minutes.

5. While the cake is baking, prepare the mousse. In a small saucepan, combine the ground poppy seeds and the port, if using, and simmer until the mixture is dry.

6. Sprinkle the powdered gelatin over the vodka and stir to combine. When the poppy seed mixture is dry, add the plum jam, melted white chocolate, and vodka with

the gelatin to the pan. Whisk to combine and pour into a large bowl. Whisk in the egg yolks and vanilla bean seeds or vanilla extract and let the mixture cool to room temperature. In the bowl of a mixer, whip the heavy cream to stiff peaks and fold it into the poppy seed mixture. Set the bowl in the refrigerator and allow the mousse to firm up but not set entirely, about 30 minutes.

7. When the cake has cooled, remove from the pan, place on a cake rack, and brush the top of the cake with the 4 tablespoons of apple vodka. Smooth the poppy seed mousse over the top and return the cake to the refrigerator to set, about 10 minutes.

8. To make the gelée, combine the cider with the gelatin in a small saucepan, and bring to a simmer. Stir to dissolve the powder and remove from the heat. Let cool. When the gelée is thick but not entirely set (stir after 5 minutes to check), pour over the cake to glaze and refrigerate until set, about 10 minutes.

9. To serve, use a knife dipped in hot water to cut slices of the cake, cleaning the blade between slices.

MARIA HINES, *Tilth,* Seattle, Washington

JOE WHINNEY, *Theo Chocolate,* Seattle, Washington (chocolate)

Individual Chocolate Ganache Cakes

Maria uses Theo's Madagascar Dark Chocolate Bar with a cocoa content of 74% for a rich, intense chocolate flavor with a hint of fruit for these cakes. You can use a variety of chocolate percentages, but you may have to adjust the sugar for a very high chocolate percentage.

YIELDS 8 INDIVIDUAL CAKES

FOR THE GANACHE
½ cup heavy cream
8 ounces semisweet chocolate,
   roughly chopped

FOR THE CAKE BATTER
2 sticks (½ pound) unsalted butter
1 cup plus 2 tablespoons sugar
6 ounces bittersweet chocolate,
   roughly chopped
6 ounces milk chocolate,
   roughly chopped

4 large eggs, at room temperature
2 large egg yolks, at room temperature
½ cup all-purpose flour
⅛ teaspoon coarse salt

Whipped cream, for garnish
   (optional)

MAKE THE GANACHE

Heat the cream in a small saucepan over medium heat. Put the chocolate in a small heatproof bowl. Once the cream comes to a simmer, pour it over the chocolate and let sit for 1 minute. Gently whisk the cream into the melted chocolate, being careful not to incorporate any air. Chill in the refrigerator.

MAKE THE CAKE BATTER

1. Combine the butter, 1 cup of the sugar, and ½ cup water in a medium saucepan. Bring to a boil, then simmer until the butter is melted. Put the bittersweet and milk chocolates in a large heatproof bowl. Pour the butter-sugar mixture over the chocolates and stir until the chocolate is melted and the mixture is well blended.

2. In a large bowl, beat the eggs, yolks, and remaining 2 tablespoons sugar with an electric mixer until the mixture is pale yellow and forms thick ribbons.

3. Fold the chocolate mixture into the eggs until well combined. Fold in the flour and salt. Refrigerate the batter for at least 1 hour or overnight.

ASSEMBLE THE CAKES

1. Reserve ½ cup of ganache, then divide the rest into eight equal parts and roll into balls.

2. Butter 8 individual ramekins and fill each one-third full with the cake batter. Place a ganache ball in the center of each mold and cover with more batter, filling each mold three-quarters full.

3. Heat the oven to 350°F. Bake the cakes until the sides are set and their tops puff up but are still soft, about 15 minutes. Let cool for 2 minutes and then invert the cakes onto individual serving plates. Gently warm the reserved ganache and drizzle over the warm cakes; serve while warm. Add a dollop of whipped cream, if desired.

ELISABETH PRUEITT, *Tartine Bakery & Cafe*, San Francisco, California

SUE CONLEY & PEGGY SMITH, *Cowgirl Creamery*, Point Reyes Station, California (cheese)

Fromage Blanc Bavarian Cream Cake with Poached Plums

A bavarian cream is composed of three specific elements: gelatin-bound custard, whipped cream, and egg whites. In this recipe, Cowgirl Creamery's fromage blanc, which is a fresh cow's milk cheese made from skim milk, is used in place of the egg whites and the custard is cooked.

YIELDS ONE 10-INCH CAKE

FOR THE CAKE LAYER
1⅓ cups cake flour
¼ teaspoon table salt
¾ cup sugar
5 large eggs, at room temperature
2 tablespoons grated orange zest
6 tablespoons unsalted butter, melted; plus more for the cake pan

FOR THE BAVARIAN
¾ cup sugar
7 large egg yolks
4½ teaspoons unflavored gelatin
3 cups fromage blanc
3 cups heavy cream
2 tablespoons fresh lemon juice
2 teaspoons grated lemon zest
2 teaspoons grated orange zest

FOR THE POACHED PLUMS
6 ripe Italian plums or whatever is in season
1 cup sugar
2 sprigs fresh thyme

MAKE THE CAKE

1. Heat the oven to 350°F. Butter a 10-inch cake pan or line the bottom with parchment and butter the paper. Sift the flour and salt together in a medium bowl. In a large bowl, beat the sugar and eggs with an electric mixer over high speed until tripled in volume and thick ribbons form, 8 to 12 minutes. Add in the orange zest. Using a rubber spatula, slowly and carefully add the flour mixture in small amounts into the batter. Stir the melted butter into the batter in three additions and mix until combined. Pour the batter into the cake pan and bake until a pick inserted in the center comes out clean, 35 to 40 minutes.

2. Allow the cake to cool in the pan on a rack for 15 minutes. Carefully run a sharp knife around the inside edge of the pan to loosen the cake. Invert the cake onto the rack, remove the paper (if using), and let cool right side up on the rack.

3. Line a 10-inch springform pan with plastic wrap, letting the sides of the plastic hang over the edges of the pan by a few inches. Place the cake with the dome side down and the flatter side up in the bottom of the pan. Set aside.

continued

MAKE THE BAVARIAN

1. Combine the sugar with ½ cup water in a medium saucepan and bring to a boil, stirring to dissolve the sugar. Remove from the heat and let cool. Combine the sugar syrup and egg yolks in a metal or other heatproof bowl or pan and set it over a saucepan of simmering water, creating a double boiler. Cook the egg mixture, whisking constantly, until it reaches 180°F, is very thick, and coats the back of a spoon, about 10 minutes. Remove from the heat and set aside.

2. In a small bowl, sprinkle the gelatin over ¼ cup warm water and let stand for 5 minutes (without stirring) to soften. Whisk the gelatin mixture into the egg mixture, adding small amounts at a time, then let cool. You can speed up the cooling process by placing the bowl over an ice bath, stirring so the mixture doesn't set.

3. In a large bowl, whisk the fromage blanc with ½ cup of the cream to soften the cheese. Fold the cooled egg mixture into the cheese mixture, then fold in the lemon juice and the lemon and orange zest. In a separate bowl and using an electric mixer, whip the remaining 2½ cups cream until it holds soft peaks. Fold the whipped cream into the cheese mixture in two batches.

4. Gently spoon the bavarian over the cake in the springform pan, smoothing the top with a spatula. Press plastic wrap on top of the filling so that a skin doesn't form, then fold over the sides of the plastic wrap hanging over the edges of the pan. Refrigerate for at least 4 hours or preferably overnight.

POACH THE PLUMS

Heat a medium pot of water over medium-high heat and poach the plums for 1 minute. Drain the plums, peel them, and carefully cut around each pit to remove them. In a medium saucepan, heat 3 cups water over medium heat and add the sugar and thyme. Cook for 1 minute. Add the plums and poach for 2 minutes. Use a slotted spoon to transfer the plums from the poaching liquid to a bowl. Let cool. Put in a container and when the poaching liquid is cool, pour it over the plums. Cover and refrigerate until ready to use.

TO SERVE

Unmold the cake by running a sharp knife around the inside edge of the pan, then release and lift off the pan sides and peel away the plastic wrap. Using 2 large metal spatulas, carefully transfer the cake to a serving plate. Spoon the plums evenly over the whole cake or, for individual pieces, spoon the plums and syrup over each cut slice. The cake will keep covered for up to 3 days in the refrigerator.

GALE GAND, *Tru*, Chicago, Illinois

JUDY SCHAD, *Capriole Farm*, Greenville, Indiana (cheese)

Goat Cheese Panna Cotta with Caramelized Figs

Panna cotta, a smooth custard, is made with cream, but Gale has also added buttermilk for a tangy flavor. Capriole's goat cheese is known for its silken texture and adds a rich, lemony taste and velvety finish to this panna cotta. Topped with caramelized figs, this is an unusual and elegant dessert.

SERVES 6 TO 8

2 teaspoons unflavored gelatin
2 cups heavy cream
¾ cup sugar

1 cup fresh goat cheese, softened
1½ teaspoons pure vanilla extract

1 cup buttermilk
4 ripe fresh figs, cut in half

1. Sprinkle the gelatin over 4 teaspoons water to soften. Set aside.

2. Meanwhile, in a large saucepan, combine the heavy cream and ½ cup of the sugar. Bring to a simmer over medium heat but do not let boil, then turn off the heat and whisk in the softened goat cheese, whisking until the pieces of cheese are totally incorporated and the mixture is smooth. Add the vanilla and the softened gelatin and whisk again to dissolve the gelatin. Whisk in the buttermilk. Strain the hot mixture through a fine-mesh strainer into a pitcher with a pour spout.

3. Lightly grease 6 large or 8 small ramekins. Pour the mixture into the ramekins and refrigerate for at least 3 hours or overnight.

4. Just before serving, caramelize the figs: Dip the cut sides of the figs into the remaining ¼ cup sugar and caramelize them with a home-use blowtorch or by placing them under a broiler, cut side up, for 1 minute.

5. When ready to serve, carefully dip the bottom of each ramekin into a baking pan of hot water for about 10 seconds. Wipe the bottom of the ramekins dry, then run a thin knife around the edge of the molds to loosen the panna cotta. Set a chilled dessert plate over the top of a ramekin, then flip the plate and ramekin over at the same time, inverting the mold onto the plate. Repeat with the remaining ramekins. Garnish with the caramelized figs and serve immediately. You can also serve the panna cotta in the ramekins, with the figs on the top or alongside.

continued

*Goat Cheese Panna Cotta
with Caramelized Figs*

GINA DePALMA, *Babbo,* New York City

JODY & LUISA SOMERS, *Dancing Ewe Farm,* Granville, New York (cheese)

Caciotta Cheese Fritters with Honey

Gina loves the high butterfat of this Caciotta, a Tuscan cow's milk cheese, which makes a satisfying airy fritter.

YIELDS 20 TO 24 FRITTERS

4 tablespoons (½ stick) unsalted
  butter, cut into pieces
1 tablespoon sugar
½ teaspoon coarse salt
Freshly ground black pepper

¾ cup unbleached all-purpose flour
3 large eggs, cold
¼ teaspoon baking powder
4 ounces Caciotta, grated
2 tablespoons finely grated Parmigiano-
  Reggiano or Grana Padano

4 to 6 cups olive oil (not extra-virgin)
  or canola oil for frying
¾ cup honey, for garnish
4 to 5 sprigs fresh thyme, for garnish

STRICTLY ITALIAN

Fresh ricotta. Real ricotta. Properly packaged ricotta. Making this cheese was the "new" plan for Jody Somers. The "old" plan was to finish veterinary school and go into equine surgery. Seemed like the right path for a Future Farmers of America® member and lover of all things animal.

But after buying a small rundown farm in Granville, New York, and slowly renovating it, Jody took a different path and headed off to Italy to learn the art of cheesemaking. He moved to Tuscany to learn the art of making sheep's milk cheeses, including ricotta and pecorino, as well as cow's milk cheeses like Caciotta. While in

Italy, Jody became friends with Luisa, and although their relationship took some time to unfold, they are now full partners in life as well as in cheesemaking.

Back in New York, Dancing Ewe's ricotta is made from 90% whey (the by-product of Dancing Ewe's pecorino or Caciotta) and 10% whole raw milk from his high-fat-content Jersey cows, ladled into a proper, imported Italian ricotta basket (to drain the moisture from the cheese) and sold fresh. This is small-scale food production at its best. So good in fact that chefs like Mario Battali and his pastry chef Gina DePalma are big fans of Dancing Ewe's cheese.

While Jody and Luisa now spend time every year in Italy seeing family and learning new cheesemaking techniques, they are also looking ahead to a time when they start producing cured meats and olive oils.

1. In a large saucepan, heat ½ cup water with the butter, sugar, ½ teaspoon salt, and pepper to taste until the butter is melted and the water is simmering. Add the flour all at once, and use a heat-resistant spatula to mix the flour and water into a thick dough. Lower the heat and cook the dough for 1 minute, spreading it along the bottom of the pan and gathering it up into a ball. Repeat this procedure until the dough appears dull and dry and has begun to stick to the bottom of the pan, about 1 minute.

2. Immediately transfer the dough to the bowl of a stand mixer, and using the paddle attachment on medium speed, beat in the cold eggs one at a time. (If you don't have a stand mixer, put the dough into a large mixing bowl and use an electric mixer on medium speed.) Allow each egg to be fully incorporated into the dough before adding the next, and scrape down the sides of the bowl after each addition. Add the baking powder and continue to beat the dough until it's completely cool and stiff, then beat in the grated Caciotta and Parmigiano-Reggiano or Grana Padano.

3. Add enough oil to a large, heavy-bottomed pot or deep fryer so that there's about 6 inches. Heat the oil to 350°F (use an instant-read thermometer). Gently drop the dough by small teaspoonfuls into the hot oil, frying 5 to 6 fritters at a time. Cook for about 2 minutes, turning the fritters in the oil often and allowing them to puff up and brown.

4. When the fritters are evenly golden brown, remove them from the oil and drain on a paper towel–lined plate. Continue cooking in batches until all the dough is used up and all the fritters are cooked.

5. Warm the honey in a small saucepan. Serve the fritters while hot with a generous drizzle of warmed honey and small sprigs of thyme on individual plates. If serving on a platter, garnish the hot fritters with the thyme and serve the warmed honey in a bowl alongside the fritters.

MARIA HINES, *Tilth*, Seattle, Washington

JOE WHINNEY, *Theo Chocolate*, Seattle, Washington (chocolate)

Chocolate Pots de Crème

Intensely flavorful and silky in texture, this French classic custard is made with more dark chocolate than most recipes and a touch of ginger. Instead of plain dark chocolate, you can use Theo's Chai Milk Chocolate bar, which perfectly complements the ginger in this recipe, but you may have to reduce the sugar a bit to suit your taste. Substitute heavy cream for half or all the milk for an even richer pudding.

SERVES 6

3 cups milk
4 ounces fresh ginger, peeled and cut into 2 pieces

9 ounces dark chocolate, 71%, cut into small pieces
6 large egg yolks

½ cup sugar
1½ teaspoons pure vanilla extract

1. Heat the oven to 350°F. Heat the milk in a large, heavy-bottomed saucepan over medium heat and add the ginger. Remove from the heat, cover, and let sit for 20 minutes to steep. Remove the ginger pieces, then return the saucepan to the stove and heat until just simmering. Put the chocolate in a large, heat-proof bowl. Pour the hot milk over the chocolate in three batches, stirring until the chocolate is melted and the mixture is smooth before adding the next batch.

2. Whisk the yolks and sugar in a large bowl until pale yellow and fluffy. Add the hot milk-chocolate mixture slowly at first to temper the egg mixture in three batches, whisking constantly. After the last addition, stir in the vanilla. Portion the mixture evenly into six 5-ounce ramekins and place in a baking pan. Add enough hot water to reach halfway up the sides of the ramekins to create a water bath.

3. Bake on the center rack of the oven for 25 minutes, or until the tops of the pots de crème are set but still quiver a little when jiggled (or a when a knife inserted comes out almost clean). Remove the ramekins from the water bath and let cool. Cover with plastic wrap, pressing it directly on top of the custard to ensure a skin doesn't form. Refrigerate for at least 3 hours before serving.

BIG VISION CHOCOLATE

Walking through the plant of Theo Chocolate with owner Joe Whinney is a very uplifting experience. Is it the pervasive chocolate scent driving this mania? Maybe it's the happy glow on all of Theo's employees' faces (from chocolate, perhaps?) or the homemade graham crackers and marshmallows being sandwiched with his chocolate for National S'mores Day. Joe is a combination of Willy Wonka for grownups and Bono of the chocolate trade. His love of chocolate and belief that the producers of its vital cacao bean should be treated with more human dignity than they have previously received make him a great messenger connected to a very popular product.

Joe makes really good chocolate, but his primary goal is to raise the perceived value of chocolate and therefore the price paid to his suppliers. Joe sees the farmers who raise cacao as the stewards of the land and the consumers who buy his chocolate as the support for those stewards. Joe gives the following example: "It takes 12 American consumers buying conventional chocolate (like Hershey's®) to keep a West African family in poverty and their children malnourished." In contrast, Joe pays on average two to three times the world price for his cacao to ensure the highest quality and to make sure the people he does business with can earn a living wage and educate their families. After extensive travels in the pursuit of cacao, Joe developed his beliefs by simply asking the question, "Would you want your kids living like this?"

At the age of 24, Joe borrowed $20,000 from his aunt Helen to start Theo Chocolate. (Theo is short for *Theobroma cacao*, the Greek name for the cacao tree.) His business model was simple: Make premium organic chocolate at fair trade practices to increase the value of chocolate by creating a direct relationship with farmers, controlling production and supply, and marketing a message as well as a high-quality product. After four successful years of production, Theo's message is being fully embraced.

Chocolate Buddha (top); Maria Hines and Joe Whinney (left)

MONICA SEGOVIA-WELSH & ANDREA REUSING, *Lantern Restaurant,* Chapel Hill, North Carolina

GEORGE O'NEAL, *Lil' Farm,* Hillsborough, North Carolina (eggs)

Snow Eggs with Green Tea Crème Anglaise

Snow eggs, known as oeufs a la neige, are made out of meringue, shaped into eggs, and poached. George's hens are raised on pasture, and their diets are naturally complemented with bugs and other nutritious critters. The eggs have enormous flavor and are used in the most suitable way here, with the whites making a light meringue and the yolks part of a rich sweet sauce.

SERVES 8

8 large eggs, separated
3 cups heavy cream
3 cups milk

2 tablespoons high-quality green tea leaves with bergamot or matcha powder (or other floral tea)

1 cup plus 2 tablespoons sugar
Coarse salt
4 tablespoons honey

1. Measure 1 cup of egg whites from the separated eggs and set aside. Put the yolks in a medium bowl and set aside.

2. Pour the cream and 1 cup of the milk into a medium saucepan and bring to a simmer over medium heat. Stir in the tea leaves or powder, remove from the heat, cover, and let steep for 6 to 8 minutes or longer if a stronger flavor is desired.

3. Strain the tea-cream through a fine-mesh strainer into a clean medium saucepan and bring to a simmer over medium heat. In the meantime, whisk the egg yolks with ½ cup plus 1 tablespoon of the sugar until the egg yolks are slightly pale yellow. Slowly whisk the hot tea-cream into the egg yolks, a little at a time, to temper.

4. Return the cream-egg mixture to the saucepan and cook over medium-low heat, stirring constantly and scraping the bottom of the pan with a wooden spoon, until the custard thickens and coats the back of the spoon, 5 to 10 minutes. Remove the pan from the heat and pour through a fine-mesh strainer into a bowl to cool. Add a pinch of salt and whisk until the custard cools down. Set aside.

5. Pour the remaining 2 cups milk into a medium shallow skillet, stir in 2 tablespoons of honey, and heat over medium heat until hot. Reduce the heat to maintain a simmer.

6. In a large bowl, using an electric mixer, whip the reserved 1 cup egg whites until frothy, then add a pinch of salt. When soft peaks have formed, slowly add the remaining ½ cup plus 1 tablespoon sugar to the whites. Increase the mixer speed and beat the whites until glossy and firm peaks form. Drizzle the remaining 2 tablespoons honey into the whites and beat just until combined.

7. Line a baking sheet with paper towels and set aside. Using two large oval spoons, such as a soupspoon or 3-ounce ice cream scoop, drop egg-shaped meringues into the simmering milk (you should have 16 meringues). You'll have to add them in batches. Poach for 30 to 45 seconds, then flip them over using a slotted spoon and cook the other side for same amount of time. They will puff up when cooked through. Remove from the hot milk and drain on the prepared baking sheet. Repeat until all the eggs are poached.

8. To serve, spoon a couple tablespoons of green tea crème anglaise into shallow bowls and top with 2 snow eggs.

continued

LIL' FARM, BIG PLANS

George O'Neal of Lil' Farm always knew he wanted to work for "just causes." His work on affordable housing projects, co-ops, and community gardens naturally led him to farming and living off the land. In his mind, part of building a community had to include beautiful gardens and landscaping in addition to buildings. But he realized he could take that one step further and also include land that could be planted and harvested. So he started Lil' Farm on 5 acres in Hillsborough, North Carolina.

The farm is a source of pasture-raised chickens that produce eggs with yolks of a strong orange hue and a flavor that would never come from the grocery store. Once George started working the land, he discovered his love for heirloom and open-pollinated produce. The farm now grows flowers, white tomatoes, purple sweet potatoes, African horned melons, and, occasionally, a "science project"—like black peanuts—that doesn't work out. George keeps plugging away with seed he gets from "old timers who love to save seed" and from other sources of "older varieties of veggies."

One of the other great benefits of Lil' Farm is the bartering that goes on with his fellow farmers. Because of this, George has eggs year-round and vegetables 10 months out of the year, giving him good leverage for trading with local cheesemakers, artisanal breadmakers, and raw-milk producers.

But bartering isn't all O'Neal does. His farm serves a CSA, two farmers' markets, and a number of North Carolina's best restaurants. And O'Neal has big plans for Lil' Farm. He would like to one day turn it into a place to teach young, inexperienced farmers, and he'd like to have a restaurant on the farm as well. There's nothing lil' about that!

JOHNNY IUZZINI, *Jean Georges,* New York City

RICK BISHOP, *Mountain Sweet Berry Farm,* Roscoe, New York (strawberries)

Strawberry–Tomato Gazpacho

Both Johnny and Rick agree that this is the most refreshing fruit soup in the heat of the summer and the best use of summer strawberries. Scientifically speaking, a tomato is a fruit, so technically this is a fruit gazpacho, but more important, both types of fruit must be perfectly ripe.

SERVES 4

2½ pints fresh strawberries
½ pound red cherry tomatoes, halved
1 small red bell pepper, seeded
1 medium cucumber, peeled, seeded, and chopped

2 tablespoons sherry vinegar
3 tablespoons extra-virgin olive oil
Coarse salt
1 slice day-old country bread, crusts removed and cut into ¼-inch dice

1 small cucumber, peeled and cut into ¼-inch dice, for garnish

1. Hull the strawberries; set aside ½ pint and cut the remaining 2 pints in half. Put the halved strawberries, tomatoes, bell peppers, chopped cucumbers, sherry vinegar, and 1 tablespoon of the olive oil in a food processor. Purée until smooth, then strain through a fine-mesh strainer into a large bowl. Season with salt and set aside.

2. In a medium skillet, heat the remaining 2 tablespoons olive oil over medium heat and add the bread cubes. Toss the bread in the oil and cook for 3 to 5 minutes, or until lightly browned. Transfer to a paper towel–lined plate.

3. Cut the remaining ½ pint strawberries into ¼-inch dice.

4. To serve, ladle the gazpacho into serving bowls and garnish each with a spoonful of diced strawberries, diced cucumbers, and a few croutons.

continued

FROM BORSCHT TO BERRIES

Everybody in New York's food business knows Rick Bishop of Mountain Sweet Berry Farm. Besides having an easy-going and fun-loving personality, Rick is a serious farmer who knows the techniques of raising great produce, from what the soil's mineral level needs to be to how much sun and cool air is required. Rick made his name growing strawberries in a place formerly known more as the Borscht Belt, the Catskill Mountains of New York.

Rick's Day-Neutral Tristar strawberries (so named because they don't require a lot of sun and are the product of three different breeds and the star of three seasons) can grow from late May until early October thanks to their genetic makeup. But these berries take a tremendous amount of care to keep them growing and disease-free, including raised beds, clean rows with straw in between the rows, and generally well-pruned plants. They also need the cool nights that only certain environments like the Catskills can provide. The hard work continues with the picking of this small fruit, as there are about 45 to 50 of these little gems in a pint versus 12 to 15 California berries per pint. Rick says all the hard work is worth it: "My French chefs and little old ladies love them because they look so good on a plate."

Rick has taken a path through technology to improve the consistency of his sweet fruits and vegetables. Sugar content provides the best way to prove Rick's ideas about growing, irrigation, soil, and sun. The key to success is a refractometer that he uses to check sugar content (called the Brix value) in the fruit. While this device is usually found in wineries, farmers have been putting it to good use to determine peak times to pick fruits and vegetables with high sugar content, like carrots. The Brix measurement can guide a farmer to control irrigation or to add minerals to the crop to speed or slow the development of sugar content. While few consumers, and even chefs, know about this aspect of farming, it gives Rick a great advantage to keeping his chefs and little old ladies happy.

Johnny Iuzzini and Rick Bishop (above)

FRANK STITT, *Highlands Bar & Grill,* Birmingham, Alabama

JASON & SHELLEY POWELL, *Petals from the Past,* Jemison, Alabama (white nectarines and peaches)

Nectarines, Peaches, and Blueberries with Sabayon

The most appealing qualities of white peaches and nectarines are their low acidity, floral fragrance, and novel color. Alabama's difficult climate requires fruit specialists, like the Powells, who know how to produce an ideal acid-sugar balance for this white stone fruit. Chef Stitt likes to poach and peel his fruit for this dish at his restaurants.

SERVES 4

½ cup sugar
1 cup sweet wine, such as Moscato
4 egg yolks

1 large egg
2 white nectarines, thickly sliced
2 peaches, peeled and thickly sliced

1 cup fresh blueberries
1 cup whipped cream (optional)

1. Make the sabayon: Combine the sugar, wine, egg yolks, and egg in the top of a double boiler or in a medium saucepan and set over a pot of simmering water. Whisk constantly until the mixture becomes thick and coats the back of a spoon, 5 to 10 minutes. Continue to whisk and cook until you see bubbles forming on the sides of the pan and the mixture develops a light "foam" on top. Alternatively, you can gauge doneness by using an instant-read thermometer, which will read 160°F when inserted in the middle of the sabayon. Remove the pan from the heat and continue to whisk the sabayon to cool it down. Refrigerate to cool completely or serve at room temperature.

2. To serve, arrange the sliced fruit in shallow bowls, top with the berries, and spoon the sabayon around the fruit. If desired, for a rich mousse, whisk 1 cup whipped cream into the cooled sabayon before adding it to the fruit.

continued

FLOWERS TO FIGS

Jason Powell remembers the day he first walked into Highlands Bar & Grill nervously holding a handful of figs. He was expecting to meet with a sous-chef or an assistant, but out strode Chef Frank Stitt himself, the ultimate local celebrity as far as Powell was concerned. They sat down together and Stitt sliced into each variety of fig, explaining as he went how he could use each one. Their tasting at an end, the chef only had one question: "When can you get them to me?"

For the last eight years, Powell has been supplying Stitt with the best blackberries, figs, blueberries, apples, pears, and persimmons available in Alabama, a little, it seems, to his own surprise. When he opened Petals from the Past nursery in 1994, he intended to sell primarily antique roses, along with some other plants you might have found in your grandmother's garden. As time went on, however, he found himself more drawn to the edible than the ornamental. No surprise, really. His father had been a fruit specialist, and Powell spent his summers as a boy traveling with him across Alabama, meeting with farmers and researchers and seeing firsthand the positive impact of the land grant extension. Education is still a key part of what he does, working with researchers to identify the best breeds of fruits for the area's difficult climate and conducting classes at the nursery for people who want to learn about growing their own fruit trees.

Petals from the Past ran a thriving pick-your-own business on the property, but soon they had so much fruit on their hands that they needed another outlet. Somebody suggested they try selling some of it to restaurants, so Powell went right to the top, taking his figs to the chef who put Alabama on the map—Frank Stitt. Now Powell delivers to him (along with half a dozen other chefs) twice a week, bringing him new varieties to try and consulting with him on which work best. He loves coming in the back door of the restaurant, right into its guts, tossing something new to the cooks and getting their feedback right away. Deep in peach country, Chef Stitt is thankful to have Petals from the Past bringing some unique and sublime fruit to his door.

DAN BARBER & ALEX GRUNERT, *Blue Hill*, New York City

RALPH ERENZO & BRIAN LEE, *Tuthilltown Spirits*, Gardiner, New York (rye whiskey)

Hudson Manhattan Rye Whiskey Chocolate Truffles

Dan, Ralph, and Alex, the pastry chef at Blue Hill at Stone Barns, all agree that whiskey makes a unique chocolate truffle. Whipped butter with chocolate is a variant to the traditional ganache so often made with cream. These truffles literally melt in your mouth. If you prefer to skip the last coat of chocolate, you can dust the truffles in cocoa powder.

YIELDS ABOUT 28 TRUFFLES

12 ounces semisweet chocolate, chopped
2 tablespoons honey

2 tablespoons Manhattan rye whiskey
8 tablespoons (1 stick) unsalted butter, at room temperature

Dutch-processed cocoa powder, for dusting

1. Melt 8 ounces of the chocolate by placing it in a heatproof bowl or saucepan set in a skillet of gently simmering water and stirring until smooth. Alternatively, melt the chocolate in a microwave.

2. Make a simple syrup: In a small saucepan, heat ¼ cup water over medium heat and, when just simmering, stir in the honey. Remove from the heat and let cool completely.

3. Mix the whiskey and simple syrup in a medium bowl. Whip the butter with an electric mixer, then add to the whiskey mixture; add the cooled chocolate as well. Mix until incorporated. Line an 8 × 8-inch square pan with plastic wrap or oil a 9 × 5-inch loaf pan. Spread the ganache into the pan, tapping to make it even. Refrigerate until set, about 60 minutes.

4. Line a cutting board with parchment. Invert the set chocolate onto the parchment (remove the plastic wrap if you used it). Cut the chocolate into 1½ × ¾-inch pieces, or about this size. Melt the remaining 4 ounces of chocolate.

5. Line a baking sheet with parchment to hold the truffles after they're dipped. In a medium shallow bowl or baking dish, add the cocoa powder, if using. Dip each truffle into the melted chocolate, making sure each is well coated, and shake off the excess. Dust with cocoa powder if desired.

continued

ADVENTUROUS SPIRITS

After owning a successful rock-climbing gym in New York City for 10 years, Ralph Erenzo decided to climb a new kind of mountain. He bought a big piece of land in upstate New York with the hope of turning it into a climbers' ranch, complete with bunkhouses, camping facilities, and a small café for hungry climbers. His neighbors did not share his vision. They shut him down.

Luckily Ralph and his pal, Brian Lee, had a Plan B. They would get a license to make wine and then quietly add a distillery to the premises. They dropped the wine license with nary a peep from the powers that be.

Then came the hard part—making great distilled products. Brian's engineering and scientific background and Ralph's travel to France and Italy to learn about making grappa and cognac were a start, but they quickly found out that there is no manual for making small batches of rye, vodka, or bourbon. So they simply dug in and taught themselves, emailing other small-batch makers, working the Web, and making trips to other distilleries to hone their skills.

Then they started testing their ideas. They got apple scraps from a local slicing plant and made some vodka. It wasn't easy: Starting with cider was a much better route to take and smarter in the long run. Then they started working with grains. Their first aged spirits were a success, and with that, their rye, whiskey, and exceptional Baby Bourbon were born.

Today, Ralph, Brian, and their small crew are the only whiskey distillery making bourbon, rye, vodka, and other distilled products in New York since the Prohibition Age.

Ralph Erenzo and Brian Lee

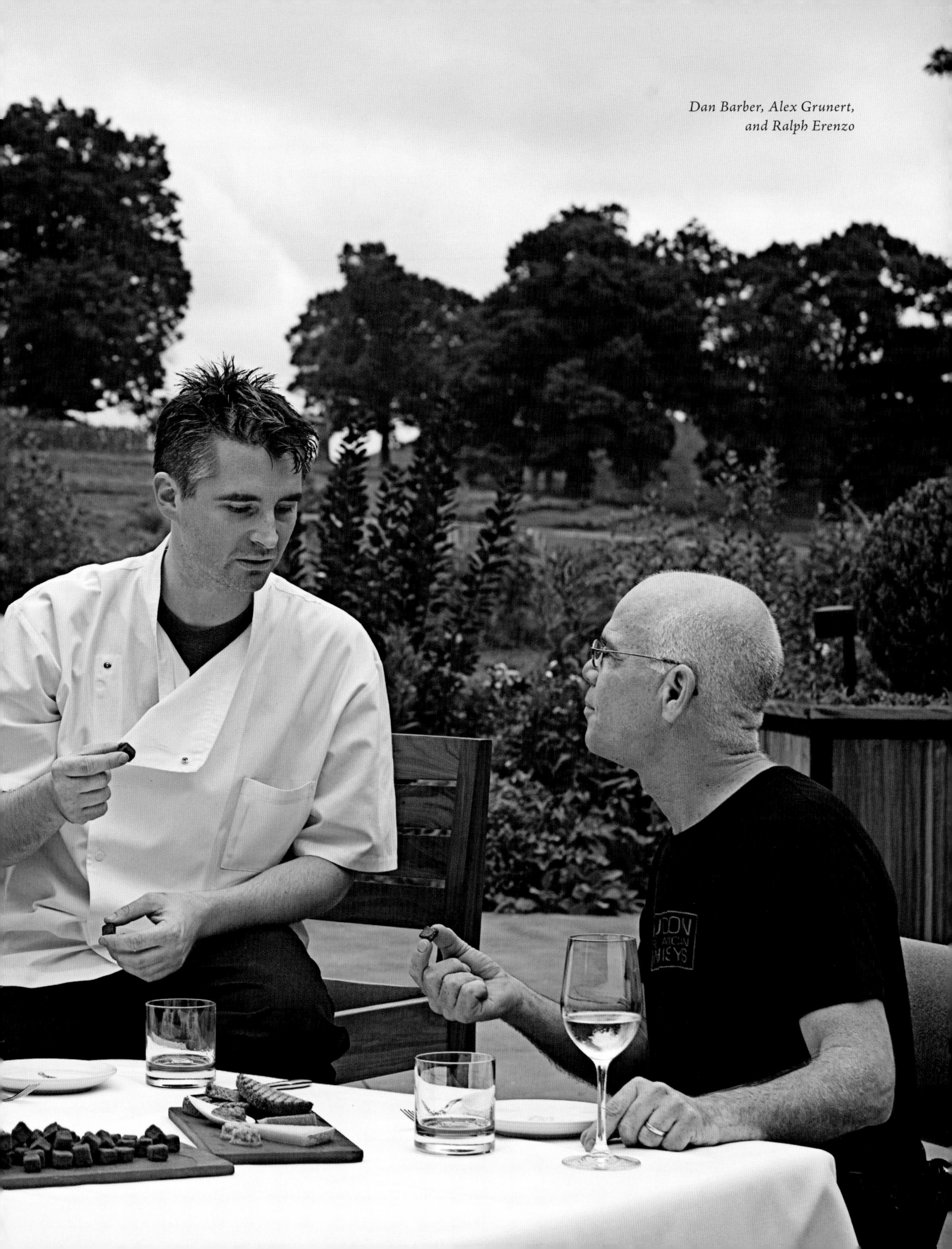

Dan Barber, Alex Grunert, and Ralph Erenzo

Recipes by Section

SIDES

DESSERTS

Hannahbells from Shy Brothers Farm

Sources

FEATURED RESTAURANTS

Animal
435 N. Fairfax Ave.
Los Angeles, CA 90036
323-782-9225
www.animalrestaurant.com

Anthos
36 W. 52nd St.
New York, NY 10019
212-582-6900
www.anthosnyc.com

applewood
501 11th St.
Brooklyn, NY 11215
718-788-1810
www.applewoodny.com

Arrows
Berwick Road
Ogunquit, ME 03907
207-361-1100
www.arrowsrestaurant.com

August
301 Tchoupitoulas St.
New Orleans, LA 70130
504-299-9777
www.restaurantaugust.com

Aureole
One Bryant Park
135 W. 42nd St.
New York, NY 10036
212-319-1660
*www.charliepalmer.com/properties/
aureole*

Babbo
110 Waverly Pl.
New York, NY 10011
212-777-0303
www.babbonyc.com

Beacon
25 W. 56th St.
New York, NY 10019
212-332-0500
www.beaconnyc.com

Beast
5425 N.E. 30th Ave.
Portland, OR 97211
503-841-6968
www.beastpdx.com

Blackbird
619 W. Randolph St.
Chicago, IL 60661
312-715-0708
www.blackbirdrestaurant.com

Blue Hill
75 Washington Place
New York, NY 10011
212-539-1776
www.bluehillfarm.com

Bolete
1740 Seidersville Rd.
Bethlehem, PA 18015
610-868-6505
www.boleterestaurant.com

Canlis
2576 Aurora Ave. N.
Seattle, WA 98109
206-283-3313
www.canlis.com

Central Michel Richard
1001 Pennsylvania Ave. N.W.
Washington, DC 20004
202-626-0015
www.centralmichelrichard.com

Charlie Trotter's
816 W. Armitage
Chicago, IL 60614
773-248-6228
www.charlietrotters.com

Chez Pascal
960 Hope St.
Providence, RI 02906
401-421-4422
www.chez-pascal.com

Craft
43 E. 19th St.
New York, NY 10003
212-780-0880
www.craftrestaurant.com

Craigie on Main
853 Main St.
Cambridge, MA 02139
617-497-5511
www.craigieonmain.com

Cyrus
29 North St.
Healdsburg, CA 95448
707-433-3311
www.cyrusrestaurant.com

Daniel
60 E. 65th St.
New York, NY 10065
212-288-0033
www.danielnyc.com

Eleven Madison Park
11 Madison Ave.
New York, NY 10010
212-889-0905
www.elevenmadisonpark.com

The Farmhouse
at Bedford Post
954 Old Post Rd.
Bedford, NY 10506
914-234-7800
www.bedfordpostinn.com

Fearing's
2121 McKinney Ave.
Dallas, TX 75201
214-922-4848
www.fearingsrestaurant.com

Frasca Food & Wine
1738 Pearl St.
Boulder, CO 80302
303-442-6966
www.frascafoodandwine.com

Frontera Grill
445 N. Clark St.
Chicago, IL 60654
312-661-0381
www.fronterakitchens.com/restaurants

Gramercy Tavern
42 E. 20th St.
New York, NY 10003
212-477-0777
www.gramercytavern.com

Hen of the Wood
92 Stowe St.
Waterbury, VT 05676
802-244-7300
www.henofthewood.com

Herbsaint Bar &
Restaurant
701 St. Charles Ave.
New Orleans, LA 70130
504-524-4114
www.herbsaint.com

Higgins Restaurant & Bar
1239 S.W. Broadway
Portland, OR 97205
503-222-9070
www.higgins.ypguides.net

Highlands Bar & Grill
2011 11th Ave. S.
Birmingham, AL 35205
205-939-1400
www.highlandsbarandgrill.com

Hugo's
88 Middle St.
Portland, ME 04101
207-774-8538
www.hugos.net

Jean Georges
1 Central Park West
New York, NY 10023
212-299-3900
www.jean-georges.com

L2O
2300 N. Lincoln Park W.
Chicago, IL 60614
773-868-0002
www.L2Orestaurant.com

Lantern
423 W. Franklin St.
Chapel Hill, NC 27516
919-969-8846
www.lanternrestaurant.com

Le Bernardin
155 W. 51st St.
New York, NY 10019
212-554-1515
www.le-bernardin.com

LeFarm
256 Post Rd. E.
Westport, CT 06880
203-557-3701
www.lefarmwestport.com

L'Etoile
25 N. Pinckney St.
Madison, WI 53703
608-251-0500
www.letoile-restaurant.com

Le Pigeon
738 E. Burnside St.
Portland, OR 97214
503-546-8796
www.lepigeon.com

McCrady's
2 Unity Alley
Charleston, SC 29401
843-577-0025
www.mccradysrestaurant.com

Michy's
6927 Biscayne Blvd.
Miami, FL 33138
305-759-2001
www.chefmichellebernstein.com/michys

minibar
405 8th St. N.W.
Washington, DC 20004
202-393-0812
www.cafeatlantico.com/minibar

Nicks on Broadway
500 Broadway
Providence, RI 02909
401-421-0286
www.nicksonbroadway.com

No. 9 Park
9 Park St.
Boston, MA 02108
617-742-9991
www.no9park.com

Osteria Mozza
6602 Melrose Ave.
Los Angeles, CA 90038
323-297-0100
www.mozza-la.com

Paley's Place
1204 N.W. 21st Ave.
Portland, OR 97209
503-243-2403
www.paleysplace.net

Per Se
10 Columbus Circle
New York, NY 10019
212-823-9335
www.perseny.com

Proof on Main
702 W. Main St.
Louisville, KY 40202
502-217-6360
www.proofonmain.com

Restaurant Eugene
2277 Peachtree Rd.
Atlanta, GA 30309
404-355-0321
www.restauranteugene.com

Rialto
1 Bennett St.
Harvard Square
Cambridge, MA 02138
617-661-5050
www.rialto-restaurant.com

Savoy
70 Prince St.
New York, NY 10012
212-219-8570
www.savoynyc.com

The Slanted Door
1 Ferry Building
San Francisco, CA 94111
415-861-8032
www.slanteddoor.com

The Spotted Pig
314 W. 11th St.
New York, NY 10014
212-620-0393
www.thespottedpig.com

Tartine Bakery & Cafe
600 Guerrero St.
San Francisco, CA 94110
415-487-2600
www.tartinebakery.com

Tilth
1411 N. 45th St.
Seattle, WA 98103
206-633-0801
www.tilthrestaurant.com

Tru
676 N. St. Clair St.
Chicago, IL 60611
312-202-0001
www.trurestaurant.com

Uchi
801 S. Lamar Blvd.
Austin, TX 78704
512-916-4808
www.uchiaustin.com

Vetri
1312 Spruce St.
Philadelphia, PA 19107
215-732-3478
www.vetriristorante.com

Vie
4471 Lawn Ave.
Western Springs, IL 60558
708-246-2082
www.vierestaurant.com

FEATURED FARMS & PRODUCERS *Farms can be visited by appointment only.*

Anson Mills
1922-C Gervais St.
Columbia, SC 29201
803-467-4122
www.ansonmills.com

Ayers Creek Farm
Gaston, OR 97119
www.edibleportland.com/2007/01/
edible_seasonal_1.html

Baffoni's Poultry Farm
324 Greenville Ave.
Johnston, RI 02919
401-231-6315
www.farmfresh.org/food/farm.
php?farm=214

Bay End Farm
200 Bournedale Rd. (farmstand)
Buzzards Bay, MA 02532
508-759-8050
www.bayendfarm.com

Benton's Smoky Mountain
Country Hams
2603 Hwy. 411
Madisonville, TN 37354
423-442-5003
www.bentonshams.com

Bluebonnet Hydroponic
Produce
12701 Ware Seguin Rd.
Schertz, TX 78154-6056
210-659-9300
www.bblettuce.com

Blue Valley Gardens
2954 North Rd.
Blue Mounds, WI 53517
608-437-3272
www.mhtc.net/~blueval/

Browne Trading Company
262 Commerical St.
Portland, ME 04101
800-944-7848
www.brownetrading.com

Capriole Farm
10329 Newcut Rd.
Greenville, IN 47124
812-923-9408
www.capriolegoatcheese.com

The Chef's Garden
9009 Huron-Avery Rd.
Huron, OH 44839
800-289-4644
www.chefs-garden.com

Cowgirl Creamery
80 Fourth St.
Point Reyes Station, CA 94956
866-433-7834
www.cowgirlcreamery.com

Creative Growers
88741 Torrence Rd.
Noti, OR 97461
541-935-7952
www.creativegrowers.com

Culton Organics
3683 Marietta Ave.
Silver Spring, PA 17575
717-285-4064
www.localharvest.org/farms/
M15563

Dancing Ewe Farm
181 County Route 12
Granville, NY 12832
www.dancingewe.com

DiStefano Cheese
5108 Elton St.
Suite E
Baldwin Park, CA 91706
626-962-6989
www.distefanocheese.com

Eckerton Hill Farm
130 Farview Rd.
Hamburg, PA 19526
www.localharvest.org/farms/M29899

EcoFriendly Foods
3397 Stony Fork Rd.
Moneta, VA 24121
540-297-9582
www.ecofriendly.com

Eden Brook Fish Co.
82 Coldspring Rd.
Monticello, NY 12701
845-791-4423
www.edenbrookfishco.com

Elysian Fields Farm
844 Craynes Run Rd.
Waynesburg, PA 15370
724-852-1076

Flora Bella Farm
Three Rivers, CA 93271
www.florabellafarm.net

Flying Pigs Farm
246 Sutherland Rd.
Shushan, NY 12873
518-854-3844
www.flyingpigsfarm.com

Four Story Hill Farm
21 Four Story Lane
Honesdale, PA 18431
570-224-4137
*www.localfoodphilly.org/wg_beef_*
pork_lamb_four_story.php

Freddy Guys Hazelnuts
12145 Elkins Rd.
Monmouth, OR 97361
503-606-0458
www.freddyguys.com

Gardner Ranch
1984 Highway 93
Sunset, LA 70584
www.gardnerranch.net

Growing Power
5500 W. Silver Spring Dr.
Milwaukee, WI 53218-3261
414-527-1546
www.growingpower.org

Hardwick Beef
Hardwick, MA 01037
413-477-6500
www.hardwickbeef.com

Heritage Meats
18241 Pendleton St. S.W.
Rochester, WA 98579
360-273-2202
www.heritagemeatswa.com

Honey Locust Farm
7 Morris Dr.
Newburgh, NY 12550
845-561-7309
www.localharvest.org/farms/M6633

Island Creek Oysters
296 Parks St.
Duxbury, MA 02332-4839
781-934-2028
www.islandcreekoysters.com

Jasper Hill Farm
884 Garvin Hill Rd.
Greensboro, VT 05741
802-533-2566
www.jasperhillfarm.com

John Boy's Farm
336 Stanton Rd.
Cambridge, NY 12816
914-646-4263
www.localharvest.org/farms/M25665

Jurgielewicz Duck Farm
Barnes Rd.
East Moriches, NY 11955-0068
631-878-2000

Kentucky Bison Co.
603 E. Main St.
Louisville, KY 40202
877-859-2426
www.kybisonco.com

Kinnikinnick Farm
21123 Grade School Rd.
Caledonia, IL 61011
815-292-3288
www.kinnikinnickfarm.com

Lil' Farm
Hillsborough, NC 27278
919-428-0204
www.ces.ncsu.edu/chatham/ag/
SustAg/csafarms.html

Link Crawfish
New Orleans, LA

Lola's Garden
Healdsburg, CA 95448

Mariquita Farm
P. O. Box 2065
Watsonville, CA 95077-2065
831-761-8380
www.mariquita.com

Mark Furstenberg
Washington, DC
www.remarkablebreads.com

Millstone Farm
180 Millstone Rd.
Wilton, CT 06897
203-834-2605
www.millstonefarm.org

Mountain Sweet Berry Farm
Roscoe, NY 12776

Munson Farms
Boulder, CO 80301
303-859-4428
www.munsonfarms.com

Norwich Meadows Farm
105 Old Stone Rd.
Norwich, NY 13815
607-336-7598
www.norwichmeadowsfarm.com

Paradise Farms
Homestead, FL 33030
305-248-4181
www.paradisefarms.net

Petals from the Past
16034 County Rd. 29
Jemison, AL 35085
205-646-0069
www.petalsfromthepast.com

Rappahannock River Oysters
P. O. Box 88
Topping, VA 23169
804-204-1701
www.rroysters.com

Satur Farms
3705 Alvah's Lane
Cutchogue, NY 11935
631-734-4219
www.saturfarms.com

Seedling Farm
6717 111th Ave.
South Haven, MI 49090
269-227-3958
www.seedlingfruit.com

Shy Brothers Farm
1325 Main Rd.
Westport Point, MA 02791
508-965-6560
www.shybrothersfarm.com

Siena Farms
113 Haynes Rd.
Sudbury, MA 01776
978-261-5365
www.sienafarms.com

Skotidakis Goat Farm
185 County Rd. 10
St. Eugene, Ontario,
Canada K0B 1P0
613-674-3183
www.skotidakis.com

Sparrow Arc Farm
Kennebunk, ME
www.sparrowarcfarm.blogspot.com

Spence Farm
Fairbury, IL 61739
815-692-3336
www.thespencefarm.com

Ted Johnson
Ogunquit, ME

Texas Quail Farm
265 Brushy Branch Rd.
Lockhart, TX 78644-4067
512-376-2072

Thanksgiving Farm
P. O. Box 840
Harris, NY 12742
845-794-1400
www.thanksgivingfarm.org

Theo Chocolate
3400 Phinney Ave. N.
Seattle, WA 98103
206-632-5100
www.theochocolate.com

Tuthilltown Spirits
P. O. Box 320
Gardiner, NY 12525
845-633-8734
www.tuthilltown.com

Viridian Farms
Dayton, OR 97114
503-830-7086
www.viridianfarms.com

Equivalency Charts

LIQUID/DRY MEASURES

U.S.	METRIC
¼ TEASPOON	1.25 MILLILITERS
½ TEASPOON	2.5 MILLILITERS
1 TEASPOON	5 MILLILITERS
1 TABLESPOON (3 TEASPOONS)	15 MILLILITERS
1 FLUID OUNCE (2 TABLESPOONS)	30 MILLILITERS
¼ CUP	60 MILLILITERS
⅓ CUP	80 MILLILITERS
½ CUP	120 MILLILITERS
1 CUP	240 MILLILITERS
1 PINT (2 CUPS)	480 MILLILITERS
1 QUART (4 CUPS; 32 OUNCES)	960 MILLILITERS
1 GALLON (4 QUARTS)	3.84 LITERS
1 OUNCE (BY WEIGHT)	28 GRAMS
1 POUND	454 GRAMS
2.2 POUNDS	1 KILOGRAM

OVEN TEMPERATURES

°F	GAS MARK	°C
250	½	120
275	1	140
300	2	150
325	3	165
350	4	180
375	5	190
400	6	200
425	7	220
450	8	230
475	9	240
500	10	260
550	BROIL	290

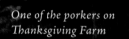

One of the porkers on Thanksgiving Farm

Index

Note: Page references in **bold** indicate a photograph

FREE PUBLIC LIBRARY UNION, NEW JERSEY

3 9549 00470 2719